CONTROVERSIES
in
CONTEMPORARY ADVERTISING

To Tim, with love, forever

CONTROVERSIES
in
CONTEMPORARY
ADVERTISING

KIM SHEEHAN

University of Oregon

SAGE Publications
International Educational and Professional Publisher
Thousand Oaks ▪ London ▪ New Delhi

For information:

Sage Publications, Inc.
2455 Teller Road
Thousand Oaks, California 91320
E-mail: order@sagepub.com

Sage Publications Ltd.
6 Bonhill Street
London EC2A 4PU
United Kingdom

Sage Publications India Pvt. Ltd.
B-42, Panchsheel Enclave
Post Box 4109
New Delhi 110 017 India

Printed in the United States of America

Library of Congress Cataloging-in-Publication Data

Sheehan, Kim Bartel.
Controversies in contemporary advertising / Kim Bartel Sheehan.
       p. cm.
Includes bibliographical references and index.
ISBN 0-7619-2635-6 (pbk.)
   1. Advertising. I. Title.
HF5823.S4854 2003
659.1—dc21   2003006412

This book is printed on acid-free paper.

03   04   05   06   10   9   8   7   6   5   4   3   2   1

Acquisitions Editor:	Al Bruckner
Editorial Assistant:	MaryAnn Vail
Copy Editor:	F. Hubert
Production Editor:	Diane S. Foster
Typesetter:	C&M Digitals (P) Ltd.
Proofreader:	Doris Hus
Indexer:	Will Ragsdale
Cover Designer:	Michelle Lee Kenny

Contents

Acknowledgments

This book could not have been written without the help and support of many of my colleagues at the University of Oregon. Dean Timothy Gleason made sure that I had the time I needed to bring this book to completion and provided answers to my legal queries on a continual basis. Dave Koranda, Rebecca Force, John Russial, and Jim Upshaw provided insights into the relationship between advertising and mass media. Charlie Frazer, Ann Maxwell, and Bill Ryan are wonderful sounding boards and munificent colleagues.

Thanks also to those who read and commented on this book's proposal: Jan Slater, Tom Reichert, Chris Cakebread, and Sally McMillan. Chris Cakebread of Boston University gave valuable insights, comments, and suggestions on the manuscript as a whole: When I mention "a colleague" in the text, more often than not it is Chris.

MaryAnn Vail at Sage was a good listener and a calming influence. Frank Hubert was a patient and thorough copy editor who generously tolerated my questionable grammar choices. Thanks to you both.

Thanks go to two scholars I've never met: James Twitchell and Michael Schudson. Both have changed my worldview in profound ways.

Thanks also to all the students who joined me in J446, Advertising and Society, at the University of Oregon. You were all my inspiration to write this book. Special thanks to former students Andrea Swanson, who introduced me to the complexities of direct-to-consumer advertising, and Eric Lammerman, who did some helpful legwork early on in the project.

Finally, my deep appreciation goes to my family for their support and assistance during the writing of this book. My husband, Tim Sheehan, is willing to talk about these issues 'til the cows come home in order to better understand the complexities of advertising today. Dr. Paul Sheehan interpreted medical language that was beyond my comprehension. My mother, Jean Bartel, and my in-laws, Jim and Anne Sheehan, never fail to ask about the book and to marvel at its progress. The four-legged family members sat in silent vigil and gave up numerous walking opportunities to see this book through. I love you all.

1 Advertising, Its Supporters, and Its Critics

Advertising is the foot on the accelerator, the hand on the throttle, the spur on the flank that keeps our economy surging forward.

—Robert W. Sarnoff

Advertising is the rattling of a stick inside a swill bucket.

—George Orwell

Advertising: We see and hear it every day. We talk about it with our friends and family; television specials are dedicated to it. When it happens during major events like the Super Bowl, we read about it and highly anticipate it. The focus of this book is advertising in general and its role in our society in particular. Like many types of mass-mediated content (e.g., television programs, popular film, music, and news stories), advertising influences our lives. Whether this influence is positive, as Mr. Sarnoff suggests, or negative, as Mr. Orwell suggests, depends on many different factors. These factors include the type of individual seeing the advertisement, the context in which the advertisement is seen, and the content of the advertising message itself. Advertising, like other types of mass-mediated content, plays a part in creating each of our own individual worldviews.

A worldview is the synthesis of our individual knowledge, experiences, and values. By influencing our worldviews, advertising is likely to generate some type of change in the way we think and feel. This process of change will subsequently result in a number of different effects not only on us as consumers but also on our worldviews and on our society. Some of these effects are intended by the advertisers and the advertising agencies creating the messages; others are not. Intended effects (or consequences) are planned and somewhat controlled by the advertisers and their agencies. These effects of advertising include having the message reach certain numbers of people who are part of a certain demographic group and/or using the message to create a specific impression or develop a certain meaning among specific consumers. Unintended effects (or consequences) are not specifically planned by the advertisers and their agencies but may occur among some members of a society. These effects include generating consumer reactions to the appropriateness of any type of advertising message, reactions to specific messages and advertising content, and/or influencing the overall worldview of individuals, such as the development of distinctive perceptions of others in society or attitudes toward consumerism in general.

In many cases, unintended effects are seen as having negative consequences. For example, an advertisement for a prescription drug might have an intended effect to empower consumers by giving them information that will allow them to be more in control of their health care. An unintended effect may be an increase in the number of patient-doctor conflicts if doctors believe that a specific advertised drug is a poor choice for their patients. In some cases, though, unintended effects can also be positive. For example, an unintended effect of prescription drug advertising is that patients are more likely to consistently take their medication because the advertising serves to remind them.

Throughout this book, we will be discussing the intended and unintended effects of many different types of advertising messages. In this chapter, we lay the groundwork for this discussion by examining definitions of advertising and the roles of advertising in our society. Since advertising is highly visible, it receives criticism from many different types of people. Therefore, we examine the role of critics of advertising in our society. Most important, we suggest that all criticisms are not created equal: Some criticisms of advertising are much more valid than others. To that end, we provide a framework for examining advertising critics and criticism.

What Is Advertising?

The word *advertise* means, in its simplest form, to give notice, to inform, to notify, or to make known (Nicosia, 1974). Dunn and Barban (1986) provide a more complex definition that suggests that advertising is a paid, nonpersonal message from an identifiable source delivered through a mass-mediated channel that is designed to persuade. This second definition differentiates advertising from other types of persuasive messages such as personal selling, which is a personal communication that is not delivered through a mass-mediated channel, and public relations, which is a form of communication that is not paid. Dunn and Barban's definition also differentiates advertising from other types of mass-mediated communication; journalism, for example, is not paid and is often not from an identifiable source. This definition also clearly states that advertising is an advocate for its sponsors, known in the industry as an advertising agency's clients. As an advocate for a client, an advertising message is biased and contains a specific point of view. As a persuasive message, an advertising message includes symbols and language that are designed to resonate with members of the message's intended audience. An advertisement is not meant to be all things to all people, and as such, the message has the potential to be problematic for those who are not part of its intended audience.

Although Dunn and Barban's (1986) definition allows us to distinguish advertising from nonadvertising messages, it does little to help us evaluate the role of advertising in our society. Specifically, it does not address the role of consumers in the advertising process. A definition of successful advertising, provided by Nicosia (1974), helps in this regard. Nicosia suggests that there are three components of successful advertising: information, reasoning, and emphasis. The first component, information, is the "news," the unique element or attribute of the product or service being sold. The second component is reasoning, which is an aspect of an advertisement that stimulates thought among receivers of the message. These thoughts could include developing interest in the message, evaluating a claim, developing a judgment regarding the relevance of the product or service to the consumer's life, creating or interpreting a general meaning of the message, or deciding to further consider the product or to purchase it. The final element in Nicosia's definition is emphasis. Emphasis considers the part or parts of the message that receive the most attention in a commercial. For example, a famous commercial from the 1950s for the pain reliever Anacin promoted that Anacin provided "fast fast fast relief." The emphasis on the word *fast* made consumers feel that Anacin was the *fastest* pain reliever available: a perfect example of the component of emphasis at work.

Nicosia's definition is important because it considers the consumer (i.e., the audience). An advertisement without an audience is nothing more than some images on paper or video. Members of an audience bring their own worldviews to the advertising message and create meaning from the messages. This simple fact—that consumers create meaning from advertisements—results in many of the intended and unintended effects of advertising.

_____ Who Is Involved in the Advertising Process?

If you took an introductory advertising class, you probably learned that three key groups are involved in the creation of advertising messages. The first group includes people at advertising agencies. These individuals develop, create, and place advertising messages. The second group includes people who work for the sponsors of the messages, also known as the clients. Not only do they pay for the messages, but the advertising messages are also created with clients' overall business and marketing goals in mind. The final group consists of people working at the media outlets such as television and radio stations, newspapers, and magazines. These individuals are involved with making sure messages run when and where they are supposed to run. However, as we consider Nicosia's (1974) definition of advertising, we must add a fourth group to this list: consumers— the people who receive the messages. These individuals either actively seek out messages (e.g., by reading print ads while researching the purchase of a new computer) or receive messages that were not sought out (e.g., by watching television during a break in a football game). A fifth group should also be considered. This group is made up of the institutions involved in the regulation of advertising messages from both a legislative perspective as well as from a self-regulatory perspective. In addition, we cannot forget the people who are the focus of this chapter: those individuals who criticize advertising and can be part of any of the groups previously mentioned. But more about them in a bit.

Advertising's Roles in Society

Given these six groups involved in advertising, it is possible that virtually everyone in the United States participates in the advertising process. Advertising performs several roles in our society: specifically, an economic role, an information role, and an entertainment role. Advertising agencies and their clients wish to operate profitable businesses that serve employees, stockholders, and other societal stakeholders well. Among other tasks, advertising agencies provide the functions of identifying which media are most appropriate for each client's message. This highlights the economic role of advertising in our society. The legal system supports commercial speech that is truthful and does not mislead. This recognizes that while advertising serves an economic purpose, it does not have free rein to communicate in order to achieve its goals. Finally, the entertainment role is important because consumers enjoy, and are likely to support, advertising that is not only informative but also entertaining: In one study, 44% of adults like advertising, with many associating "liking" an ad with being entertained by it (Shavitt & Lowrey, 1998). Each of these important societal roles will be discussed in turn.

Economic Role

In the United States, we would rather have prosperity than penury. Prosperity is defined as success or well-being, whereas penury is scarcity. Prosperity is one of the products of business, which creates products and services that the public wants and sells the products and services to consumers at prices they can afford. One of advertising's key economic roles, then, is to facilitate the selling process. Advertising helps to sell products and services by providing consumers with ideas and styles of living that can be achieved by using the products and services. These ideas are often seen as superior to the consumers' "status quo" (Nicosia, 1974).

Additionally, the economic role of advertising finds that advertising supports a free press. A free press is necessary for an informed citizenry and for the survival of a democracy. In 2000, for example, total spending on advertising in the United States was $243.7 billion, almost a 10% increase from the previous year (Coen, 2001). The percentage of spending that goes directly to media outlets (approximately 90%) supports a range of content and programming and underwrites the costs of providing content to consumers. While the economic recession and the September 11 terrorist attacks had a negative effect on advertising spending in 2001, spending on advertising is still large relative to many other industries in the United States and is the primary area of financial support for the media. This will be discussed more in Chapter 3.

This economic role has several benefits to our society. Advertising is one way that consumers find out about products and services to purchase, and consumer purchasing allows advertisers (i.e., businesses that produce products and services) to maintain and pay a workforce. Advertising is a key element in the launch of new products, which often stimulates economic growth. Advertising advances competition, which results in the lowering of prices that consumers pay for goods and services (McDonald, 1992). Advertising also increases government revenues because jobs produce taxable income, and greater sales increase sales tax revenues. The economic role of advertising is a far-reaching and important element of our capitalist system.

Information Role

At its most basic level, advertising presents information to help consumers make decisions regarding the purchase of products and services. Consumer decision making involves some degree of information processing. The amount of information processing a consumer undertakes for a given purchase varies based on several factors: the type of product or service to be purchased, previous consumer experience with the product category, the level of competition, and the amount of information consumers have available for analysis.

As a group, Americans believe that advertising is informative. In a recent study, almost half of consumers said they trust the information provided by advertising and information from advertising helps them make purchase decisions (Shavitt & Lowrey, 1998). A study by a research company, Wirthlin Worldwide (1999), found that 87% of respondents to a recent survey agreed with the statement: "Before I make a major purchase, I spend a lot of time finding out as much information as I can about which brand is best."

Advertising has a great deal of influence, but remember that it is only one of the many channels that consumers use to make decisions. In the Wirthlin study, respondents reported that in addition to advertising, they used network television news reports, newspaper and magazine articles, and the World Wide Web to find out about products and services. Advertising was seen as having the greatest influence on less expensive consumables, such as over-the-counter medications and athletic shoes, and somewhat less influence on more expensive consumer durables, such as automobiles and major appliances (Wirthlin Worldwide, 1999). Thus, it is important to recognize that advertising plays an information role in conjunction with other sources of consumer information.

Entertainment Role

The final role, and the most recent role associated with advertising, is entertainment. At its basic level, the entertainment role is important when considering that people cannot be bored into buying something. In fact, it is unlikely that people can be bored into doing anything at all.

Consumers may complain about commercials interrupting the television programs they enjoy, yet a recent study showed that one in five adults enjoys commercials on television as much as the shows where they appear (Powell, 2001). In fact, the younger someone is, the more likely he or she is to be entertained by commercials. Think about commercials for soft drinks, a category that targets youth. What are Coke, Pepsi, and Mountain Dew selling us? Yes, they are trying to get us to purchase the actual beverage. However, when you think about it, very little of the content in soft drink commercials provides information about the products themselves.

Soft drink ads do not focus on flavor, on the quality of ingredients, or on unique packaging. Instead, soft drink commercials seek to provide consumers with little entertainment breaks designed to create an overall liking of the specific beverage among consumers. Coca-Cola advertising, for example, features the antics of a family of polar bears enjoying the product. To state it differently, soft drink manufacturers strive to out-entertain potential purchasers with their advertising (Arthur, 1995).

The national daily newspaper *USA Today* has a regular feature about advertising called Ad Track, which measures how well people like various television commercials. *USA Today* recently reported that respondents to Ad Track strongly related how well they liked a specific product or service to the entertainment aspect of its advertisement. Entertaining ads were employed for products ranging from batteries to soft drinks. Among the 41 campaigns surveyed in 2001 by *USA Today*, men and women agreed that the best liked commercials were the advertisements that entertained them (Howard, 2001). The importance of the entertainment role, then, cannot be underestimated.

The Role of Critics in Society

Every institution in our society has its critics. Journalists are often highly critical of our government; entertainment reviewers evaluate and criticize new movies, books, and music; and students evaluate their professors at the end of each course. Frequently, criticism leads to a rich debate, either in person or through the media, about the validity and veracity of the criticism. Pick up any newspaper, for example, and read the editorial page: You will often find numerous points of view on the different subjects being debated. You will also find a debate on the debates themselves: reactions to criticism previously printed that may praise or ridicule the author or his or her point of view. The Internet has certainly increased the amount of debate, but whether the level of the debate has increased is, well, up for debate!

Like any institution, advertising has its critics. Any group in the public eye, and specifically those who provide messages to large numbers of people, is a likely target for criticism. Advocates for advertising, like anyone else who is criticized, have two choices: ignore or address the criticism. Although it is easy to ignore criticism, it is generally not a good idea because it is important to determine whether consumers, as potential purchasers of a product, share the views of the critics. If so, continuing to use messages that are problematic for valid reasons may be damaging to the brand, and perhaps to future brands, and to the overall corporate image of clients.

As an advertiser, then, you must be prepared to address objections from people who do not share your views about the messages you create. This is often not easy, and may be uncomfortable, but it provides an opportunity to communicate with the public (which consists of current and potential consumers) and to educate them about advertising in general and your advertising in particular.

Some critics are straightforward and open to debate, and others are confrontational in their beliefs. Some critics may not be directly accessible and may even be anonymous. Many people are difficult and frustrating to debate: Some will never change their views, no matter what is said. It may be in your (and your client's) best interest not to engage these types of people in a debate, as it is generally more effective to concentrate on people who will listen with open minds. People who listen with an open mind may not initially agree with your position, but they may be willing to reconsider their beliefs if given more information (Shannon, 1998).

Nevertheless, it is important to anticipate what critics may say about advertising and to respond accurately to criticism. Open discussion allows everyone to be heard and different ideas to be considered. It also starts a debate that can generate ideas for the future and can assess possible compromises that are acceptable to all sides (Shannon, 1998).

Types of Advertising Criticism

Advertising criticism comes in several flavors. The first type is criticism of the long-term or overreaching effects of advertising. This type of criticism examines advertising's effects on consumers after prolonged, continual exposure to specific types of messages or images. It has been suggested that much of the criticism on advertising's effects is speculative, based on an intuitive assessment that is often literal minded and on a previously developed conviction that advertising is manipulative and dangerous (Irving, 1991).

Some general areas of criticism based on advertising effects include

- The role (or lack of a role) of consumers in the advertising process. Some critics of advertising believe that consumers have been left out of the process and believe that advertising talks down to consumers instead of making them equal partners in decision making. These critics tend to believe that the advertising industry is very limiting in how it views people in general. We examine this issue later in this chapter.

- The appropriateness of advertising. Other critics believe that the glut of product advertising in the marketplace is detrimental to society and question the amount of advertising that consumers are exposed to today. In addition, they question whether certain types of products should even be advertised or sold in the consumer marketplace. We examine a range of controversial products in Chapters 11 to 15.

- The role of advertising as a force that undermines our culture. An ongoing debate examines whether advertising reflects our lifestyle (i.e., advertising mirrors society) or creates our lifestyle (i.e., advertising shapes society). Advertising certainly has the power to reflect, cultivate, and amplify values and behaviors in our culture. However, how the values are selected and whether the selected values are appropriate are concerns to some critics.

- The profane nature of advertising. Advertising is often provocative to attract attention and break through message clutter. However, there is also a submessage that says the ruder and more shocking you can be, or the more controversial the imagery in the ad, the more successful the advertising and its creator (Reinhard, 2001). This type of criticism tends to be focused on a specific commercial or campaign and is often based on the personal taste of the critic. There is a saying that states "about taste we cannot argue." This is because taste is a very personal matter of choice (Reinhard, 2001). We will discuss issues of taste further in Chapter 6.

Different Types of Criticism

A column by critic Debra Goldman in the trade magazine *AdWeek* provides a good example of the difference between issues with taste and issues with advertising effects. Goldman examined pop superstar Britney Spears's appearances in many different media, including her Joy of Pepsi commercials. Goldman (2002) writes,

> One is the sober concern that all that cleavage and bumping and grinding sends the wrong message to the legions of prepubescent girls who make up her most devoted audience. . . . And there's contempt for the empty slickness of her packaging. But nothing seems to incite Britney rage like the Virgin Thing. Her claim of chastity, which was perfectly plausible when she embarked on pop stardom at 16, has become more incendiary as her bra-cup size has increased and her act has become more suitable for a strip club. The sheer brazenness of using a claim of sexual innocence to sell titillation drives Britney's critics nuts. (p. 12)

Goldman's critique did not mention previous media criticism regarding taste and Ms. Spears (e.g., her questionable clothing choices, her grating vocal styling, or that she is "selling out" to appear in Pepsi commercials). Instead, Goldman outlined some longer term effects of the Britney Spears phenomenon—that is, the problem of providing conflicting sexual imagery to young girls. It raises the level of debate from issues merely of taste to substantive issues of marketing, pop culture, and its effects on youth.

How to Evaluate Criticisms of Advertising

Think of the times you have been criticized in the past. What is your first reaction? Often, the initial response to criticism is to immediately try to give your side of the story or to try to belittle the critic. However, it is important to first understand the validity of the criticism. This will help you understand what type of response you should give to the criticism, as well as how much energy you should put into your response.

You should evaluate six areas about the critic and criticism. These are:

1. The critic's credentials

2. The recency of the criticism

3. The type of harm identified

4. The objective reasoning used

5. The critic's view of the role of the consumer

6. The usefulness of the criticism

Each of these will be discussed in turn.

The Critic's Credentials

Because advertising is so accessible and because people are exposed to so much advertising, many ordinary consumers consider themselves experts on the subject. However, it is probably safe to assume that certain types of criticism will reach more people and have more impact than other types. For example, criticism coming from an editor or a reporter for a national publication like *Advertising Age* or *USA Today* or from an academic researcher publishing in *The Journal of Public Policy and Marketing* might be more important to consider than the criticism voiced by someone like your Aunt Dorothy.

To evaluate the critic's credentials, look first at his or her affiliation. Where does he or she work? Is it a mass media outlet, a college or university, or some other well-recognized institution? Is it a group you are familiar with or one you have never heard of? What are the basic values of the institution? Is it well respected? The more well-known and respected an institution, the better the chances that the criticism will be valid.

Next, you should ask yourself whether it is appropriate for the critic and/or his or her institution to address the topic at hand. For example, a children's advocacy group like the PTA may be an appropriate group for addressing issues of product placement in children's TV programming and may have valid criticisms that should be addressed. A toy manufacturer with a small budget that is shut out of product placement opportunities may not be an appropriate entity to address such issues because its criticisms may be based on self-interest rather than any desire for greater societal improvement.

You can also evaluate the past writings of the critic. Looking at the critic's past writings will help you determine whether the current criticism is an area of his or her expertise. Think about film critics: We should have more confidence in a movie review by Roger Ebert, who sees many movies a week, than in a review by your next-door neighbor, who sees two movies a year (Kirk, 1996).

There are many sources available at the library to help you learn about critics, their affiliation, and where criticisms were published. You can also use an online search engine such as google.com or yahoo.com to find information about critics (Cameron, 2002).

Recency

Recency examines when the criticism was published. If the criticism is recent (i.e., published within the last 6 months), then it may be more valid than older criticism. This is because there might have been changes in the topic area that makes the older criticism obsolete. For example, the tobacco settlement that went into effect in 1999 forbids tobacco advertisers from using cartoon characters in their ads. Therefore, criticism of tobacco advertising that argues against the use of cartoon imagery must be viewed from a less than recent perspective.

Advertising is a fast-moving business: Some advertisers change their messages every few months, with few campaigns airing more than a year or two. Because of this, recency may be more salient for evaluating advertising criticism than any other aspect discussed here.

Potential for and Type of Harm

Assess the criticism to identify what the critic sees as the specific problem with the advertising message and the harm that such a message will cause. Types of harm can range from a minor annoyance (e.g., frequent airings of the same commercial during a short time period) to a major danger (e.g., running television advertising for beer during a time with high viewership among children). Criticisms about messages resulting in the latter types of harm need a different, more thoughtful response than criticisms about the annoying nature of advertising. In addition, examining the nature of harm should examine the likelihood of the harm occurring—that is, whether there is a rare chance it might occur, that it might occur under some circumstances, or that there is a likely chance the harm will occur. The more likely the chance that the harm will occur, the more important that attention should be paid to the criticism. As part of this assessment, you should try to evaluate the range of effects that a single message might have. This will help you to frame a response that says "yes, that might occur, but what is much more likely to occur is . . ."

Knowing the potential for harm may help determine whether the critic's reasoning is valid. It should also help both you and the critic develop a prognosis of how to address the problem. One way to evaluate this is by considering whether the harm is direct or indirect. Direct harm includes situations where consumers are deceived and thus may be losing money by purchasing bad products. As we will discuss in Chapter 4, deceptive advertising is illegal and is monitored by the Federal Trade Commission. Thus, as an advertiser, you should be able to measure (or prove) whether the messages you create are not deceptive.

Indirect harm is a bit more difficult to evaluate. It includes psychological harm to individuals and families, such as the creation of unhealthy desires and the development of attitudes toward issues such as materialism, waste, environmental destruction, and social injustice. Indirect harm is much more difficult to monitor and measure than direct harm. In addition, it is difficult to place the total blame for indirect harm solely on advertising. Because of this, responding to indirect harm can frustrate many advertisers. Although such harm should not be downplayed, it may be a better use of time and energy to accept some responsibility for the harm, recognize the role that mass media as a whole play in the harm, and move on to other issues in the criticism.

Objective Reasoning

Objective reasoning is the logical framework used by the critic to present his or her argument. One of the first things to evaluate with regard to objective reasoning is whether the criticism is a fact or an opinion (Ormondroyd, 2001). A fact is a piece of information that can be verified. An opinion is a thought or idea that may or may not be based on facts and includes a degree of interpretation on the part of the critic.

Facts are universal. Opinions are individual and are deduced from facts. For example, one set of facts shows that many ads directed toward men during sports programming on television often feature men acting aggressively in athletic situations. Another set of facts shows that violence against women is increasing in our society. No scientific correlation shows a linkage between these two facts, but some critics are of the opinion that the two are linked. Therefore, the opinion that advertising in sports programming supports violence against women has not been verified by research but is rather an interpretation of two sets of facts.

When you evaluate the reasoning and the facts, ask yourself whether the assumptions made by the critic are reasonable and whether they are supported by evidence. Is the author's point of view objective and impartial and is the language free of emotion-arousing words and biases?

Also evaluate whether the argument is logical. Is the information organized and presented in a rational way, where the points interrelate and build upon one another? Are the main points clearly presented? Is there a sense of balance, or is the critic saying the same thing repeatedly? If the critic is merely stating his or her opinion in different ways without presenting supporting rationale, then he or she is likely to be presenting a weak argument.

View of the Consumer

How does the critic view the consumer: as an active, involved receiver of information or as a passive vessel that messages enter via osmosis? During the 1940s, a group of scholars known as the Frankfurt School saw individuals in mass capitalist cultures as having lost all powers of critical perspective (Irving, 1991). Many critics still view consumers in this way and believe that, as consumers, we are powerless over advertising. Advertisers bend our will to manipulate us into buying things we do not want.

This perspective is strengthened by some individuals' belief in subliminal advertising, which was a popular concept during the 1950s and 1960s in the United States. The idea that advertising is subliminal suggests that it works beneath the consciousness level of individuals. Discussions about subliminal advertising began with experiments in movie theaters, where a cinema owner interspersed messages saying "drink Coca-Cola" and "eat popcorn" into the movie. The owner's findings that sales of soft drinks and popcorn increased because of the messages were later discredited (Sutherland, 1993). More recently, a scholar named Wilson Bryan Key argued that advertising art directors insert tiny visual imagery into ads to subliminally stimulate desire. In the last 25 years or so, numerous studies have shown that the advertising industry does not use subliminal imagery because it does not work (Sutherland, 1993). We will discuss more about subliminal imagery in Chapter 5.

An active consumer, in contrast, is a pragmatic participant in communications. Active consumers critically evaluate messages and learn as much as they can about purchases from several sources, not just advertising. Researchers have investigated how we attend to messages, and it is apparent that as individuals, we choose what to attend to, what to process, and what to avoid (Sutherland, 1993). We pay the most attention to interesting stimuli (the entertaining role), although we do pay a minimal amount of attention to uninteresting stimuli. Even this minimal amount of attention, known as *shallow processing*, occurs at the conscious level, further discrediting ideas about subliminal advertising.

The idea of an active consumer is present in what is known as the uses and gratifications approach to the study of mass media messages. Individuals are sensitive to messages that resonate with them: messages about protection, gratification, needs, and desires (Irving, 1991). Among these desires is the real need to have pleasure in our lives, and owning things gives us pleasure. We derive individualized meaning from messages based on our own complex personalities, and it cannot be assumed that there is a single universal interpretation of a single message among all consumers. Consumers appropriate ads to use for their own purposes and amusement, and they insert ads into their own subcultures so that they ultimately affect their worldviews (Fiske, 1986).

Obviously, we are not going to be active consumers for all types of purchases: If we did exhaustive research before we purchased soda from a machine, for example, we would spend all our time on these simple purchase decisions. Therefore, consumers develop *heuristics*—that is, rules that help us streamline the decision-making process. Heuristics often involve individualized brand preference and/or brand loyalty; that is, positive experiences with brands in the past result in subsequent purchases of the brand. Actively invoking these rules, though, provides additional evidence that the active consumer model is indeed the appropriate model. We will investigate passive and active consumers in more detail in Chapter 2.

Usefulness

Finally, evaluate whether the criticism helps to improve the practice of advertising. Does the critic offer suggestions on how advertising can be changed to address the issues that he or she raises? Realistically, the institution of advertising is here to stay. Both professionals and critics should focus on improving the messages seen by consumers while maximizing the results for clients. Good criticism tries to provide guidelines or solutions to address how the unintended effects of messages can be reduced or even avoided

Responding to Criticisms of Advertising

As mentioned earlier, criticism should not be ignored. Even if you do not respond to the critic immediately, it is important to evaluate the criticism. If it is valid, it is also important to address the criticism in the future. As a student, you may wish to practice debating criticism to develop the evaluation skills suggested earlier. In any event, it is important to remember the following points when responding to criticism:

- Listen to the concerns of the critic. Understanding what causes another person to have a specific belief demonstrates respect for his or her beliefs and gives you time to construct an effective and appropriate response.

- Give the critic new information. Critics form opinions based on the information that they currently have; giving them more information may help them reevaluate their opinions.

- Prepare a persuasive response. Focus on areas where people agree with the overall goals of advertising and find ways to show them how advertising achieves such goals.

- Know when, and when not, to be defensive. Sometimes, ignoring critics makes their opinions sound valid. When opponents use inaccurate information, answer them with statistics and other information. Know when to back down. If you seem to be attacking a popular person or an institution, the perception can seriously damage the perception of advertising.

- Encourage open and civilized debate. The practice of advertising is not perfect. Creating advertisements that are informative, entertaining, and persuasive will assist in the economic success of clients and of business.

Summary

In this chapter, we introduced concepts of advertising and described, albeit in broad strokes, the role of advertising in our society. Obviously, this is a big topic that the rest of this book will spend time addressing. The next chapter will address the idea of a consumer culture, which is one of the chief areas of concern among advertising critics. We will discuss the worldview presented by advertising and how that worldview is at times in conflict with the worldviews of others. We will also discuss brands and their roles in society. We will then devote chapters to the relationship between advertising and mass media (Chapter 3) and advertising and regulatory systems (Chapter 4) and delve more deeply into subliminal advertising (Chapter 5).

We then spend several chapters discussing advertising directed to and featuring specific groups (men and women, minorities, elders, and children) and discuss the range of criticism that has been directed to issues such as stereotyping and message content. Then, we will discuss certain advertising for specific products and services that has come under scrutiny, as well as the Internet's influence on such issues. We end with a discussion of the future of advertising and suggest a vision of the future where strong messages can be heard and acted upon by consumers.

You now have the tools to begin to evaluate these criticisms as you come up on them, so do not hesitate to refer to this chapter as you read this book.

2

Are Goods Bad?

Living in a Consumer Culture

It is not enough to show people how to live better: there is a mandate for any group with enormous powers of communication to show people how to be better.

—Marya Mannes

In the United States today, individual as well as corporate wealth are important social goals. The economic role of advertising, discussed in Chapter 1, was recognized as an essential factor in modern commerce more than 70 years ago (McDonald, 1992). An examination of advertising's specific effects on the economy shows that advertising increases consumer demand for products and services in the short term and also encourages competition based on increased demands (McDonald, 1992). In addition, advertising affects the prices of goods and services. In the short term, advertising can create the conditions for consumers to pay higher prices for the value that brands provide. In the long term, advertising influences lower prices because the increase in competition causes increased production efficiencies and results in overall cost reductions for products (McDonald, 1992).

Advertising's role in encouraging the purchase of products and services can create what some critics call a "consumer culture" in our society. In this chapter, we define and discuss the idea of a consumer culture in the United States. We also begin to discuss the concept of the brand and evaluate the importance of brands in our society and in a consumer culture. Brands are developed through advertising messages that create a shared meaning between consumers who see the advertisements and the product or service featured in the advertisement. The phenomenon of making meaning among consumers in society is also discussed in this chapter.

The Consumer Culture

We often hear that people in the United States live in a consumer culture. What exactly does this mean? First, let us look at the definition of culture. As defined by McCracken (1988), culture is the ideas and activities by which each of us, as individuals, constructs our world (p. xi). Culture can be seen as a way to interpret everything we interact with; stated differently, culture is the lens through which the world is seen (McCracken, 1988). For example, hold up the index and middle fingers of your right hand. What does this sign say to you? Depending on your cultural background, this may be a sign of peace, a sign of victory, or an obscene gesture. The answer depends on your cultural references—that is, on the way you see the world. Cultural references are learned simply by experiencing them. We also learn about culture in a myriad of different ways such as by observing how others interact, by being taught at school, and by being exposed to various aspects of the culture through the mass media.

What is a consumer culture? The word *consume* has three basic meanings: It can mean to ingest, to use up, or to completely destroy. Michael Schudson, in his book *Advertising, the Uneasy Persuasion* (1984), describes a consumer culture on its basic level as a society in which people own many consumer goods (p. 7). Looking back to the definitions of consume, we see that this first meaning focuses on the "ingestion" portion of the definition.

At a more complex level, a consumer culture has been defined as a society in which human values have been "grotesquely distorted so that commodities become more important than people or, in an alternative formulation, commodities become not ends in themselves but overvalued means for acquiring acceptable ends like love and friendship" (Schudson, 1984, p. 7). This second conceptualization of a consumer culture encompasses the "completely destroy" part of the definition of consume; that is, a consumer culture can be one in which the idea of consuming totally overwhelms and ultimately destroys other aspects of the culture. For example, a consumer culture suggests to us that if we want to be attractive to others, we should buy *this* perfume, or if we want to have an exciting love affair, we should drink *that* beer. Our attractiveness or our ability to be loved has nothing to do with who we are internally but rather with what we buy and how those purchases are seen by people external to ourselves. This idea is also known as *commodification*—that is, the process of "stripping an object of all other values except its value for sale to someone else" (Twitchell, 1999, p. 93). For example, the Christmas holidays have become commodified because many in society no longer view the holiday exclusively as a religious celebration or as a way for individuals to personally reaffirm their belief system. Instead, Christmas has turned into a festival of gift giving. Rather than reaffirming a set of religious values, our self-worth can be affirmed based on how good the gifts are that we give and receive.

A consumer culture can be problematic in some ways because the value created and celebrated by the culture is based primarily on objects and on the process of purchasing objects. For example, in a consumer culture, being loved or feeling attractive has nothing to do with your personality, your intelligence, or your personal set of values and beliefs but only with what you purchase and consume. In addition, a consumer culture tends to ignore the substantive value of products and services (e.g., a product's attributes) and primarily values intangible aspects of purchasing and owning products and services.

For example, a winter coat should keep you warm when it is cold outside. However, if you look in a fashion magazine like *Vogue* or *Glamour,* you will rarely see this attribute featured in coat advertising. Instead, many advertisements for winter coats feature the image that owning the coat conveys to others. For example, the GAP ad (Figure 2.1) features a coat and is clearly intended to communicate a sense of fashion and style, not warmth. Therefore, a consumer might buy one of these coats not because it is the best choice for cold winter weather but because she will feel differently, and likely better about herself, when she owns the coat.

Figure 2.1   This advertisement suggests that coats should be purchased because they are trendy and affordable not because they are warm.

The value of the economic role of advertising has been questioned because the dominance of this role can lead to a society where the purpose of advertising is to promote consumption as a way of life (Schudson, 1984). Of course, we all have to purchase certain goods and services to live our lives. However, other goods fall more into the "want" category than the "need" category. Advertisements for the "want" categories of goods have been questioned since they may make people yearn for things they do not have and want things they do not need to live their lives. Examples are luxury goods (e.g., a diamond necklace), frivolous goods (e.g., shoes with built-in roller skates), and goods that people buy when other, less expensive products would serve the same purpose (e.g., an automatic cat litter box cleaner).

When considering such criticism, the basic question you should ask yourself is: What kind of power does advertising really have? Can advertising make us forget or sublimate our basic needs (e.g., warmth in the winter) and create needs that do not exist? If so, then we are truly living in a consumer culture (reflecting the "completely destroy" aspect of consuming). If not, then the relationship of advertising to our culture is likely to be more complex than many critics would have us believe. Advertising may be a focus of our culture, but it is not the overpowering and overwhelming force suggested by critics. Instead, it is based more on the "ingestion" concept of consuming. Ingest means to take in and make a part of you, and in some ways, that is what advertising does best: It allows consumers to associate meanings with products and services and to internalize those meanings for future use.

Advertising: Informational and Transformational

As we mentioned in Chapter 1, consumer decision making is a complex phenomenon that involves various degrees of deliberation and contemplation on the part of a consumer. If you have ever bought a car or a computer, you probably did a lot of research on different brands and options before pulling out your credit card. If you have bought a house or watched your parents buy one, you know that quite a bit of information, research, and analysis is needed to make that specific purchase. Consumers tend to be highly involved in decision making for high-ticket items. However, "involved" decision making is not the sole provenance of expensive consumer goods. Have you recently purchased a greeting card? How long did you take to make that decision? Even for relatively inexpensive products, we sometimes take a long time to make just the right choice to meet our specific needs.

Americans tend to find advertising generally informative and useful in guiding their own decision making (Shavitt & Lowrey, 1998). Indeed, the information-providing aspect of advertising suggests that advertising does a good job at communicating what a product can actually do and what kind of performance consumers can expect when they purchase the product. Advertising also informs consumers about new products: A majority of consumers responding to a recent survey reported that keeping them up-to-date about products and services is an important value of advertising (Mehta, 2000).

Advertising provides consumers with new uses for old products: Arm & Hammer saw baking soda sales increase when they publicized how their product could keep stale odors out of refrigerators. Comparative advertising, which offers information that compares the attributes of one product with a similar one, often provides objectively measurable information on attributes or price. Consumers can use that information to determine which products or services are most suitable for them. Finally, advertising provides information about important health benefits. For example, knowledge of the importance of fiber in one's diet came primarily from advertising by cereal companies (Smith, 1997).

Figures 2.2 and 2.3   Kmart describes their look as "full on sexy," and Herbal Essence promotes their "totally organic" experience,

When we are purchasing products like computers and cars, advertisements that provide specific information about a product's attributes, also known as *informational advertisements*, are important in decision making. Obviously, though, we can all think of commercials that provide minimal information about a product's or service's attributes. Instead, a second group of advertisements, *transformational advertisements*, provide information that suggests how we as consumers will feel if we buy the product or service. Advertising can transform us—that is, suggest that our lives will somehow be different and better—if we purchase the advertised product or service. For example, recent advertisements for a range of products, including Kmart clothing (Figure 2.2) and Herbal Essence shampoo (Figure 2.3), suggest that purchasing the products will make you feel sexy.

Buying California pistachios (Figure 2.4) and Bud Light (Figure 2.5) will make you the life of the party. Buying the product transforms us into a better version of ourselves; the advertisements give us clues to help us determine what that better version of life will be.

Advertising and Brands

Take a moment to reread that last paragraph. Notice we said that California pistachios, not just any variety of nuts, make you feel sexy. Bud Light, not just any kind of beer, helps you have friends. The messages of

Figures 2.4 and 2.5   The benefits of products like pistachios and beer to one's social life

these advertisements demonstrate the power that advertising has in creating a brand. What is a brand? By definition, a brand is "the name and/or symbol used to identify a product or service and distinguish it from the competition" (Vanden Bergh & Katz, 1999, p. 526). Brand equity, a component of a brand, is a product quality based in the mind of consumers. It consists of both the tangible and intangible attributes of the brand.

Let's face it, many products have the same basic qualities. In blind taste tests, many people cannot tell the difference between Coke and Pepsi. Is a box of Kellogg's Corn Flakes fundamentally different from the store brand? Some people would say "yes," some people would say "no," and others would say "it depends." Often, products are seen as different only because advertising suggests to us that they are different.

If two products do not differ materially—that is, in terms of the actual function of the products—they can be made to differ in terms of attributed qualities, which is also known as *image* (Schudson, 1984). The process of branding, then, is the assignment of attribute qualities that distinguish one brand from all others. Brands are not necessarily valuable to every consumer for every purchase. In some situations, consumers seek what are known as *satisfactory products*. Satisfactory products are "good enough" to do the job that consumers want or need them to do. For example, many consumers see sugar as a satisfactory product. Consumers buy it to use in baking or to put in their morning coffee. It has one major responsibility: to sweeten. Name-brand sugars (e.g., C&H and Domino) are priced higher than store brands, but for many consumers, any sugar, even a low-priced sugar, is usually good enough to do the job.

Brands become valuable when consumers want or need products that are better than satisfactory. For example, one consumer may not care about the brand of sugar that she buys, but she may care about her brand of shampoo. Some consumers would never purchase a bargain shampoo because, although it may do a satisfactory job of washing their hair, satisfactory may not be sufficient for individuals who pride themselves on their shiny, flowing locks.

Brands provide consumers with a range of different benefits that make brands more than satisfactory to consumers. These benefits include:

• Benefits in terms of product quality. Some consumers believe advertised brands are higher in quality than unadvertised brands (Mehta, 2000). Brand advertising promotes and encourages the development of quality products (Schudson, 1984) because advertisers do not want to risk spending money to develop a brand image for a product that will not perform up to expectations. In fact, an old adage of the advertising business says that advertising can only sell a bad product once, since consumers will not buy a bad product a second time.

• Benefits in terms of perceived value. Some consumers perceive that brands are a better value than nonbranded items (Shavitt & Lowrey, 1998). If a brand image consists of certain attributes (e.g., long-term customer service or 24-hour assistance), consumers can factor these attributes into their purchase decision making.

• Defensive benefits. Brand advertising can be defensive in that it can try to prevent consumers who are currently satisfied with the brand from switching to other brands (Schudson, 1984). An example of this would be a commercial featuring a homemaker who tried a bargain brand and regrets the negative influence it has on the cleanliness of her dishes or the softness of her clothing. Additionally, consumers can use advertising to defend their own choices and to minimize what is known as *cognitive dissonance*. Cognitive dissonance is an internal conflict about a decision that occurs after the decision is made. After an individual purchases a product, he or she may question whether the purchase was the best choice or whether the purchase should have been made at all. An example of advertising that attempts to address cognitive dissonance is automobile advertising. Most automobile manufacturers recognize that recent purchasers of cars use the advertising for their car to affirm their choice and confirm that the purchase decision they made was a good one.

How Branding Works

Branding works when advertisers and agencies find images and attributes within the product or service that resonate with target consumers. You may recall a famous old advertisement for the Avis Rental Car Company. Their ads positioned themselves as the number two company, second to Hertz, and said that when you are number two, you try harder. This idea of being number two resonates with consumers because many people can think of a time when they were working hard and trying their best, and they appreciate the effort that it can take.

Advertising that transforms has been criticized because it suggests that important qualities and values can only be achieved through purchasing specific goods and services. You cannot have a fun, carefree life without Coca-Cola. You are not a good parent unless you take your kids to McDonald's or buy Jif peanut butter. You are not a safe driver unless you drive a Volvo. In particular, it is this use of intangible attributes having little to do with product performance that causes critics to become alarmed about advertising. Creating such emotional connections between product and purchaser is seen as manipulative and inherently unfair.

Schudson (1984) argues, however, that it is ridiculous to believe that advertising should be based on product attributes that will only appeal to the rational side of an individual. He states, "People's needs have never been 'natural' but always cultural, always social, always defined relative to the standards of their societies" (p. 145).

Schudson suggests that the cultural lens through which we view the world also encompasses the products and services that we consider purchasing. Since we are viewing the world through this cultural lens, it is difficult to make decisions based on the rational attributes of a product. The cultural lens allows us to create meaning from the products and services that come into our view. Stated differently, we derive meanings about the world not only from the products we see but also from the messages surrounding the products and from our experiences in the world that may or may not include the products.

Advertising and Meaning

Consumer goods have a significance that goes beyond their "utilitarian character and commercial value" (McCracken, 1988, p. 71). All of us find meaning in a world that McCracken calls "culturally constituted"—that is, a world that we as individuals and consumers experience every day. The beliefs and assumptions of our culture shape this world. Earlier in this chapter, culture was defined as the lens through which the world is seen. Culture can also be described as the blueprint for all our activities because our culture determines what actions we take to create and fashion our worldview. For example, culture influences how you act in the classroom. In a large lecture class, you might never think about shouting out ideas without first raising your hand. In fact, you might not think about speaking at all! But in a smaller, more informal discussion section, you might feel very comfortable speaking your mind, and the culture may influence you to speak without raising your hand and to debate others in the class, including the instructor.

Our culture is made real in many ways: by our relationships, by our educational system, and by products and services that we purchase. In our society, we often view products and services by virtue of what they can do for us. However, we also view products and services in other ways, such as in terms of whether they are masculine (e.g., cars or a gray flannel suit) or feminine (e.g., boats or a pink shirt). We may feel more comfortable buying products that align with our own perception of gender: Some men may not feel comfortable in a pink shirt, and some women may feel awkward in a gray flannel suit. We also view products and services in terms of how they signal our status in society: Some products clearly signal that the wearer belongs to the upper class (e.g., a Rolex watch); other products suggest that the wearer is young and trendy (e.g., a Swatch).

We can take a single product and use advertising to create a meaning that changes the product from one that is used by babies (e.g., Pampers) to one that is used by the elderly or the sick (e.g., Depends). We can take another product and create meaning through advertising that changes the product from a cooking ingredient to a refrigerator deodorizer. These different meanings are only partly related to the attributes of the product itself, as much of the meaning is resident in our culturally constituted world.

Advertising transfers meaning from the world to the product. It brings meanings from the world and the product together in a single message or a series of messages so that a consumer can perceive what is called the "essential similarity" between the world and the good (McCracken, 1988, p. 77). Thus, when the consumer takes some meaning from the world and registers the symbolic equivalence of the meaning in an advertisement, he or she will attribute the properties from the world to the product. The advertising relates to the product properties of the world that are familiar to the consumers, and these properties may or may not be known to the consumer.

Good advertisers know how to analyze which properties of a specific product or service will resonate best with consumers. To do this, advertisers must develop a deep understanding of the meanings that are resident in each consumer's culturally constituted world. All choices made in the advertisement contribute to transferring the properties of the cultural world (the setting of the advertisement, the clothing people wear, what the people look like, etc.) to the product or service being advertised. For example, young adults in our society sometimes have tattoos or body piercing, and you rarely see their parents with similar body decorations. An advertisement for bottled water directed to younger audiences, then, may feature youth with body piercing. In advertisements directed to their parents, the adults featured in the advertisements would be unlikely to have body piercing, unless you wanted to suggest that the water provided a "fountain of youth." This representation might be risky, however. If the consumers have

Figure 2.6 Target's advertising positions the discount retailer as trendy and hip.

a negative view of youth with tattoos or body piercing, they may not wish to be as "youthful" as the message suggests. Additionally, tattoos and body piercing may not suggest youth to some consumers. The meaning may instead be associated with other groups, such as Hell's Angels or crusty old sailors. Thus, the connection between the product and the meaning may not resonate with the consumer group.

The discount retailer Target wants to attract young, trendy people to their stores. An advertisement for Target uses attractive young people, bright colors, and an eye-catching graphic style to appeal to younger Target audiences (Figure 2.6).

As in all advertisements, this transference must be done in such a way that the consumer easily interprets the connection between the cultural world and the good. If the connections are too vague or unclear, the consumer is likely to become disinterested in the message. The transference cannot be too explicit: The advertiser can only suggest the essential similarity, and consumers must create the meaning themselves. The other benefit to being less than explicit is that the images are not so youth oriented that others would be alienated from shopping at Target.

Active and Passive Consumers

This process of making meaning, then, suggests that we are indeed active consumers, which is one of the two perspectives briefly mentioned in Chapter 1. McCracken (1988) states that the process of making meaning can only be done by active consumers. Indeed, he insists that as active participants, we "are kept informed of the present state and stock of cultural meaning that exists in consumer goods" (p. 79). McDonald (1992) addressed the notion of an active consumer somewhat differently. He said that although advertisements may have their own "energy charge," messages have no value at all unless consumers choose to give them value (p. 98). An individual brings his or her own context to an interaction with an advertisement, and this context created by the individual plays a dominant role (McDonald, 1992).

The meanings that we as consumers develop from advertisements, and subsequently from the products and services that we decide to purchase, have several results. First, the meanings help to create our own worldviews. The right way to behave in different situations can be suggested by the products and the meanings in their advertisements. For example, it might not be appropriate to serve M&Ms at a fancy dinner party, but it might be acceptable to serve a candy like Rocher. Beyond these simplistic meanings, these messages serve to help us define what is childish (M&Ms; Figure 2.7) and what is adult (Rocher; Figure 2.8) and perhaps what is mundane (M&Ms) and what is more aspirational (Rocher).

We use products, services, and their meanings to define and orient ourselves. "One of the ways individuals satisfy the freedom and responsibility of self-definition is through the systematic appropriation of the meaningful properties of goods" (McCracken, 1988, p. 88). For instance, we will choose different products to purchase if we wish to be seen as "conservative" in contrast to "cutting edge."

In many normal situations, then, we use products, services, and their meanings in a way that is not particularly problematic; that is, we use them to help us make sense of a very complex world. However, it is possible that the transfer of meaning can go wrong. McCracken refers to these bungled transfers as *consumer pathologies*. One of the strongest criticisms of advertising is that some consumers build their lives solely around the products and services that they purchase. For example, you have probably seen either in a magazine or on the street a young adult dressed in designer clothing from head to toe. Some of us might see this as someone we wish to emulate, who is confident in the choices that he or she made and perhaps who is also financially well off. However, some people would see this individual as someone who defines his or her self-worth solely from the fact that he or

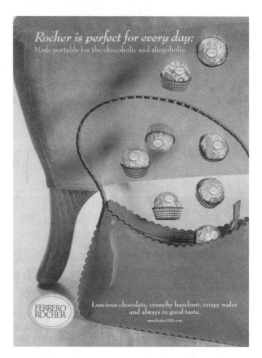

Figures 2.7 and 2.8   The ad for M&Ms features speckled chickens, while the ad for
                           Rocher shows upscale accessories.

she wears designer labels, and deduce that this individual may be more
insincere and shallower than others who may not be so involved with
consumer goods.

The idea of a consumer pathology such as the one just described suggests
to some people that advertising is manipulative. Does nondesigner clothing
keep us warm and covered just as well as designer clothing? Do people need
to spend amounts of money equivalent to a month's rent on a single outfit?
Your answers to these questions would depend on your context (i.e., your
worldview). Different situations for a single individual might result in different answers to these questions.

However, some critics believe that the only reason consumer pathologies
occur is that advertising is manipulating consumers: Advertising makes us
buy things we do not need. We would not have choices as consumers if
advertising did not suggest that designer clothing has a value that makes it
imperative that certain people purchase the clothing. Advertising and manipulation are complex concepts, and we address them in the next section.

Consumers and Manipulation

Much of the criticism directed at the advertising industry suggests that
the biggest problem with advertising is that it is manipulative. What exactly

does that mean? And is it true? Given the previous discussion on the creation of meaning and the role of active and passive consumers in society, it becomes a more complex topic for consideration.

What does manipulation mean? In its simplest form, manipulation suggests that one entity (e.g., an advertiser) can use a method (e.g., an advertisement) to make another entity (e.g., a consumer) do something involuntarily (e.g., buy a product). Compare this process to the definition of persuasion, which is the advocacy of a specific point of view of one entity (e.g., an advertiser's commercial) provided to another entity (e.g., a consumer) for the second entity to debate and evaluate. Persuasion is an important concept in our culture because, in a democracy, multiple voices and points of view regarding specific issues need to be heard (Nicosia, 1974).

The influential scholar John Kenneth Galbraith wrote a criticism of the manipulative effects of advertising in his book *The Affluent Society* (1957). In this book, he discusses the dependence effect—that is, the creation of consumer wants by the same entities that also satisfy those wants. Galbraith argued that companies create specific products and services and then use advertising to create desires among consumers that the products they have created can satisfy. In the affluent society, goods become highly important and valued more than many other aspects of society (Galbraith, 1957).

Galbraith suggested that advertising uses two techniques to manipulate consumers. First, advertising creates a propensity to consume (Galbraith, 1957). Consuming is seen as the quick, easy way to solve problems and attain the "good life." As part of this propensity to consume, manipulation can cause consumers not to evaluate advertising messages in a rational way. Instead, the advertisement has the ability to create the "illusion that it will satisfy conscious or unconscious desires that it may not, in fact, satisfy" (Phillips, 1997, p. 18).

Second, Galbraith (1957) argued that advertising directs the choices that consumers make, and some of these choices may be correct, but others may be incorrect. To illustrate, Phillips uses the example of Marlboro cigarettes. The advertisement says that smoking Marlboros will make purchasers feel manlier. However, the side effects of smoking in general are likely to make that person feel less than manly (Phillips, 1997). This type of effect could also be viewed as part of the deceptive nature of manipulation.

It is important to note that manipulative advertisements differ from explicitly deceptive advertisements in that deceptive advertisements clearly state erroneous facts. For example, if laundry detergent A advertised that it got stains out better than laundry detergent B and a scientific test proved otherwise, detergent A would be explicitly using deceptive tactics in its advertisements. In contrast, manipulative advertisements do not make "the connection between product and desire explicit" (Phillips, 1997, p. 18). Marlboro cigarettes, for example, do not directly state in their ads: "You'll feel more manly if you smoke Marlboros." In reality, many consumers would probably rationally deduce that statement to be untrue.

Advertisements that implicitly *suggest* a meaning can have a stronger effect on our desires than advertisements that explicitly *state* a meaning. A suggestion, rather than an explicit statement, has the potential to outmaneuver any rational decision making we do as consumers. Often, these suggestions involve power drives that each of us has within, such as sex, love, status, and fear (Phillips, 1997). These power drives are so strong that they have the potential to undermine rational processing.

Let us consider, for a moment, some questions. What does the idea of manipulation have to do with the concept of passive and active consumers? As we stated earlier, passive consumers can be manipulated, whereas active consumers can be persuaded. Put another way, if you think consumers are passive, you believe that advertising can make people do things. If you believe consumers are active, you believe that people do things with advertising (McDonald, 1992).

Do you think you are a rational consumer? Most individuals would say that they are. As a rational consumer, how often have you personally been impelled to purchase something? If advertisers really knew how to make us buy large quantities of many different things we really do not want or need, wouldn't they have done that by now? Wouldn't stores be crowded every single day of the year with people purchasing goods?

Many people have pondered the question of whether advertising can truly manipulate people. Repeatedly, scholars conclude that traditional advertising is only part of a consumer decision-making process. In research involving adults, it is clear that people make decisions based on numerous inputs: a client's marketing activities (which include advertising but also include public relations, personal selling, promotions, contests, and other activities), personal experience with a product, and level of dissatisfaction with one's current brands. While an advertising message can create awareness and eventually develop knowledge and interest in a brand, it is only one of many factors that leads the consumer into the store to make the purchase.

Much of the advertising that consumers use is nonintrusive—that is, advertising that consumers actively seek or scan when they have a specific need or interest but ignore at other times. When this happens, consumers are using selective perception. A good example of selective perception involves ads for feature films. If you want to go to a movie, you are likely to open a newspaper to check the ads with the movie listings and start times. If you are not going to a movie, you are likely to ignore such ads (Fletcher, 1992).

Intrusive advertising, on the other hand, is advertising for products and services that you are not currently searching for, and much of the time, we screen intrusive advertisements out. For example, television programs feature many car advertisements in any given week, but the only ones some consumers remember are the ones for the brand of car they own. This is selective processing in action.

Advertising provides information that consumers make into meaning, and consumers balance that information and its meaning against their own interests and values before making a purchase. In her book *EVEolution*, trend forecaster Faith Popcorn said "you can't browbeat a woman into buying something she either doesn't want or doesn't need. In fact, you cannot browbeat a woman into much of anything, unless it is to never buy your product again" (Popcorn & Marigold, 2000, p. 33). Popcorn's statement illustrates that consumers must be in the right mood to receive advertising and develop a meaning from the message. When consumers are answering surveys about advertising or watching television, they may not be in the right frame of mind to be receptive to messages. But when the rubber hits the road (i.e., when consumers are in stores making a decision), it is likely that snippets of advertising messages will return to them and assist in the decision-making process (McDonald, 1992).

A further point against the manipulative aspect of advertising can be found in the high failure rate of new products. Many marketers introduce new products with huge advertising and marketing budgets, yet in an average year, as many as 90% of new product introductions fail (Phillips, 1997). On the other side of the coin, some products become phenomena without any advertising support at all. One example is the Beanie Baby craze that in the United States lasted from 1995 to 1998 or so. During that time, Beanie Babies were one of the hottest products on the market, with consumers waiting in line overnight to purchase the new editions as they came out. Moreover, all this happened without spending a cent on advertising.

Manipulation also implies that the advertising message is somehow sneaking up on us, and we are unprepared for the full frontal assault by advertising. Most advertising does not do that. We are conditioned, a necessity in our culturally constituted world, to recognize the difference between advertising and other types of mass-mediated content. We can easily tell the difference between an advertisement for Pampers and today's episode of *Days of Our Lives* and between a print ad for Budweiser and the latest NFL box scores. "Humans are a very rich, lively and independent form of life; historically they have shown a very great ability to overcome environmental forces far stronger than ads can ever exercise" (Nicosia, 1974, p. 302).

Why, then, do critics and others in society continue pursuing the idea of advertising as a manipulative force? McDonald (1992) suggests that this myth of a passive consumer is in part the responsibility of the advertising industry itself, which talks about advertising making an impact, people receiving impressions, and messages being hammered home. These phrases all suggest that advertising is doing things to people. The persistence of the myth of the passive consumer may also be seen in studies showing that consumers are highly skeptical of advertising (Phillips, 1997). In trying to explain this skepticism, Twitchell (1996) has said that "we have a tendency to consider advertising in the way we consider many other cultural events, like politics, law and religion, as somehow 'out there' beyond our control"

(p. 110). However, the process of making meaning, described earlier in this chapter, suggests that advertising can make suggestions, but it cannot control us. In fact, the opposite is true: We as consumers are in control because we make the meaning of the messages ourselves.

Additionally, advertisers want to take (at least partial) credit for the successes of their clients: They want to draw a direct connection between the presence of an advertising message and subsequent increases in sales or changes in attitude. However, unless the advertiser is operating in experimentlike conditions, where there is a high degree of control over all the different variables that might influence a decision, it is very difficult to prove the exact effects of advertising on sales and attitudes.

This is not to say that advertising has no effect. Advertising can have effects on consumers, but only if consumers choose to look at the advertisements. Advertisements can be selected for perception by an individual only if the executions stand out—if they signal to the individual consumer that the advertisement features a message that will be important enough for the consumer to spend a bit of time observing, processing, and making meaning from the message. McDonald (1992) suggests that advertising executions will stand out if any of the four following conditions exist:

1. The advertised product or service is different or special.

2. The product or service is advertised in an unusual or striking way.

3. The product's or service's advertisement is personally relevant to the consumer.

4. The consumer is familiar with the advertisement.

McDonald (1992) suggests that the best advertising will often meet all four conditions.

Summary

In this chapter, we discussed the concept of a consumer culture and how as consumers we create meaning from the messages advertisers provide. We also examined whether these messages in traditional advertisements could be manipulative of "reasonable consumers" exposed to these messages. Certainly, part of the meaning of the message will derive from the context in which the message appears.

The discussion presented in this chapter takes the Federal Trade Commission's (FTC's) concept of the reasonable consumer into effect, and it is important to note that the effects of advertising may vary with different consumers and different brands. The positive effects of advertising on sales are shown only when the sender of the messages understands the needs of some group of consumers and relates to such needs by developing relevant messages. (Nicosia, 1974). Certain populations are more vulnerable to advertising messages that may be misleading or otherwise problematic. We will discuss those more in future chapters. We have also focused on traditional advertising: those 30-second television spots and full-page magazine ads that we inherently know are paid, persuasive communication.

The content of the mass medium in which the advertisement appears, also known as the advertising environment, can help consumers create meaning from the advertising message. Consumers reading an advertisement in the *Wall Street Journal*, for example, may create a meaning that is entirely different from the meaning of the same advertisement in the *National Enquirer*. In our increasingly complex communication environment, we also are exposed to newer, nontraditional types of advertising that tend to blur the lines between the advertisement and the content surrounding it. In the next chapter, we will investigate the relationship between advertising messages and the mass media where they appear.

3

The Chinese Wall

Advertising and Mass Media

The function of the press in society is to inform, but its role in society is to make money.

—A. J. Liebling

A recent issue of a fashion magazine had a special section featuring information about fashion and style. In the section, each full-page advertisement faced a full page of editorial featuring fashion and beauty tips. However, upon reading each one-page story, it quickly became apparent that the "hero" of each editorial was the product featured in the advertisement opposite the story. An ad for the Chrysler PT Cruiser (Figure 3.1), for example, was accompanied by a story (Figure 3.2) about chic shopping areas in Los Angeles. Not surprisingly, the Chrysler PT Cruiser is recommended as the best way to visit these exciting shopping areas.

No doubt, you have seen this type of content, called an *advertorial*, in different media. In their longest form, these blends of editorial and advertising content are called *infomercials*, which are entire program-length television shows dedicated to a single product. To more closely examine this blurring, in this chapter we review the relationship between mass media and advertising. This is an interesting and complex relationship that is highly symbiotic: Each institution relies on the existence of the other to exist in society. However, at times, conflicting values can create considerable tension in the relationship.

Functions of the Mass Media

The Constitution of the United States guarantees a certain number of freedoms for American citizens. Not only is freedom of speech a fundamental

Figures 3.1 and 3.2   An ad for the Chrysler PT Cruiser side by side with its complementing page of "editorial" in a recent magazine advertorial

right of all Americans, but the United States was founded under the precept of freedom of the press. The framers of the Constitution believed that an uncensored press is a necessity in a democracy. Today, freedom of the press is in a privileged position that holds great importance for all members of society.

A theory known as *social responsibility theory* recognizes the important role that the media play in the lives of citizens. Social responsibility theory suggests that the press is responsible to society to operate for the social good; for example, the mass media have a social responsibility to provide an open forum for diverse viewpoints. Another part of the social responsibility of the media is that they should exhibit responsibility while covering events of public importance and reporting controversial events.

In pre-Revolutionary America, the mass media were limited to printed pamphlets and a few newspapers that reported on the issues of the day. Primarily, these media were political in nature, with the purpose of encouraging democracy and keeping citizens informed on issues that affected the burgeoning democracy in the United States. Since 1776, the role of the mass media in our society has been expanded. Today, mass media have both content functions and economic functions, as detailed in Theodore Peterson's ideas of six functions of mass media. These six functions are:

1. Servicing the political system by providing information, discussion, and debate on public affairs

2. Enlightening the public to make it capable of self-government

3. Safeguarding the rights of the individual by serving as a watchdog against government

4. Servicing the economic system primarily by bringing together the buyers and sellers of goods and services through the medium of advertising

5. Providing entertainment

6. Maintaining their own financial self-sufficiency so as to be free from the pressures of special interests (Siebert, Peterson, & Schramm, 1956)

Social responsibility theory suggests that all these functions are not equally important. Most important are the first three functions because these contribute the most to a democratic society. Social responsibility theory also suggests that the fourth function, servicing the economic system, should not take precedence over the first three functions. Social responsibility theory also asserts that the mass media should strive to provide "good" entertainment—that is, entertainment that can enhance society and help to accomplish societal goals.

Social responsibility theory also suggests that not all media would have to complete the sixth function. Certain individual media should be exempt from providing financial self-sufficiency if it helps them better accomplish the first three functions (Siebert et al., 1956).

Examining the Chinese Wall

The term *Chinese Wall* has been used to describe the relationship between the content function (i.e., news and entertainment) and the advertising function of the mass media. The term was first used after the 1929 stock market crash. At that time, the term described new regulations that provided a separation between brokerage firms and investment bankers. This separation was necessary to avoid conflicts of interests between brokerage firms' objective analyses of stocks and bonds and investment bankers' desire to have a successful stock offering. As a group, the regulations were known as the Chinese Wall because they were meant to create a barrier between the two operations that would be as effective as the Great Wall of China (Wayman, 2000) and presumably avoid future stock market crashes.

Today, we often hear the term Chinese Wall used to describe the separation between the editorial functions and the advertising functions at a media outlet. With a Chinese Wall in place, there is presumably a mechanism at mass media outlets that guards against any potential conflicts of interest between the advertising function and the editorial function. However, the existence of the Chinese Wall and the degree to which it is successful in doing its job are matters of debate among those involved in mass media.

David Shaw (1987) found evidence of the Chinese Wall when he reported that newspapers were less likely than at any other time in history to be concerned with how advertisers were portrayed in their pages. He says that a "high, thick wall has arisen between the news/editorial and advertising departments at most responsible papers, and editors, publishers and advertising executives alike speak of this wall as a largely unbreachable barrier, akin to the separation of church and state in our society" (Shaw, 1987, p. 1). He mentions, however, that other media were less likely to have a strong wall. Television, for example, was highly dependent on audience ratings and advertising income; thus, television executives were likely to consider advertiser needs differently from newspaper executives. Magazines were also more sensitive than newspapers to advertiser demands, especially in terms of editorial content and taste.

Those professionals involved with the creation of media content worry that the weakening and possible fall of the Chinese Wall can damage audiences' perceptions of a medium's credibility, impartiality, and integrity. However, for many media executives, these concerns must be balanced against the real-world necessities of paying bills and maintaining audience levels. The debate, then, has been characterized as a conflict between the values of informing the public and of maximizing profits (Brown & Barnes, 2001).

Advertising and the Chinese Wall

In the early days of television, right after the end of World War II, network television shows were produced by advertising agencies for a single sponsor. Programs such as the top-rated *Texaco Star Theatre* (hosted by the popular Milton Berle) and the *Goodyear TV Playhouse* had the imprint of their sponsors on the shows (Jacobson & Mazur, 1995). Today, we have a vestige of such sponsored offerings with a program such as the *Hallmark Hall of Fame*. However, these single-sponsor programs are rare and tend to occur now as special presentations rather than weekly programs.

The multiadvertiser model became the norm in the 1950s, and as the number of single-sponsor shows declined, the percentage of revenue generated from advertising in the media increased. Today, between 50% and 80% of revenue generated by television, radio, magazines, and newspapers is from advertising. Compare this to 1960, when less than 50% of the revenue of all media was generated from advertising.

Given this growth in the interrelationship between mass media and advertising, concerns are expressed over the influence that one institution can have over the other. Probably, the dominant concern that is voiced in society is that advertising has too much influence over the mass media and mass-mediated content. In this chapter, we investigate this concern and provide evidence that the mass media also exert considerable influence over advertising content.

Advertising's Influence Over Television Content

As mentioned, there are concerns in society regarding advertising's influence over mass media. Specifically, some critics perceive that both entertainment and news programming content can be biased in favor of those entities that support the media with their advertising dollars. Twitchell (1996) suggested that the greater the mass medium's reliance on advertising, the greater the advertiser's control of the content. What are the results of this control? To some, advertiser control results in huge amounts of "fluff" in our media choices as media executives select content that appeals to the most people. To others, it suggests that journalism is no longer a value-free discipline and can no longer be objective in the content it presents (Twitchell, 1996).

One role of the media planner in the advertising agency is not only to determine in which media advertisements will appear but also to determine specific placement for the advertisements in terms of specific television programs, sections of the newspaper, editorial adjacency in magazines, and the like. For television programs, many advertisers have explicit (i.e., written) guidelines about what types of programs are best for their products. Today, many advertisers provide written guidelines for their agencies to follow. However, many other advertisers avoid preparing written guidelines, perhaps to avoid allegations that advertisers try to influence programming. However, even if there are not written guidelines for a client, there tends to be a code known by media buyers as to which types of programming are appropriate and which types are not. For example, many fast-food companies wish to avoid airing in programs where there is bloodshed on the screen because this may not be a particularly appetizing environment for their products. Some conservative companies wish to avoid advertising in programs with high sexual content.

Regardless of whether a client has an explicit or implicit code, the activities of media buyers make their clients' preferences in programming perfectly clear to television executives, who are able to use that information in programming decisions. For example, they may choose to develop programs that avoid the types of controversy that could alienate advertisers, resulting in what has been called censorship based on economics (Jacobson & Mazur, 1995). Evidence of censorship based on economics is clearly available today. Large package good companies such as Procter &

Gamble (P&G) spend a huge percentage of their budgets on network and nationally syndicated television programs. P&G tends to be conservative and controversy averse in its selection of mainstream media; in the past, the company avoided airing commercials in programs such as *The Jerry Springer Show* (because of its reputation for being "shock TV"), the *Dr. Laura Show* (for controversial content regarding homosexuality), and *NYPD Blue* (for occasionally airing partial nudity) (Gibbs et al., 2001). The chairman of P&G, John Pepper, has urged network television programming executives to increase the amount of family-friendly programming. Pepper also spearheaded an awards program that compensated programming executives and companies for creating high-quality family fare.

Entertainment programming on television is not the only programming that can be influenced by advertisers. Some critics have observed that advertisers may have some influence over news content. In particular, news programs have been accused of avoiding controversial or damaging coverage of companies that are major advertisers on their stations (Bagdikian, 1983). For example, news reports have avoided exploring controversial subjects such as automotive safety and insurance rates, fearing a backlash by advertisers in these categories. Interestingly, this preferential treatment is not limited solely to corporate advertisers. During the 1992 presidential campaign, for example, candidate Ross Perot spent a majority of his advertising money on ABC. Compared to his coverage on CBS and NBC, Perot received more favorable coverage of his candidacy from ABC (Twitchell, 1996).

A new trend is for network television stations to develop marketing alliances with major partners. This causes concern among some critics about network TV news' objectivity in covering their partners' activities. For example, CBS and Kmart had an agreement to cross-promote products, as did NBC and Sears. Critics ask whether the news departments of NBC and CBS can be expected to report fairly on the business practices of Sears and Kmart, given these marketing ties (Mandese, 1994).

Advertising's Influence Over Public Television

The Public Broadcasting System (PBS), which includes the PBS television network as well as National Public Radio (NPR), has been criticized for its increase in commercial content (also known as underwriting). Critics have expressed concern that this increase could lead to the same issues as on network television: questionable choices made in reporting that favor advertisers.

The Public Broadcasting System was created through an endowment during the Johnson administration, when the Public Broadcasting Act was signed in 1967. PBS was designed to be free of commercial values. Through the first 20 years of its existence, corporations funded about 30% of PBS budgets, and corporate sponsors and underwriters were identified with only a simple tag that read something like "this program is brought to you today by United Air Lines." A plain screen on television would name the sponsor.

In 1992, then-President Reagan slashed the subsidy for Public Broadcasting. Since then, the proportion of corporate and private funding has increased significantly. Evidence of this increase is seen in the type of sponsorship messages currently seen on PBS. Today, advertisers or underwriters can describe products and show them visually on television as long as they do not use price advertising or urge consumers to go out and purchase the products. For many sponsors, there is little to distinguish a PBS underwriting announcement from an advertisement on a program such as *Meet the Press*.

Certainly, public broadcasting has not shied away from hard-hitting analysis of contemporary society. The show *Frontline*, for example, frequently exposes corporate wrongdoings and aired a documentary that was critical of automotive giant General Motors (GM). In response, GM called such programming a "hostile environment" for advertising messages. This suggests that even on PBS the potential to economically censor exists, although there may not be evidence that this has indeed happened (Jacobson & Mazur, 1995).

Advertising's Influence on Print Media

Advertising's influence on content does not extend only to television; in fact, magazines have probably come under greater attack for pandering to advertisers than any other medium. Magazines consider and often consult their advertisers when developing stories, looking for sources, and selecting products and services on which to report. While products that are not advertised are also covered, the balance between advertiser-focused and non-advertiser-focused content has been examined, and problematic relationships have been identified. For example, an investigation of the magazine *Self* in the 1980s showed that only advertisers received editorial coverage in the publication. After this relationship was reported in the press, the editor was fired and the magazine changed its policy.

A single advertiser may also exert pressure over the magazines in which it advertises. In 1993, automaker Chrysler wanted to be sure that its advertisements ran in a suitable editorial environment. Chrysler instituted a prenotification policy, which said that any magazine wishing to run Chrysler advertising would have to provide summaries of articles with sexual, political, or social issue content that might appear in the magazines where Chrysler's ads were scheduled to run. Chrysler could then decide whether the scheduled ad would run or be pulled. Of more than 100 magazines, about half agreed to the policy.

Other examples in the magazine realm include:

- Car manufacturers have refused to advertise in automotive "buff" magazines such as *Car and Driver* that have either criticized the manufacturer's business practices or that did not give good product reviews to the company's products (Twitchell, 1996).

- Under pressure from gown advertisers, bridal magazines refuse to take ads from companies that sell used bridal gowns (Twitchell, 1996).
- Some magazines refuse to accept ads for products that help you stop smoking, fearing repercussions from tobacco advertisers (Twitchell, 1996).

Several pieces of research exist to support the anecdotal evidence just presented. One study found that about 40% of magazine editors had been told by either an ad director or a publisher to take an action that compromised what they believed to be the publication's editorial integrity. Only one half of these individuals said that they refused the request. Consumer magazine editors were much more likely than business publication editors to turn down requests to compromise editorial content (Howland, 1989). A smaller study found that 47% of farm magazine writers believed that the magazine's efforts to please advertisers made it difficult to work without any kind of vested interest. Half of the respondents said that pressure from advertisers was a problem in some cases (Hays & Reisner, 1990).

It is important to note that examples exist of situations when individual media did not back down from controversial content or pander to advertisers. *Fortune* magazine published a cover study about IBM's then chair and CEO, Louis Gerstner, who was described in the story as "arrogant, brusque and obsessed with status." Although the article also praised his management style, IBM pulled ads from the publication. This reaction has not made *Fortune* more cautious; the publisher announced that if the publisher loses the course set out for the magazine, then the franchise begins to decline (Pogrebin, 1997).

Advertising's Influence Over Newspapers

Regardless of the findings by Shaw (1987) discussed earlier in this chapter, newspapers are also concerned with advertising's influence over editorial content. A study of 150 editors by professors at Marquette University found that almost all the editors acknowledged some degree of interference by advertisers. Almost 90% of the editors specifically stated that advertisers attempted to influence story content, and more than one third of the editors said that advertisers succeeded in influencing the content. The worst culprits were automotive, real estate, construction, and restaurant advertisers (Soley & Craig, 1992).

Advertising and Editorials

The use of advertorial sections has been increasing. These features, combining editorial content and advertising, have been accused of badly blurring the lines between the advertising and editorial functions in both magazines and newspapers (Cameron & Ju-Pak, 2000). The growth in the number of advertorials is tied to the increasingly competitive markets that newspapers and magazines face. Advertorials are a way to generate revenue from new advertisers by providing editorial content that is complementary to their advertising message. Newspapers, for example, will often produce special sections on fashion or home improvement that feature a range of advertorials, and the types of magazine advertorials are limitless.

Advertorials are problematic for some because of the intentional blurring of the advertising and editorial lines (Singer, 1991). Sometimes these sections are clearly labeled as advertorials, but other times they are not. Although the American Society of Magazine Editors (ASME) encourages magazines to label advertorials as such, there is no specific regulation that compels print media to do so. Readers may misinterpret advertorials as editorial content, which may create higher credibility for the message. The message changes from "advocacy" to "news." However, advertorials can confuse readers about the origins of the information they provide and could compromise editorial credibility. Others suggest that advertorials, specifically unlabeled ones, cause information pollution at best and are potentially deceptive at worst (Cameron & Ju-Pak, 2000).

Advertising and Corporate Ownership

Some critics believe the increase in advertising's influence may be due to corporate ownership of media. For example, the *Washington Post* company owns *Newsweek* magazine, which generates significant revenue from advertising by tobacco companies. Many people wonder whether the *Washington Post,* arguably the most influential newspaper for our governmental lawmakers, has the ability to cover the tobacco industry accurately, given the parent company's ownership. AOL Time Warner owns a range of properties, including the magazine *Entertainment Weekly* and Warner Brothers movie studios. In a vein similar to the *Washington Post* question, critics wonder whether *Entertainment Weekly* can provide unbiased reviews of movies produced by Warner Brothers.

Since the mid-1990s, we have seen some changes in the apparent influence that advertising has over the mass media. Earlier, we referred to Chrysler's efforts to ensure quality environments for their messages. In 1997, Chrysler eliminated the policy previously mentioned after magazine editors and designers said the policy amounted to censorship. Editors also suggested it was unfair of Chrysler to place the fear of economic consequences on the magazines. Additionally, ASME and the Magazine Publishers of America (MPA) agreed that advertisers should not have an advance look at any content in order to limit possible economic censorship (Kelly, 1997). However, as this book is being written, many media are struggling due to a downturn in the economy. How this affects the Chinese Wall is yet to be seen.

Mass Media's Influence on Advertising _____

We have seen how advertisers can influence mass media content, and now we turn to the other side of the Wall. Do the mass media have influence over advertising content? There is certainly anecdotal evidence to support that they do. However, these instances rarely receive the coverage and publicity that advertising influence does. The media's ability to serve as a screen for advertising messages, as well as the increase in media concentration, suggest that advertising as an industry is not quite as powerful as the mass media might want the public to believe.

Mass Media as a Screen

Any mass medium serves as a screen for advertising and thus has the power to affect advertising messages. In the print media, for example, editors determine whether specific advertisements are appropriate to appear in the publication, and they have an influence on the specific placement of advertisements in the publication. Magazine editors, in particular, are often concerned with ads appearing in their publications. They are especially concerned that the advertisements placed "far forward" in the magazine complement the magazine's editorial, and they work to ensure that the ads in the front reflect the values and the quality of the publication.

With television, the screening process is much more formalized. The major broadcast and cable television networks have a department known as standards and practices that is responsible for determining which commercials can and cannot air on network television.

Standards and practices is an outgrowth of the trusteeship model of mass communications, which suggests that broadcasters have a responsibility to operate in the public interest given their access to a scarce resource, the airwaves (Dessart, 2001). The network standards and practices department is set up to make sure that all nonnews matter that airs complies with legal, policy, factual, and community standards. The formalized process is important for consistency in decisions, especially since broadcast messages, including ad content, come into individual's homes "unforeseen, often unbidden, and sometimes unwelcome" (Dessart, 2001).

Standards and practices departments are outgrowths of significant content restrictions that were in place in the early days of broadcasting. For example, early in the history of radio, networks did not allow either product price mentions in advertising or the announcement of the locations of stores that sponsored radio programs. In the 1920s and 1930s, radio networks would arrange to have an organist available during live broadcasts to drown out such language in a live broadcast. By the late 1930s, networks established more formal procedures to ensure that advertising policies and federal law were followed (Dessart, 2001).

At one time, the standards and practices departments received reinforcement by portions of the National Association of Broadcasters' (NAB) code that contained advertising standards and time limits for nonprogram content, such as commercials. Various portions of the NAB code have since been examined for their legality, and today, the code is not in existence. Therefore, the network standards and practices departments bear the sole responsibility for evaluating content.

These standards and practices departments have sizable jobs: They not only evaluate advertising that the networks plan to run, but they also review the content of network-produced or purchased programs as well as any theatrical movies that the networks plan to air. The people working in these departments are busy evaluating a wide range of content for imagery, language, and appropriateness for the time period when it airs and the target audience it will reach. In addition, standards and practices assign the ratings that appear at the start of every television program.

In terms of advertising review, standards of imagery, language, and time period appropriateness are evaluated in ways similar to programming content. If a movie studio wishes to run an ad for an R-rated movie, for example, the standards and practices departments must evaluate the content of movie advertisements and determine the time periods when this advertisement would be allowed to run. They are involved with regulating potentially deceptive advertising standards and can request substantiation for claims and statistics used in advertising. Often, the network's guidelines exceed legal requirements in this regard. In addition, the standards and practices department evaluates and makes recommendations on revisions to controversial statements or imagery in advertisements. The networks exercise broad discretion to accept or reject commercials based on taste. No network will air a commercial unless its standards and practices department has approved it.

The existence of standards and practices departments has been criticized for several reasons. Many believe that these departments represent anachronistic paternalism at best and most often a form of censorship (Voigt & Melillo, 2002). Advertisers are concerned that television networks, with their mix of news and entertainment, erroneously claim the publishers' right to exercise their judgment as to what is appropriate for broadcast to the American public. The networks may be overstepping the constitutional boundaries, specifically when it comes to advertising in entertainment programs. Network advertising and sales executives worry that the very process of examining advertisements prior to airing leads to pettifoggery (i.e., disreputable tricks or quirks of law) and rigidity that may limit the types of commercials that appear.

The inconsistency of the process concerns advertisers. There is no national standard that all networks use; the standards are unique to each network. What this means is that a spot approved by ABC might not be approved by NBC (Limberg, 2002). Additionally, since several individuals hold these positions at each network, the judgments about ads depend on the individual doing the judging, and decisions may be inconsistent within a single network (Voigt & Melillo, 2002). This results in the perception of a double standard.

The ABC network once banned a public service announcement (PSA) about skin cancer sponsored by the American Academy of Dermatology that depicted a skin cancer diagnosis and treatment. The spot ended with a skin cancer victim removing his artificial nose and cheek. ABC refused to air the spot, citing reasons of taste. However, during the same month, ABC ran commercials promoting an upcoming film release titled *The Mummy*, which featured a rotted corpse with a missing nose (Hranchak, 1999). In this case, some argue, economics overruled taste.

Local broadcast media outlets rarely have their own standards and practices departments, yet the screening process exists even when a standards and practices department does not. For example, a radio station pulled an advertisement for an ultraquiet Miele dishwasher. The ad featured an actual recording of a Miele dishwasher to demonstrate how quiet the machine was, and the commercial featured several seconds of silence. The station pulled the ad because they were worried that listeners would switch stations during the silence, thinking the station had gone off the air. The screening function, then, limited the advertiser's campaign effectiveness ("Silent Dishwasher Ad Too Quiet," 2000).

Media Concentration

The idea of media concentration suggests that one side of the Chinese Wall may be getting stronger, resulting in undue pressure and influence on the other side of the wall. With media concentration, the editorial side is strengthening while the advertising side is weakening.

The idea of media concentration suggests that mass media outlets are no longer single, independent entities in their markets. Instead, they are part of vast vertically and horizontally integrated entities that can influence advertising in many ways, but perhaps most often in financial ways.

Vertical Integration

Vertical integration refers to one entity owning multiple outlets of a single medium. For example, according to their corporate Web sites, the Gannett Company owns more than 100 different newspapers, and Clear Channel Communications owns 1200 different radio stations. Today, 76% of newspapers are chain-owned, and 50% of all television stations are network affiliates (Morton, 1995). Proponents of chain ownership suggest that it is valuable because it minimizes risk and promotes diversity. However, the increase in ownership has been a concern among journalists, programmers, and advertisers.

Journalists are concerned that corporate owners of large media chains have lower standards for journalism and also devalue local coverage. Radio programmers worry that corporations exert influence over music choices. Both journalists and programmers are concerned about downsizing local staffs, the increase in transient management that is uncommitted to local markets, and the increased potential for high turnover in writers, news anchors, and announcers, as rising stars are frequently transferred to more important outlets. Moreover, these concerns also apply to advertisers: Any of the situations just mentioned could affect the quality, size, and involvement of the medium's audience.

Smaller, minority-owned outlets can be highly affected by chain ownership. According to a study by the Black Broadcasters Alliance, the number of minority-owned radio stations decreased from 127 in 1997 to 100 in 1998. The majority of the stations that were sold off and had a format switch were black-owned stations (Black Broadcasters Alliance, 2002). If this trend continues, no black-owned stations may exist by the end of the first century of the new millennium. Important audience members (and target markets) may be disenfranchised by such an occurrence.

Advertisers are also concerned with the diminishing of competition caused by the emergence of chains. As chains grow, they acquire more funds to continue to purchase additional outlets. In the case of newspapers, chains can buy out smaller papers, resulting in one-paper markets. In the case of radio, two or three chains can own most of the airwaves in a single market. This lack of competition can result in higher advertising rates for most advertisers. This may keep local advertisers from running ads in the local media that they most rely on and have supported for many years.

Horizontal Integration

Horizontal integration refers to a single entity owning a variety of different outlets and content providers. AOL Time Warner, for example, was created from two distinct mergers. Time and Warner Brothers merged in the last decade of the 20th century, and then this new entity merged with American Online (AOL) in 2000. As with vertical integration, horizontal integration causes concerns among many different groups of people, which cite concerns with market domination and access. For example, the AOL Time Warner merger was criticized for creating a company that would have a national monopoly of content (Hu, 2000). The merger was also criticized because AOL could easily dominate the online industry, forcing high rates for advertising and for online access (Wilcox, 2000). Content producers expressed concerns that Time Warner would not carry certain types of programming, resulting in a limited selection for advertisers. Cable companies worried that Time Warner would deny certain cable companies access to Turner programming such as CNN (Wilcox, 2000). Disney, a company that has certainly not shied away from horizontal integration, complained that the merger would cause consumer choice to diminish (Hu, 2000). Critics suggested that the merger would stymie future development of new technology, including interactive television (Hu, 2000).

The growth and penetration of vertically integrated companies have the potential to produce the worst kind of corporate journalism, where the news is "dumbed down" for the lowest common denominator of consumers of the entire media package (Welch, 2000). This is tied to a continuing concern with how the mass media operate—specifically, their overreliance on aggregating and selling audiences. For example, television chooses which programming to air based not only on the number of people who watch a program but also on the demographics of the group. Even if a network could sell out a program and make a profit, it might choose to cancel a program if it thinks another program could get a different, better audience (Baker & Dessart, 1998) This could be problematic if advertiser-sponsored programs are eliminated or rescheduled to make room for a different program with different demographics. Demographic groups that are not as "attractive" to some advertisers, such as older people or minorities, may not have access to the types of programming they would like to have.

Criticisms of the AOL Time Warner merger may be a bit early and somewhat unfounded, but they do suggest some of the longer-term concerns that arise when companies merge. In hindsight, we can see that the AOL Time Warner merger did not result in a corporate domination of content, either online or offline. Time Warner Cable reaches only 12% of cable homes, and AOL does not block ads from competitors (Hu, 2000). The huge size of the market in the United States and the diversity of choices available to consumers make any part of the content market nearly impossible to monopolize, even if there are companies like AOL Time Warner that are the largest content producers for a particular market (Welch, 2000).

Summary

In this chapter, we examined whether advertising influences mass media content or whether mass media content influences advertising. It is clear that the relationship between the two institutions is highly symbiotic, and examples of influence are seen on both sides. Advertising supports a free press. However, advertising may exercise too much influence in exchange for such support.

What will happen in the future? Perhaps this symbiotic relationship will become even stronger with the increase in the reliance that American consumers place on the Internet. The lines between advertising and content messages truly blur in the online environment. Marketers create their own Web sites, which are a mix of advertising and content, and search engines sell the top places to the highest bidder. We also see partnerships between credible news sites and online retailers that make it easy for us as consumers to get all the information we need but cause concerns about the actual credibility of information online.

Thus, the Chinese Wall still stands but is not nearly as strong as it once was. However, it does represent one of the many regulatory processes that closely examines the content of advertising that we as consumers are exposed to every day. In the next chapter, we will look further at advertising's regulatory structure in the United States and examine the multiple forces that have input on the advertising that we create and see.

4

Checks and Balances

Government and Self-Regulation of Advertising

That government is best which governs the least, because its people discipline themselves.

—Thomas Jefferson

Morris Hite once said that advertising lives in a fish bowl (Hite, 1988). It is the most visible of all commercial practices, and no other business, communications medium, art form, or enterprise has so many watchdogs. In Chapter 3, we examined how the mass media play an influential role in regulating advertising messages (and vice versa). In this chapter, we evaluate other regulatory mechanisms that are much more formalized than the Chinese Wall relationship described in Chapter 3. Specifically, we examine the roles of the government (via the First Amendment of the Constitution and the Federal Trade Commission) and of the industry (via self-regulation) in regulating advertising messages. We also examine a recent lawsuit that does not fall under traditional jurisdictions.

Advertising Regulation in Context

The Industrial Revolution in the United States began the process to provide a proliferation of products to consumers. The Industrial Revolution also saw the creation of brands, which gave consumers reasons to try and/or prefer one brand to another. The growth in the number of products offered to consumers and the rise of the brand in society led to what is still an important catch phrase for consumers in society today: Caveat emptor, or let the buyer beware. Caveat emptor is a Latin phrase and a legal principle.

As a legal principle, it suggests, for example, that buyers should examine and check for themselves the goods that they intend to purchase because the seller is generally under no duty to disclose anything to the buyer. The legal doctrine affords sellers much protection from purchasers' claims that the seller did not disclose the true condition of the products being sold.

During the latter part of the 19th century and the beginning of the 20th century, the federal government was quite circumspect in its policy toward advertising and other business practices. The federal government wanted to protect consumers from fraudulent and abusive marketing practices but also wanted to make sure that the economic wheels of the country kept turning during this evolutionary period. Thus, there were minimal attempts to regulate advertising or to regulate business growth as a whole.

As the influence of business and marketing in our society grew during the 1950s, the federal government recognized that it was time for increased legislative involvement in regulating messages. This involvement, while continuing throughout the 20th century and into our current one, waxes and wanes with different administrations. Recently, government involvement has been heightened with new concerns about information technology, the Internet, and e-commerce (Russell & Lane, 2002).

Advertising and the First Amendment

The role of government is not to suppress, destroy, or disable advertising. Advertising is one of the least expensive techniques for distributing goods and provides a huge service to the U.S. economic system (Nicosia, 1974). This is not to say that government is not involved at all in advertising practices. The government has a twofold responsibility when it comes to advertising. First, the government has recognized that advertising speech is part of a category known as commercial speech, which receives some protections under the First Amendment of the Constitution. However, the government is charged not only with protecting commercial speech (i.e., protecting advertisers' and advertising agencies' right to communicate information) but also with protecting consumers from speech that can cause them harm, such as deceptive advertising. Let us first look at what types of protection are available to those creating commercial speech today.

First Amendment Protection of Advertising

The First Amendment states that "Congress shall make no law respecting an establishment of *religion*, or prohibiting the free exercise thereof; or abridging the *freedom of speech*, or of the *press*; or the right of the people peaceably to *assemble*, and to *petition* the Government for a redress of grievances" (emphasis added). From an advertising perspective, the most important element of the First Amendment is the idea of freedom of speech:

Citizens of the United States have the right to speak freely without government involvement. How does advertising come within the scope of the First Amendment? The current state of advertising's First Amendment protection is the result of a process involving a series of interpretations of the First Amendment in light of different types of advertising messages.

In the first half of the 20th century, the U.S. Supreme Court ruled in the case of *Valentine v. Christensen* that advertising was not entitled to any First Amendment protection. What that means is that if some entity had an issue with some type of advertising communication, the advertising message could be banned legally. Beginning in the 1960s, though, the Supreme Court began to recognize that certain types of advertising messages should be protected, especially advertising that contained information important to consumer decision making. Today, First Amendment law has evolved to where it is evident that the right to communicate information of public interest is not unconditional or unlimited in commercial settings. However, when commercial advertising for a legal product or service is not false or misleading, it generally comes within the protection of the First Amendment. This protection is afforded to advertising messages regardless of the fact that messages may be objectionable on the grounds of taste or other aspects that do not violate the law.

To that point, the Constitution (and specifically the First Amendment) has been interpreted as providing three levels of protection for speech. The first level, the highest protection, is afforded to political, artistic, and cultural speech. This type of speech is completely protected because it is either necessary for the functioning of a democracy (as in the case of political speech) or it has the greatest chance of being stifled (as in the case of artistic and cultural speech). The First Amendment, then, protects museums and galleries that wish to display controversial works of art. It also allows political candidates to have unfettered messages about themselves and their competitors, which we will discuss in Chapter 14.

The next level, commercial speech (which includes advertising), has some protections (see the next section). The third level—obscenity, libel, or "fighting words"— has minimal protections because the Supreme Court has recognized that there are certain well-defined and narrowly limited classes of speech that can be prevented and/or punished without constitutional problems.

Commercial Speech

The legal system in the United States has been involved with the advertising industry primarily by reviewing proposed regulations on commercial speech and evaluating whether the speech has protection under the First Amendment. A 1993 Supreme Court opinion summarized the general principles underlying the protection of commercial speech:

The commercial market place, like other spheres of our social and cultural life, provides a forum where ideas and information flourish. Some of the ideas and information are vital, some of slight worth. However, the general rule is that the speaker and the audience, not the government, assess the value of the information presented. Thus, even a communication that does no more than propose a commercial transaction is entitled to the coverage of the First Amendment. (*Edenfield v. Fane*, 1993)

The Supreme Court uses a standard known as the Central Hudson test to evaluate the constitutionality of a ban on advertising messages. This test was named after a famous 1980 Supreme Court case, *Central Hudson Gas & Electric v. Public Service Commission of New York*. In this case, Central Hudson wanted to advertise electronic appliances that they sold to consumers. During this time in society, though, the United States was facing an energy crisis. Therefore, the Public Service Commission was opposed to Central Hudson's advertising because the commission did not want consumers purchasing products that might increase overall energy use. For example, if consumers did not yet own an electric dishwasher, purchasing a new one would add to their total energy consumption. By banning Central Hudson from advertising the products, consumers would be less likely to consider purchasing new products that would increase their energy consumption.

Based on the Central Hudson case, the Supreme Court asks four questions when considering whether banning or otherwise regulating advertising is constitutional or unconstitutional.

1. Is the advertisement for a legal product or service, and is the message misleading? If the answer to either of these questions is no, then the advertisement will not have First Amendment protection. If the answer to both of the questions is yes, then the next question will be considered.

2. Is there a substantial government interest in banning or regulating the speech? To phrase this question somewhat differently, is the advertisement promoting something that the government, for whatever reason, is hoping people will not do or buy? If a substantial government interest is found, then the next question will be considered.

3. Does a regulation on advertising advance the government interest? For example, will banning an advertising message substantially help the government achieve its goals? If the ban will advance the government interest, then the final question is asked.

4. Is the ban or regulation no more extensive than necessary? That is, the Court considers whether the ban or regulation will place constraints on a company so that it would be unable to succeed or if there is a reasonable fit between the ban and the government interest.

There is considerable case law on the First Amendment and advertising, which we will not delve into here. However, we can illustrate how the Central Hudson test works with one particular case: *44 Liquormart v. Rhode Island.*

A retail liquor store, 44 Liquormart, ran a series of newspaper advertisements that featured a number of different products, including products that contained alcohol (e.g., beer) and products that did not (e.g., pretzels). In these ads, 44 Liquormart featured brand names and occasional images of products that contained alcohol (e.g., a six-pack of Budweiser beer) but did not feature prices for these products. However, the ads featured the store's low prices for products such as peanuts or pretzels.

The state of Rhode Island, where 44 Liquormart was located, had a law that prohibited price advertising for alcohol products. The retailer was fined for breaking this law, although 44 Liquormart's ads did not contain prices for alcohol products. Commissioners on the Rhode Island Liquor Control Administration levied the fine because they perceived that the ads contained an implied suggestion that liquor prices were very low at 44 Liquormart, just like the advertised prices on pretzels, peanuts, and other snacks. Thus, the ads provided an implied price of alcohol products, even if they did not explicitly give the price, which was in violation of the law.

So let us use the Central Hudson test to determine the constitutionality of this law that banned advertising for alcohol products where prices (even if not for alcohol products) were featured. The first question in the Central Hudson test asks whether the product is a legal product and whether the ads were misleading. Although not legal for everyone, liquor is a legal product for adults to purchase. In addition, the ads contained information about products sold at 44 Liquormart that included truthful information about prices for appropriate products. Therefore, the ads were truthful ads for legal products.

The second question of the Central Hudson test asks whether there is a substantial government interest in banning the advertising message. The state of Rhode Island has a substantial interest in promoting temperance (Linder, 2002), given health care costs, drunk driving issues, and the like. This begins to suggest that a ban may be constitutional, but further questions must be addressed.

The third question of the Central Hudson test asks whether a ban on the advertising message would promote the government interest. It could be argued that banning any type of price-implied advertising of alcoholic beverages would promote the government's interest because associating liquor with bargain prices might induce higher alcohol consumption. The third question, then, also suggests that a ban may be constitutional, and the fourth question must be assessed.

In this case, the fourth question of the Central Hudson test was the one that was problematic for the Supreme Court. This question asks whether the ban on advertising is no more extensive than necessary to achieve the government's interest. The Supreme Court held that the ban on 44 Liquormart's advertising was unconstitutional, concluding that there was not a reasonable fit between the ad prohibition and the goal of cutting alcohol consumption. Justice John Paul Stevens, writing for the Court, indicated that:

> It is perfectly obvious that alternative forms of regulation that would not involve any restriction on speech would be more likely to achieve the State's goal of promoting temperance. Higher prices can be maintained either by direct regulation or by increased taxation. Per capita purchases could be limited, as is the case with prescription drugs. Even educational campaigns focused on the problems of excessive, or even moderate, drinking might prove to be more effective. (Linder, 2002)

Therefore, the Supreme Court felt that Rhode Island should have done more to address issues of temperance before a ban on price advertising for liquor products was appropriate.

An Uneasy Relationship

From the perspective of advertising practitioners, the First Amendment is beneficial in that courts seek to balance the interests of both the senders of messages and the receivers of messages, taking into account the content of the messages and the medium itself (Vanden Bergh & Katz, 1999). Additionally, the Central Hudson test uses a prescriptive method to evaluate advertising messages in a consistent way. Practitioners believe that the test works well with traditional advertising messages that can be isolated and evaluated separately from other marketing activities.

However, there is still an unclear definition of commercial speech beyond that of traditional advertisements appearing in recognized traditional media (Vanden Bergh & Katz, 1999). The growth of the Internet, which is an international medium, has created new concerns and issues with advertising and persuasive messages. Many have asked whether unsolicited commercial e-mail, or spam, is protected by the First Amendment, given that it is often intruding into a private place: someone's computer mailbox, which is often in their home.

Additionally, some critics of the Supreme Court have suggested that the Central Hudson test is confusing and applied inconsistently. The Central Hudson test is an example of ad hoc balancing; that is, the Court looks at the individual situation and balances the choices (Wood, 2000). Critics argue that instead of finding a reasonable balance on a case-by-case basis, a decision regarding the protection of commercial speech for legal products and services should be definitively created by the Supreme Court.

Finally, some scholars do not believe that commercial speech should have any protection under the First Amendment whatsoever. Speech for profit-making goals should not be seen as equivalent to speech for democratic goals. The profit orientation of commercial speech may represent a coercive influence, which in turn should deprive advertisers and their agents of any constitutional protections for freedom of speech. Advertising's primary role is to generate profits for the advertisers, and so there cannot be a connection between protecting speech and "any vision, or attitude, or value of the individual or group engaged in advocacy" (Baker, 1976, p. 34).

However, the volumes of case law addressing protections for commercial speech suggest that it will be difficult to take away the current level of protection from advertisers and marketers anytime in the near future. In addition, there are several other groups involved in analyzing and regulating messages in the broad media "fish bowl" where advertising lives. Next, we examine the role of the Federal Trade Commission in regulating advertising.

Advertising and the
Federal Trade Commission

The Federal Trade Commission (FTC) was created in 1914 and is sanctioned by the government to prevent unfair competition as well as to monitor and deter false, fraudulent, misleading, or deceptive advertising in interstate commerce. False and misleading advertising falls under the FTC's jurisdiction because it is seen as an unfair trade practice. Today, the FTC's role has evolved to one that regulates advertising messages to ensure that consumers make product choices based on complete, truthful, and nondeceptive advertising (Russell & Lane, 2002).

False and Deceptive Advertising

The FTC clearly defines false and deceptive advertising. Advertising is deceptive when there is a representation in the advertisement (e.g., a description, an image, or a promise) or an omission in the advertisement (e.g., leaving out an important piece of information) that is likely to mislead consumers to their detriment. Two points merit additional clarification. First, the FTC uses the notion of a reasonable consumer in determining whether advertising is deceptive. Thus, an advertisement could be problematic if an average or reasonable consumer would be misled by the message. A single voice complaining that an advertisement is deceptive may not warrant sanctions by the FTC if that individual is not deemed a reasonable consumer. Second, the idea of consumer detriment focuses primarily on some type of economic detriment. Specifically, if an individual purchases a product based on deceptive information provided in an advertisement, the

FTC would find that he or she was misled to his or her detriment because the individual suffered a monetary loss from the purchase. If the advertising was misleading but no one purchased the product, the advertising may not warrant sanctioning because an obvious detriment is not evident. To summarize, the FTC uses a three-part test to evaluate deceptive or untruthful advertising:

1. There must be a representation, omission, or practice that is likely to mislead the consumer.

2. The act or practice must be evaluated from the perspective of a reasonable consumer.

3. The representation, omission, or practice must be material—that is, likely to affect a consumer's choice or use of a product or service (Russell & Lane, 2002).

It is important to note that advertisers are responsible for claims that are reasonably implied from their advertisements, as well as claims that are expressly stated. These requirements apply to all objective claims, including those made using consumer testimonials (Russell & Lane, 2002).

The FTC becomes aware of deceptive advertising from a range of sources, including consumers, other advertisers, or the FTC staff, and they have the power to investigate any claim of deception from any of these sources. Investigations of advertising charged with being deceptive generally begin with the collection of substantiation from advertisers. Substantiation is the advertisers' support for claims that are made in advertising messages, and advertisers must prove that the claims made in their advertisements are truthful. For example, if laundry detergent A advertises that its product makes white shirts brighter than laundry detergent B, laundry detergent A may have to provide some type of scientific evidence that its product produces the advertised results.

The FTC's Powers

The FTC has several tools that can be used to address deceptive advertising. If the FTC finds that an advertisement is deceptive, the advertiser may be asked to sign a consent decree. The consent decree is a document that does not admit to deception, yet acknowledges that the advertiser will stop running the sanctioned advertisement (Russell & Lane, 2002). If an advertiser chooses not to sign the consent decree or if an ad that is found deceptive continues to run after the consent decree is signed, the FTC has several additional courses of action. The FTC can fine the advertiser, order the advertiser to stop running the advertisements (a cease-and-desist order), and/or require the advertiser to run corrective advertisements. Corrective advertisements have to clearly correct the deceptive message earlier aired.

In addition to these sanctions, advertisers may also be asked to redress consumer injury. Specifically, advertisers may have to refund money that consumers paid for products or services with deceptive advertising messages or pay for damages inflicted by the product. This latter redress is only invoked if there is a violation of a cease-and-desist order (Rotzoll & Haefner, 1996).

Another Uneasy Relationship

The FTC's strongest power over the advertising industry is its sanctioning power. The FTC can stop deceptive advertising and demand economic reparations from advertisers that are found in violation of FTC regulations. However, many criticize the FTC as an ineffective regulatory group. There are several reasons for this assertion, and criticisms of the role and the functions of the FTC are widespread and, at times, at opposite ends of the spectrum.

For example, the FTC has been criticized as being a server of "efficient markets rather than a guarantor of public rights and responsibilities" (Cross, 2000, p. 203). This means that the FTC will favor business and economic profits over the rights and concerns of individuals. In contrast, though, the FTC has been criticized for having commissioners "appointed by the federal government" who are primarily from the legal professions and not necessarily experts in business, advertising, or behavioral science (Nicosia, 1974). Therefore, commissioners' lack of business sense makes their abilities to provide adequate regulation questionable.

The FTC's method in evaluating cases and claims has been met with criticism. For example, the FTC has been criticized for only looking at the verbal components of claims made in television advertising (e.g., dialogue, voice-overs, or words appearing on the screen). It has been suggested that this is because the FTC is populated by lawyers and other legally trained staff, whose orientation and training focus on words, not images. These individuals may ignore visual imagery, which can often be just as misleading as the verbal components (Richards & Zakia, 1981). This ties into an additional criticism of how the FTC evaluates messages. The FTC focuses solely on the explicit content of the language, not the meanings that people create from the language. The FTC does not monitor the emotional and psychological impacts of advertising messages, and the FTC has been faulted for not expanding their definition of injury to include emotional injury, not only material injury.

The FTC has been challenged to expand their scope not only in terms of types of injury but also in terms of the range of messages they evaluate. Currently, only national ads come under the FTC's jurisdiction of regulating and protecting interstate competition (Clark, 1988). Thus, several categories of advertisements fall outside the scope of the FTC. For example, the FTC cannot examine categories such as lottery ads because lotteries are state entities and the purchase of tickets must be within a single state. They also do not examine local advertising, which is often retail advertising. Many local retailers are faulted for misleading advertising, particularly regarding small-print disclosures for high-ticket items such as cars and appliances. Often, retail advertisers will offer very low down payment prices for high-ticket items, yet will have high interest terms, which are only disclosed in small print at the end of a commercial or print advertisement. Consumers often overlook such information, may be misled by the low down payment message, and may suffer material harm when they agree to expensive repayment programs.

The FTC has also been criticized for having too broad a scope, given their size, which has been decreasing steadily since the 1980s. (Jacobson & Mazur, 1995). The FTC's jurisdiction now includes regulation of commercial messages on the Internet. The Internet's influence on commerce within the United States and outside its boundaries is becoming a huge force, yet many believe that the FTC is not sufficiently staffed to handle the responsibility of regulating the Internet.

Finally, procedural issues are a cause for concern. The body of complaints seen by the FTC is of actual or alleged abuse or violations of the law because the FTC does not investigate an advertisement until a complaint is made (Nicosia, 1974). Since what they see is at the "dark end" of the spectrum and not a random sample of advertisements airing in the media, they are limited in their ability to provide prescriptive assistance to make all advertising better. When the FTC does get involved in areas outside the legal domain, it has little influence to instigate change. For example, the FTC has been involved in investigating violent content directed to children when there are not any laws prohibiting such messages (Phillips, 1997). Thus, compliance with recommendations on such advertising is not as successful as anticipated.

The FTC is not the only governmental agency that regulates and monitors advertising. Several other government groups are also involved, but these groups tend to serve specific categories, and we will discuss them in more detail in the appropriate chapters.

Advertising and Self-Regulation

Self-regulation is when an industry polices itself. For many industries, self-regulation is based on professional codes of ethics or conduct that are enforceable by a regulating body (e.g., the American Bar Association's code of conduct for lawyers who belong to the bar). The advertising industry has no such enforceable code, primarily because advertising is a business of communication, and as we just discussed, communication is protected by the First Amendment. Therefore, free speech guarantees may be compromised if there is any type of legally enforced code of conduct in the advertising industry.

The National Advertising Review Council

First Amendment protection does not mean that the advertising industry itself is not involved in regulating those involved in the practice of advertising. The industry has a specific entity designed for self-regulatory purposes. In 1971, a self-regulatory structure, the National Advertising Review Council (NARC), was established through the joint efforts of the Association of National Advertisers (ANA), the Association of American Advertising Agencies (AAAA), the American Advertising Federation (AAF), and the Council for Better Business Bureaus (CBBB). The NARC is composed of two groups. The National Advertising Division (NAD) is the main group that receives, evaluates, and acts on complaints from the public, from agencies and other business concerns, and from internal staff members, although complaints come primarily from within the advertising industry. The staff of the NAD seeks to evaluate the merits of the issues raised in advertising complaints by checking the information using accepted standards of truth and accuracy. Therefore, the NAD functions much like the FTC in this regard.

The NAD's evaluations of complaints, and their recommendation as to how problematic messages might be changed or whether ads should be withdrawn, are sent directly to the advertiser that is the focus of the complaint. If the advertiser does not wish to comply with the NAD's recommendation, the advertiser can appeal to the second group that comprises the NAD. This group is the National Advertising Review Board (NARB), a five-person panel that is made up of three representatives from client organizations, one advertising agency representative, and one public member. They evaluate appeals as well as any other types of issues that the NAD cannot resolve. They also can refer problematic cases directly to the FTC.

Still More Uneasy Relationships

Self-regulatory agencies like the NARC can be very useful; former FTC Chairman Robert Pitofsky complimented the NARC stating that self-regulation "can deal quickly and flexibly with a wide range of advertising issues and brings the cumulated experience and judgement of an industry to bear" (Federal Trade Commission, 1999, p. 6).

However, numerous criticisms of industry self-regulation in general, and of the NARC in particular, exist. The most serious criticism is that the NARC has no real power: It cannot impose fines, and advertisers do not have to cooperate with its recommendations (Clark, 1988). One advertiser said that it refused to comply because "no one, other than the NAD, had questioned its advertising" (Clark, 1988, p. 138).

Another problem is that most consumers are unaware that such a program exists (Rotzoll & Haefner, 1996). Most of the complaints tend to be one advertiser complaining about the actions of another. This is seen as problematic since advertisers may use this process as a way to keep competitors in check (Clark, 1988). Clark further argues that the analysis of comparative claims used by the NARC is too stringent, preventing small businesses from taking on large ones because they don't have the resources to prove claims to the point of acceptability by self-regulatory agents.

The Advertising Agency and Legislation

You may have noted in the previous discussions that the advertiser, which is an advertising agency's client, is seen as the responsible party in matters of debate on advertising content. Constitutional law, the FTC, and self-regulatory systems recognize that advertisers are ultimately responsible for the content of the messages that they pay for. Agency contracts with their clients tend to absolve agencies legally from any blame from the message, and most liability issues are handled in these contracts (A. Cuneo, 2000). In these contracts, advertising agencies are protected from lawsuits involving the accuracy of claims provided to them by clients, and they are absolved from responsibility if consumers suffer damages if something goes wrong with the product after it is purchased.

Recently, though, an agency was the subject of legal action. In this case, the agency produced an advertisement that was acceptable from a legal perspective but unacceptable for other reasons. The situation involved athletic retailer Just for Feet and the Saatchi & Saatchi advertising agency.

The Just for Feet Fiasco

In 1999, the retailer Just for Feet ran an advertisement during the Super Bowl that offended many people. The commercial presented the story of a barefoot African runner being pursued by a group of people in a Jeep-type vehicle. After the runner drank water presumably laced with some type of drug, the group in the Jeep captured him and forced him to wear a pair of running shoes (available from Just for Feet) .

New York Times writer Stuart Elliott said that the commercial was appallingly insensitive, and others called the commercial racist and culturally imperialist (Shallitt, 1999). Just for Feet then sued its agency, Saatchi & Saatchi Business Communications in Rochester, New York, for more than $10 million in damages for advertising malpractice (A. Z. Cuneo, 2000, p. 23).

In Just for Feet's lawsuit, the retailer claimed that the finished execution of the Super Bowl spot was nothing like the concept that the agency originally presented to them. When executives at Just for Feet saw the commercial, they told agency personnel that they were uncomfortable with the spot.

However, executives at Saatchi & Saatchi "reassured them that the spot would be well received based on their experiences with such ads" (A. Z. Cuneo, 2000, p. 23). When asked about the possibility of producing a different spot, agency executives responded that it was too late to create something in time to air during the Super Bowl.

Lawyers and executives at Saatchi & Saatchi argued that a charge of malpractice was ridiculous because advertising as a business has "no explicit guidelines and standards, and therefore, it cannot have committed malpractice" (A. Z. Cuneo, 2000, p. 23). Additionally, executives at the agency pointed to the commercial's acceptance by the Fox network's standards and practices department (Fox was airing the Super Bowl that year). The system of checks and balances had worked because the commercial had passed through a major screen that is set up to keep blatantly unacceptable advertising off the air. Finally, many in the advertising industry responded to the controversy by reiterating what the FTC and the NARC support: The client is ultimately responsible. The client approved and paid for the commercial and therefore needs to take responsibility for any repercussions that may occur from the message. Furthermore, client personnel from Just for Feet needed to stand up to their agency if they truly did not want to run the advertising it recommended.

However, not all agency personnel agree with these opinions. Some agency executives believed that while clients cannot be compelled to do advertising that is illegal, immoral, or in bad taste, agencies should tell clients of any risks that may be inherent in the running of the advertising. In the Just for Feet example, Saatchi & Saatchi should have alerted their client that certain groups might perceive the message as in bad taste. Others say that advertising agencies claiming no responsibility for offensive messages are the same as agencies admitting that they have no expertise.

Writing in *Ad Age* magazine, advertising professor John Eighmey called on agencies to take more responsibility for the meaning of the messages they create when he wrote: "Advertising accidents can be prevented. Each of us has to have the courage to question our pre-conceived notions, and to expand our own view of the world. Advertising should be about breaking barriers, not reinforcing them. Let each one of us who loves advertising pledge to do this now" (1999, p. 24).

Just for Feet filed for bankruptcy protection at the end of 1999 and was subsequently acquired by FootStar in 2000. Although this marked the end of the lawsuit, the door has been opened to future advertising malpractice lawsuits.

Summary

In this chapter, we examined the various groups involved in the regulation of advertising messages and investigated how the advertising agency's role is interpreted and may be open to interpretation in the future. There is not a single, perfect way to evaluate and regulate advertising, and this is probably a positive thing. No single entity has complete power over advertising messages today. The Constitution, the FTC, and self-regulation are complementary regulatory bodies that can address a range of issues at different levels and set reasonable examples for the industry to follow. The focus tends to be on what Rotzoll terms "hard" issues—that is, explicit information and messages contained in advertising (Rotzoll & Haefner, 1996). The Just for Feet lawsuit, however, provides an initial way that the "soft" issues may be addressed in the future, which is not necessarily through litigation but from improved agency/client communication and agreements as to standards that should apply to the creation of advertising.

This chapter focused on traditional advertising messages. In the next chapter, we will look at nontraditional messages that increasing numbers of advertisers are using to circumvent the cluttered advertising environment and that can showcase brands in new and different ways. Although these nontraditional messages have not come under the same level of scrutiny that traditional advertising has, this may change in the future, and the concepts discussed in this chapter would apply to these nontraditional messages also.

5

Beyond Subliminal

The Pervasiveness of Persuasion

All that I desire to point out is the general principle that Life imitates Art far more than Art imitates Life.

—Oscar Wilde

Persuasive communication exists in all areas in our society. Have you ever tried to talk a professor into giving you a better grade, tried to avoid getting a traffic ticket, or negotiated with a vendor at a yard sale? These are all examples of persuasive communication: You are advocating your own admittedly biased point of view to convince someone to change his or her mind.

In Chapter 2, the difference between persuasion and manipulation was discussed. We hope we made clear that advertising is persuasive. Still, as advertisers, we need to acknowledge that persuasive communication can have a strong influence in our society. In addition, we must acknowledge that the messages we create are biased and that we are advocates for our clients.

Given this advocacy position, the role of persuasive communication in our society is important to consider. We must recognize that some people may be uncomfortable with persuasive communication, so we must acknowledge and evaluate their suggestions on how to use persuasive communications ethically.

_____ Persuasive Content and Subliminal Messages

Most advertising messages are a mix of informational and persuasive content. The persuasive aspect of such messages comes in two forms. First, the advertiser chooses specific attributes of each product or service for inclusion in the message. Often, such selected attributes are those that will be important or meaningful to consumers. Second, the message may indicate how consumers will think or feel once they have decided to purchase or use the product. Consumers make the decision about what to buy based on how the product or service, as described, will address their own needs and wants. Advertising that does not present such a point of view would be ineffectual, then, and truly wasteful of both the advertiser's and the consumer's time and money (Nicosia, 1974).

It is commonly recognized that most consumers recognize that traditional commercials, such as those we see on television and hear on the radio every day, are advocacies for products and services. Today, however, critics are increasingly concerned about the types of persuasive messages that "slip in under the radar"—that is, those that consumers do not register as being traditional advertisements. Instead, persuasive messages can be presented in ways that have been described as "sneaky" or "subliminal."

Some people believe that advertising works subliminally; that is, advertising places a message under an individual's margin of consciousness. In turn, messages can create some level of anxiety that can be relieved only by purchasing a product or service to address the anxiety. This product or service is presumably one we would not normally buy (Twitchell, 1996). As we discussed in Chapter 2, the myth of subliminal advertising has been in existence since the 1950s and persists to this day.

Have you ever looked for sexual imagery in an alcohol ad featuring a photograph of ice cubes? This idea originated with the best-known proponent of subliminal advertising, Wilson Key. Key wrote a series of books that suggested that advertising agencies, specifically art directors, embed advertising with symbols that represent sexual and death-related imagery to create feelings of anxiousness, which leads to increased drinking. Somewhat in response, the Federal Communications Commission (FCC) created a policy in 1974 that stated if TV stations knowingly ran subliminal advertising, they could be found in violation of the public trust and risked having their licenses revoked (Teinowitz, 2000). However, even this action did little to diminish the public's perceptions that subliminal advertising does exist. Even the denial of professionals will not reduce the public's view that subliminal advertising exists. A recent study of advertising professionals found that 95% of respondents denied use or knowledge of use of subliminal advertising in the profession (Rogers & Seiler, 1994). Indeed, most respondents said that they did not use it because there was no evidence that it worked (Rogers & Seiler, 1994).

Smelling a Rat

In the 2000 presidential campaign, the subliminal advertising controversy was reinvigorated with a television spot in support of then-candidate George W. Bush. The spot criticized then-Vice President Al Gore's prescription drug plan, and the word *rats* appeared on the screen for about one thirtieth of a second. The word was highlighted as part of the word bureaucrats. It was seen by an engineer in Seattle, who videotaped the ad, replayed it using slow motion, and timed how long the word appeared on the commercial. He then forwarded his findings to officials in the Gore campaign. The Gore campaign alerted the media soon after this happened (Mishra, 2000).

The Republican Party said that ad used a "visual drumbeat" to reinforce the advertisement's central message about the Democrats' policy toward prescription drug payments. Republicans identified bureaucrats as the gate-keepers for such payments. The Republican Party denied that they were try-ing to use subliminal techniques to suggest that bureaucrats were rats (Teinowitz, 2000). However, the FCC, referring back to their 1974 policy, sent letters to 216 television stations that may have broadcast the adver-tisement, giving the stations one week to express their opinions on whether subliminal advertising was used in this spot (*New York Times*, 2000). If executives at the stations knew that the commercial contained the word *rats* prior to airing it, the FCC would be able to charge the stations with accept-ing deceptive advertising. This could lead to a letter of admonishment or the revocation of the station's license (*New York Times*, 2000). In responses from 179 stations that aired the ad, 162 said they were not aware the ad flashed the word *rats*. In contrast, executives at the balance of the stations questioned whether the word placement was truly subliminal because they said they could clearly read the word. The FCC closed its investigation without trapping any rats.

Active and Passive Consumers Revisited

Why does this fascination with subliminal advertising continue? There are several reasons. First, many critics still believe in the idea of the passive consumer. As discussed earlier, passive consumers believe that they are powerless against advertising. The term *subliminal*, literally meaning "beneath the surface," supports this idea of a lack of control among pas-sive consumers. To put it simply, if we do not know an advertising message is there, we cannot know how to avoid it or make it go away. Additionally, the phenomenon known as the *third person effect* may come into play. The third person effect states that although individuals believe that they are active consumers and processors of information, they will say they know others who have been affected by the subliminal strength of advertising.

Active consumers would not be susceptible to subliminal advertising because by nature they are actively involved with absorbing the information that they see and hear in advertisements. In addition, it is contradictory to suggest that individuals can perceive anything presented below their thresh-old of perception: They can either consciously perceive messages or they cannot (Vanden Bergh & Katz, 1999).

Today, the idea of subliminal advertising has started to take on a new meaning. Specifically, subliminal advertising has begun to refer to advertis-ing that is sneaky in that a persuasive message appears in a place where we do not expect to see one. A message that does not have the traditional context of a television or magazine advertisement may be more persuasive than the norm. Furthermore, the environment in which the message appears can enhance its persuasiveness. One specific area that is of concern to many is the idea of product placement.

Product Placement

Product placement is defined as a paid product message aimed at influencing a movie or other media audience through the planned and unobtrusive entry of a branded product into the medium's content (Balasubramanian, 1994). In a way, product placement is a hybrid of advertising and publicity because it involves using movies or other media content to incorporate brands in return for money or some other promotional consideration (Gould, Gupta, & Graner-Krauter, 2000). Advertising agencies are often involved in placing clients' products in television shows and feature films. Other times, a specialist firm acts as a liaison between agency and studio and obtains scripts far in advance so advertiser can evaluate a range of potential product placements (Balasubramanian, 1994).

Product placement in films and television programs is a new spin on an old technique. In the early days of television, brand names were in the program title (e.g., the *Texaco Star Theatre*). There has always been a tradition of sponsored content: Shakespeare's sonnets were written for hire, and James Bond novels mentioned brand names of cars (Campbell, 2001). While the use of products in the title of programs has never been a concern to the FCC, the Commission discouraged program tie-ins through product placement before the 1960s. The networks themselves voluntarily adopted standards that kept brand name products out of TV shows in a 1960 amendment to the Communications Act (Balasubramanian, 1994). These standards were relaxed in the 1980s. Today, paid product placement appears in all manner of media, including films, television, novels, and more. Product placement is seen by many advertisers as a targeted and cost-effective way to reach consumers (Wells, 2001).

Product Placement in Film

Ever since a little alien had a snack of Reese's Pieces, the level of product placement in movies has been increasing. Movies are expensive to make, and there is no guarantee that box-office receipts will make a profit for the film studio or even recoup the costs of making the film. Once the movie is made, additional funds are needed to promote the film: Movie marketing costs sometimes equal the cost of the film, and product placement subsidizes these costs (Balasubramanian, 1994). Today, about 15% of revenue

Figures 5.1 and 5.2   A range of products and services has been placed in feature films.

from feature films is generated from product placement (Twitchell, 1996). Some recent examples of film product placement include:

- The Robert Altman movie *Dr. T and the Women* featured Titleist golf clubs, provided by Titleist free of charge. Producers wanted this product because it was the choice of LPGA golfers (Bamberger, Kim, & Mravic, 2000).
- Nike products have appeared in films with sports-related story lines such as *Love and Basketball*, *Bring It On*, and *What Women Want* (Bamberger et al., 2000).
- Apple computers have been used on camera by stars in action movies, including *Independence Day* and *Mission Impossible*.
- Internet service provider America OnLine was featured in the film *You've Got Mail* (Figure 5.1).
- A Wilson volleyball (Figure 5.2) was an important character in the Tom Hanks film *Castaway*.

Product Placement in Television

Television product placement runs the gamut from characters in sitcoms using products (e.g., Jerry Seinfeld and Pez) to story lines and even entire shows built around advertisers. The Chinese Wall between entertainment programming and advertisers has never been strong, and today, it is more like a revolving door. Here are some examples of recent product placements on television:

- In an episode of *The West Wing*, the presidential staff had a working dinner with food from fast-food retailer Panda Express (Cebrzynski, 2002).
- Cosmetics giant Revlon was incorporated into a 3-month story line on the soap opera *All My Children*. A character in the soap opera went to work as a "spy" at Revlon, a major competitor to the Enchantment cosmetics company owned by popular daytime character Erica Kane (played by actress Susan Lucci).
- One fourth of the clients of the Interpublic Group ad agency funded the six-episode NBC show *Lost*. During the show, participants drank Dasani bottled water (a Coke product) and used survival items packed in crates featuring the logo of a home improvement store Lowe's (Wells, 2001). Paid advertisements for the same clients also ran during the program.
- The CBS show *Survivor* features a plethora of paid placements, including Snicker's bars, VISA cards, and Doritos.

It is anticipated that we will continue to see product placement influencing programming content. In fact, ABC TV planned a reality show for the fall 2001 season called *The Runner,* where sponsors designed how product placements were woven into the series ("'Runner' Test," 2001). The program was put on hold after the September 11 terrorist attacks but may appear in a future season. The growth of interactive TV will also increase the range of product placements in programming. For example, plans are in the works that will enable you to use your computer to click on video images and order clothes and other furnishings from shows you watch.

Product Placement in Other Content

Product placement does not stop with traditional media content. Today, we are seeing product placements in many different places. Here are some recent examples:

- Italian Jeweler Bulgari commissioned best-selling writer Fay Weldon to write a novel in which their product was prominently featured. The novel, *The Bulgari Connection,* was published in November 2001. Originally, it was produced as a party favor and was scheduled to have only 750 copies printed. It is now available in both the United States and the United Kingdom (Campbell, 2001).

- Ad agency Fallon Worldwide helped client BMW produce five short films featuring their product that now can be downloaded from the Internet (Wells, 2001). Well-known filmmakers such as Ang Lee and Guy Ritchie directed the films.

• Characters in video games wear clothing and accessories from a company known as Quiksilver (Bannan, 2002). Today, much of video game advertising is a bartered product placement: Characters in video games wear Quiksilver products, and the video games are sold in Quiksilver retail stores.

Intended Effects

Like any decision involving a persuasive message, there are clear effects intended by the message in the medium selected as well as unintended effects or repercussions to the message that may or may not have been anticipated before the message aired. There are several intended effects to product placement.

The Von Restorff Effect

The Von Restorff effect suggests that any technique that increases the novelty of particular products or leads them to be unexpected enhances the recall of those products (Balasubramanian, 1994). Therefore, placing a familiar brand in an unexpected context will have positive effects in terms of product awareness and recall. People recognize and/or recall brands promoted in movies, and some researchers have found that prominent product placements perform better than television ads in creating brand recall among consumers (Gould et al., 2000)

Increased Authenticity of the Content

Product placement increases the realism and authenticity of the story being told (Bamberger et al., 2000; Bannan, 2002). In pre-product placement days, TV shows might have a character drinking out of a silver can labeled *soda*, and such images do not ring true with viewers. It is much more realistic to have the soda can labeled with the name of an actual beverage, and enhances the viewing experience for all involved. In addition, there is some advantage to blending products into the story line; the persuasive message does not interrupt the flow of the story, and consumers may get less annoyed at interruptions. Research has shown that of all consumers in the world, U.S. consumers are more accepting of and likely to purchase products shown in movies than consumers in other countries (Gould et al., 2000).

Indirect Product Endorsement

Products seen in TV programs and films receive an indirect endorsement from the characters that use the product on the screen. For example, Tom

Cruise wore Ray-Ban sunglasses in the films *Risky Business* and *Top Gun*, and he has been continually associated with the brand for many years. Such an endorsement has several benefits. It can reinforce positive feelings among users as to why they bought and use the product ("I wear the same sunglasses that Tom Cruise wears!"). Additionally, the endorsement may influence nonusers to think about purchasing the product ("I can be like Tom Cruise, at least in terms of the sunglasses I wear!"). Finally, the image of the endorser can be transferred to the product and to the user's self-perception.

Developmental Support

Product placement allows for revenue streams that may permit more films, books, and Web sites to be developed and supported. Author Fay Weldon believes that sponsorships similar to hers (for the book *The Bulgari Connection*) could help struggling writers earn a decent living so they can spend more time working on their craft.

Unintended Effects

Every planned action, or effect, tends to result in unintended effects. Advertisers do not intend advertising messages to be harmful because that would not be in the best interest of the brand. Any mass-mediated message that relies on interpretation of meaning by consumers has the potential to generate unintended effects. As an advertiser, it is important to try to anticipate unintended effects, assess the impact of such effects, and examine how to minimize these effects if necessary. Some of the unintended effects for product placement that have been identified are outlined next.

Content May Be Compromised

Increased involvement by advertisers in all type of content may lead to the content being controlled solely by the products and their producers (Wells, 2001). This may affect the content in several ways. First, creativity could be stifled because product producers will have definite ideas of how their products should and should not be used in TV, films, and the like (Campbell, 2001). For example, Bulgari might not have wanted their jewels to be used as a murder weapon or worn by drug dealers (Bruno, 2001). This concern is strengthened by observations that the individuals on the advertising side who deal with product placement tend to be media buyers and planners, persons not particularly trained in program decision making (Wells, 2001).

The Wall Is Torn Down

Product placement represents the continued blurring of entertainment and selling (Rothenberg, 2001). The interests and opinions of target audiences of media content become less important. Viewers, listeners, and readers have been "relegated to the back seat while advertisers call the shots" ("'Runner' Test," 2001, p. 20). There is an associated concern with books and other types of previously nonsponsored content now becoming crassly commercial, which can ultimately destroy the credibility of such content.

Controversial Products
Circumvent Advertising Restrictions and Bans

Placement of certain types of products, such as cigarettes, in mediated content is seen as a way to circumvent other media bans that exist for the product (Gould et al., 2000). Products placed in adult-oriented films and programs can be viewed by inappropriate audiences to which they are not directed. For example, underage viewers can see products like alcoholic beverages, cigarettes, and guns. The context of the message is also a concern; for example, some feature films have presented smokers as powerful and successful people, which is problematic for opponents of smoking. The American Lung Association and the Canadian Cancer Society say that there should be a new movie rating system that includes tobacco use in the calculation to reduce the number of young people exposed to such messages (Wake, 2002).

Recently, the film *In the Bedroom* featured main character Sissy Spacek smoking Marlboros throughout the film. The studio releasing the film also distributed publicity stills with her smoking and with a pack of Marlboros placed beside her. The activist group Smoke Free Movies, which aims to sharply reduce the film industry's usefulness to Big Tobacco's marketing efforts, refers to the effects of product placement as dramatizing smoking and glamorizing the Marlboro brand by associating it with a star like Sissy Spacek.

_____ Thinking About Product Placement

After intended and unintended effects have been identified, the next logical step is to think of ways to maximize the intended effects and minimize the unintended effects. This deceptively simple statement does not emphasize the challenge that advertisers face in making the correct decisions.

In this book, we will not purport to tell you the right and wrong decisions to make because every client and every set of circumstances are different. However, we will provide you with areas to consider when making such decisions.

Consider Environment of Placement

The attitudes of the audience toward the content will affect their attitudes toward product placement (Weaver & Oliver, 2000). This suggests that placing products in television, where ratings and other data clearly indicate program popularity, may be a safer choice than product placement in feature films. With a feature film, audience reaction is unknown until the film is released. If negative attitudes are prevalent, the product's image may be damaged.

Consider How to Measure the Impact of Placement

From a pragmatic perspective, it is difficult to figure out the cost-benefit trade-offs or measure the persuasiveness of product placements (Balasubramanian, 1994). Therefore, the overall effects, positive or negative, are difficult to envision before the release of a film or the start of a television program. However, it is a good idea to determine ways to assess the effects of product placement advertising to determine if your client is getting its money's worth and if the benefits outweigh any potential detriments. Such techniques could include consumer surveys, focus groups, or interviews, which ask people to recall name-brand products in the content they view.

Evaluate Current Legislation

The FCC has sponsorship rules that must be considered during the placement of products in television programs. Specifically, programs must include an announcement stating clearly which sponsors paid for products that are featured prominently in the programs. Products that are furnished as "backdrops" for scenes do not have to be disclosed (Avery & Ferraro, 2000). Recently, legal scholars have been debating whether product placements fall under commercial speech regulations. If the courts rule that product placement messages have limited protections, then placement of some products (e.g., cigarettes, alcoholic beverages) in some programs may not be possible.

Avoid Misleading Messages

Advertisers should evaluate whether placements are misleading. Recently, some agencies have negotiated product placements in films not only for their client's products but also for products of their client's competitors. Specifically, the client's product would be seen used by the hero of the film, with the competitor's products used by the villain. This type of placement could imply a negative connotation about a competitor that some suggest is misleading (Avery & Ferraro, 2000).

Consider Placement-Participation Combination

A recent study showed that the most effective communication occurred when product placement was accompanied by paid commercial advertisement for the same product. Obviously, this type of combination will work best in television and not so well in film placement (Weaver & Oliver, 2000).

Summary

In this chapter, we examined the phenomenon of subliminal advertising and provided evidence to dispel myths that exist to this day about such advertising techniques. We then discussed product placement in television, film, and other mass-mediated content and provided ways for advertisers to examine such choices.

The next section of the book will examine people in advertising—specifically, portrayals of different types of people (men and women, minorities and majorities, elders and children) and the content of advertising messages to these different groups. We will continue to identify intended and unintended effects of such portrayals and messages, as well as provide concepts advertisers should consider in decision making.

6
Advertising Choices

Influences of Stereotypes and Taste

I am sure I can't define good taste any more successfully than our highest courts can. Indeed, when one goes to the theatre or to the movies, he must wonder if there are any bounds at all. Compared to that, advertising language has almost the moral purity of a Gregorian Chant.

—A. J. Seaman

Much of the actual "work" of advertising and advertising agencies involves choices: choices regarding whom to target, which media to purchase, or whether the magazine advertisement will be single page or a spread. To create an advertisement, advertising professionals make dozens of choices. All these choices made during the development of an advertising campaign help in the creation of the meanings of the advertisement. Thus, all choices can be important, and all choices can potentially have societal effects that go beyond the goal of the advertising message itself.

In this chapter, we discuss two specific choices advertising agency creatives make during the development of advertising campaigns and examine how advertising professionals select specific imagery and messages that can shape societal beliefs. First, we investigate the role of stereotypes in advertising messages and in society. Second, we examine how some agency personnel choose to "push the envelope" in terms of propriety by selecting messages and imagery that may be perceived by some as inappropriate and in poor taste. We look at how questions of taste are viewed by the public and can be addressed by advertising creatives.

Stereotypes in Advertising

The term *stereotype* originated as a printing term: A stereotype was originally a metal printing plate that was cast from a mold of a raised printing surface. It is much closer to what we think of as a photocopy today. In that way, then, the term stereotype is value free: It denotes neither a positive nor a negative characteristic. Today, we define stereotypes as one group's generalized and widely accepted beliefs about the personal attributes of members of another group. The essence of a stereotype is the perception that every person who belongs to the group is a generic exemplum of a type rather than a unique individual (Taylor & Stern, 1997, p. 48).

We use the term stereotype today in a descriptive way that may have either positive or negative connotations (Taylor & Stern, 1997). These connotations derive from the quantitative and qualitative components of each specific stereotype. The quantitative aspect comes into play when we consider that most stereotypes originate because some proportion of a specific population is reflected in the stereotype. For example, take the following two statements:

1. Children love to play with toys.

2. Women love to shop.

If we think of the definition of a stereotype given earlier, we see that both statements could be defined as stereotypes. However, individuals would rarely describe the first statement as a stereotype but more as a statement of fact. The second statement might be seen as a stereotype because it treats all women as a generic exemplum of a type (shoppers). The problem, though, is that the second statement is not completely true. You have probably met at least one woman who does not like to shop. In fact, we could probably state that both statements are false because there may be a child somewhere that does not love to play with toys. To state the phrases correctly, we would have to say that *most* children love to play with toys or *some* women love to shop. As we quantitatively assess the proportion of the population that meets the statement, we can judge the quantitative component of the stereotype. By not including some indication of the size of the specific group, then, the statement suggests stereotypical behavior.

The qualitative aspect involves the context under which the statement is made. The term stereotype has a negative connotation today. If we are celebrating the freedom and carefree nature of childhood, we see the first statement positively and may not think of it as a stereotype. If we are suggesting that shopping is a wasteful and unproductive activity, we might see the second statement about women as stereotypical. When we see the characterization in a negative context, the stereotype takes on an unfavorable nature. When a characterization is used in a positive context, we may not always see it as a stereotype (Dobzynski, 2000).

We can better evaluate the quantitative and qualitative aspects of stereotypes in the advertising context and the roles of stereotypes in society by thinking about stereotypes from three different perspectives:

1. The range of stereotypes presented in advertising messages

2. The valence of stereotypes presented for a specific group

3. The frequency of the portrayals of each stereotype

We will discuss each of these individually.

Range of Stereotypes

If you watch television for half an hour, you will be able to develop a list of what you would consider stereotypes in both the programming content and the content of commercials. For example, a recent five-commercial block on a single television program presented the following stereotypes: the supermom, the computer geek, the trendy youth, the good dad, the dumb blonde, and the frat boy. It is likely that these descriptors have painted an image in your mind of the specific people in the advertisements and may even suggest the types of products that were advertised in the commercials featuring the characters.

Why do advertisements use so many stereotypes? Advertisements present brief dramatic stories with a message (i.e., a selling message) in a very short time period. For example, television commercials take place in 30 seconds, and most print advertisements fit into a single page of a magazine. Since stereotypes are considered the "coin of the realm of the dramatic arts" (Lerner, 2001, p. 16), using stereotypes in advertising messages quickly sets the stage for the messages: Stereotypes convey characters and images quickly and clearly.

Although the term stereotype has a negative connotation today, some stereotypes present positive images of a specific group of individuals, whereas other stereotypes present negative images. We will discuss some of these images in the upcoming chapters. At its best, advertising presents a range of images of one group of people. Therefore, people viewing the commercials do not think of individuals in that group as being one-dimensional but rather see individuals in the group as all being alike. For example, women between the ages of 20 and 30 are seen frequently in advertisements for a range of products and services. A variety of portrayals of this group are seen: executive, mom, student, artist, and so on.

Women over age 40, though, are seen much less frequently in commercials. When they appear, older women are often portrayed as suffering from medical problems. Although some older women do fit this category, many others do not. Since a limited range of portrayals of older women is presented, we do not get a true picture of older women in society from advertising messages.

30% Die hard
25% Knockout
45% Softy

100% Cotton

Nothing says you like cotton.
Comfortable, breathable, completely washable.
Just make sure the label says cotton.

cotton

Figure 6.1   Images of a woman with a baby in a stroller
and at bath time suggest "mom" to many.

Valence of Portrayals

Valence refers to the emotional significance of any given portrayal. To state it another way, we often connect positive or negative values to stereotypes. We choose the value depending on the context in which the specific stereotype appears and given the other types of images we see. For example, when you look at the advertisement in Figure 6.1, whom do you think the woman is? An advertisement featuring a woman depicted like the woman in Figure 6.1 (jogging with a baby jogger, playing with a child at bath time) would probably suggest "mom" to many viewers. Such an image appearing in a magazine like *Good Housekeeping* is likely to be perceived positively by the magazine's readers because many readers can personally relate to the image of the mom as nurturer. When the stereotyped attributes are positive, they can make a very quick linkage between an emotion (the pride of being a good mom) and an action (buying clothes and other products made out of cotton). Thus, advertisements suggest behaviors for people who see themselves as emulating the stereotype (Lerner, 2001).

When we think of stereotypes as negative, we are thinking about the context, or the qualitative aspect. Many believe that stereotypes are problematic because they have the ability to reduce people or objects to classes based on inferences that are made from an individual or social context (Vanden Bergh & Katz, 1999, p. 67). For example, if a working woman picks up *Good Housekeeping* in the dentist's waiting room and sees a number of "good mom" portrayals in the advertisements, she may think that society believes her place is in the home, not in the office. She may feel that society chastises her for breaking with tradition by working full time, or she may feel guilty for not being as good a mom as the ad suggests she could be. In this way, the portrayal may be negative.

Frequency of Portrayals

The idea or concept of a range of portrayals is very important to consider when contemplating stereotypes. A single advertisement or any onetime portrayal of a group will not create a stereotype. The continued reinforcement of information about a group develops the stereotype. In post–World War II America, for example, the majority of adult women were homemakers. In a 30-year period, though, the number of working women increased to 50% of all adult women. As women accepted and reveled in their new roles outside the home, advertising continued to portray women as homemakers and rarely recognized that women had roles other than the traditional role at home. Advertising messages continue to portray women in this homemaker role, even when statistics prove the quantitative aspect of the stereotype to be untrue. Such portrayals continue to irk many women to this day.

If we see a range of portrayals for a single group and we are consistently exposed to a range of portrayals, stereotyping is generally not a problem. It is when we see a single portrayal consistently, to the exclusion of other images, that the stereotype moves to an exemplum—that is, a single-faceted representation of a group. An incessant recurrence of a single depiction throughout mass media content, coupled with the paucity of compensating images, marks the depiction as a stereotype. Seeing one single, consistent portrayal of a group of people can affect how we perceive all members of the stereotyped group, either while we are creating advertising messages or when we encounter members of the group in the real world.

Let us consider the "good mom" stereotype again. In terms of the frequency of the portrayal, we would ask how often we see the "good mom" stereotype relative to other depictions of women in advertisements. If the only image we see is the "good mom" stereotype, we may come to think that women should only be found in the home. This could have the effect of limiting the roles of women in society.

As illustrated earlier, the individual most powerfully affected by a stereotype is the person targeted by the stereotype. Studies have shown that if you have knowledge of how others stereotype people who are part of your own demographic group, you will start acting that way. An experiment exposed selected groups of individuals to stereotypical imagery about their groups (e.g., blonde women are stupid, elders are forgetful) and then had them perform a series of intellectual and physical tasks. Those exposed to stereotypical images of their groups did worse on the tasks than those who were not exposed to the stereotypes (Begeley, 2000). This study suggests that if no one reminds you of a stereotype about your specific group, you will not be affected by the stereotype.

The real power of stereotypes is their ability to change the behavior of the person holding the stereotype. Begeley illustrates this with an observation about women. He suggests that one stereotype of women shows them strongly affected by premenstrual syndrome (PMS), a hormonal fluctuation that naturally occurs during a woman's monthly cycle. Begeley (2000) writes, "if you think women are ninnies ruled by hormonal swings, you don't name them CEO" (p. 67).

How Stereotypes Work

How do stereotypes work in our society in general? Two specific theories help to describe the process by which stereotypes create imagery among groups of people. These two theories are known as cultivation theory and expectancy theory.

Cultivation Theory

How have stereotypes become so powerful? George Gerbner's *cultivation theory* attempts to describe the power of media in our culture. Media are:

> the most ubiquitous wholesalers of social roles in industrial societies. Mass media form the common mainstream of contemporary culture. They present a steady, repetitive and compelling system of images and messages. . . . This unprecedented condition has a profound effect on the way we are socialized into our roles. (Gerbner, 1993b, p. 25)

Specifically with regard to imagery on television, Gerbner suggests that there is a pattern of setting, casting, social typing, actions, and related outcomes that cuts across most program types and defines the world of television (Gerbner, Gross, Morgan, & Signorelli, 1986, p. 19).

The medium of television is seen as one of the strongest cultivation agents in society. Perse suggests that television creates an idea of mainstream life that homogenizes the outlooks and social reality beliefs of viewers in a direction consistent with television context. What we see on television, then, becomes a strong part in our worldview. Television can do this because it is consistent in its deviation from reality (Perse & Ferguson, 1994). For example, people who watch a lot of television are more likely than others to express sex-stereotyped beliefs such as men are breadwinners and women are nurturers. This is because television consistently provides such stereotypical images to its viewers (Perse & Ferguson, 1994).

Expectancy Theory

Recall that we earlier suggested that one power of a stereotype is that it makes someone act differently. This is captured in *expectancy theory*, which suggests that advertising portrayals build or reinforce expectations and influence social reality. If advertising stereotypes specific groups of people in certain ways, persons in the group will start to act that way because it is expected of them. You could take this to the next step and say that if we present a stereotype (e.g., good mom) and associate a product with it (e.g., Jif peanut butter), we can make a somewhat effortless connection and a meaningful advertising promise: If a woman wants to be a good mom, she will buy Jif peanut butter.

If expectancy theory is valid, then the use of stereotypes hinders one's view of any individual as a complete person. The mass media's use of stereotypes suggests that the mass media will rarely portray men and women (or African Americans, Caucasians, or Hispanics) as complete people with full and meaningful lives (Lerner, 2001). The "good mom" stereotype, for example, suggests that women have a very specific purpose in their lives focused on the home and the family. In reality, a good mom may also be running a Fortune 500 company while keeping children healthy. However, the time and space limitations of advertising do not allow this complete representation to be provided in a single message.

Obviously, such stereotypes can affect how each of us feels about ourselves: whether we are doing what is right, whether we will be accepted by others, and whether we are fulfilling the roles expected of us in society. Expectancy theory also suggests that we develop a worldview of different groups of people who are not like us (whether they are younger or older, a different gender or a different race, or simply living in a different part of the country) through the images we see in the media, including advertising. Depending on our lifestyles and how much media we are exposed to, we may see a wide range of images of different groups of people or a very limited range of portrayals of the group.

How Stereotypes Affect Advertising Messages

Do stereotypes work in advertising? The answer is: It depends. If people in the target audience relate positively to a stereotypical portrayal, the portrayal may help sell the product. If people in the target audience create opinions about groups of people other than the group that they are in, and these opinions put the stereotyped group into a negative light, a stereotyped portrayal could be problematic. Although we can all recognize stereotypes that are blatantly offensive, how we view other portrayals depends on the taste and sensitivity of members of the target audience. For example, many advertisements targeted to women portray husbands and fathers as incompetent around the home. Women may laugh at these portrayals, but men viewing the same commercials may be less amused.

Today, a new type of advertising, called *recursive advertising*, turns stereotypes on their ears. Athletic shoe manufacturer Reebok's campaign for its women's product line features women watching a televised football game while a man cleans up after them. In another spot, a group of men entertain during a women's basketball game time-out. These ads are meant to poke fun at other advertisers' use of stereotypes or marketing techniques (Voegele, 2002). While the spot makes fun of traditional female-male roles, we must ask whether such advertising really does anything to change them. Does this type of advertising merely promote the traditional stereotypes that currently exist? Is it, as Reebok suggests, really a woman's world?

In the next several chapters, we will discuss portrayals of men and women, minorities, children, and elders in advertising. At the end of each chapter, we will provide ways for you to think about portrayals as you develop advertising campaigns both in school and in the future. From this chapter, though, you should be able to tell that as an advertiser, you will probably not be able to avoid using stereotyping, but you should be sure that you present a range of images in your body of work. Throughout the chapters ahead, we will continually admonish you not to take the easy way out. Rather, think about unique and interesting images of all types of people that will resonate with individuals in your target audience. Take women out of the kitchen, strip men of their pinstripe suits, and try to present imagery that is more complex in the ads you create. One way to do this is by recursive advertising, and another way is to get outside and look at the huge variety of people on the street during any given day. Understand more about the complexities of these individuals and use that knowledge to create better advertising that resonates with target audiences.

Of course, advertisers are always concerned with breaking through the clutter. Certainly, recursive advertising gets attention if for no other reason than it causes us to reevaluate the stereotypical ideas that we each have in our minds and memories. Advertising, as you know, is challenged to be fresh, to be exciting, and to attract attention, as well as to convince fickle media audiences not to turn the page or change the channel. This leads to all kinds of techniques that some may find problematic, particularly with regard to taste and advertising.

Sensitivity, Taste, and Advertising

Advertisers have an obligation to be aware that many consumers may find the use of certain stereotypes questionable and possibly even offensive. This use of stereotyped images edges onto the slippery slope of sensitivity and taste in advertising messages. In general, advertisers need to routinely examine and evaluate imagery and language that they use to determine how consumers are affected by the messages, both in terms of the meaning consumers derive from the messages and the overall appropriateness of the strategic approach. In particular, any messages that may cross the fuzzy boundaries of good taste should be closely evaluated.

How do we know when this boundary is crossed? Bob Garfield, a popular writer at the trade magazine *Advertising Age,* wrote that "there is nothing crass about commercialism: there are only times when commercialism seems crass. This is why there are no billboards in cemeteries" (Garfield, 2001a, p. 29). Images that are shocking, disrespectful, or out-and-out disgusting must be evaluated within the context of where they will appear. The sensibilities of the target audience who will see the message must also be considered. This recognizes that a message that is completely appropriate to one target audience (e.g., men aged 18 to 24) may be inappropriate for another (e.g., women aged 65 and older).

Today in the United States, the September 11 terrorist attacks on the World Trade Center and Pentagon are still very much in the news and on the minds of citizens. In the first few days after the terrorist attacks, no commercials aired on television. The round-the-clock coverage of overwhelming news of grave proportions led network executives to conclude that any advertising at all would be inappropriate. When "normal" advertising resumed in the middle of September, it came with a heightened sensitivity among both consumers and advertisers. After the attacks, for example, Americans (including advertisers) were uneasy with ads that featured humorous situations because it felt uncomfortable to laugh during such a tragic time. Additionally, the initial wave of advertising seemed to feature a new idea of what would be appropriate and what would be inappropriate in future messages. The terrorist attacks also produced a resurgence in patriotic advertising. Automakers offered 0% financing to "keep America rolling"; athletic clubs offered discounts to new members to help "keep America strong." Many companies donated some of their profits to relief causes. Such appeals generated a range of responses from consumers and critics alike. On one side, many believed these messages suggested that advertisers were patriots working to help the flagging economy. On the other side, many felt that using patriotism to sell products after the attacks was in poor taste (Valenti, 2001). In fact, surveys showed that Americans were wary of advertisements that traded on tragedy (Smith, 2001).

The challenge to any discussion of sensitivity and taste is that each individual has his or her own ideas of what constitutes "good" and "bad" taste. If you ask any number of different individuals what they consider tasteful or distasteful, you are likely to get unique answers from each of them. Van Bakel (2001) suggests that advertising mirrors a culture, and thus, it should reflect the dominant tone of a culture. When cultural icons include such controversial individuals as Eminem and Tom Green, the dominant tone can become quite crude (Van Bakel, 2001). Concepts of taste also vary from culture to culture. In France, for example, advertisements contain nudity. However, such imagery is likely to be seen as questionable in the United States and would be forbidden in many Middle Eastern countries.

This is not to say that certain individuals and groups do not try to quantify good and bad taste. A few years ago, the *Wall Street Journal* attempted to draft guidelines for *Journal* advertisers that would describe the types of imagery that cross the line of decency and taste. In addition, the *Journal* considered creating a review board to screen submitted advertising to see if advertisements met the guidelines. Many organizations, including the Association of American Advertising Agencies (AAAA), the American Advertising Federation (AAF), the Association of National Advertisers (ANA), the Magazine Publishers of America (MPA), and the Newspaper Association of America (NAA), all agreed that the *Journal's* plans were not feasible. This decision was based on the perception that decency and taste are more a matter of individual choice than industry policy (Elliott, 2001).

Advertising tends to be the first medium to jump on national trends (Valenti, 2001). It is one way that advertisers can find ways to push the envelope and break through the clutter. Given this, how can advertisers make good decisions and wise choices about taste in terms of imagery, depictions, stereotypes, and the like? Keith Reinhard, chief executive officer of DDB Needham Worldwide, gave a speech at a recent meeting of advertising agencies that provided ideas for agency personnel to consider with regard to taste. Specifically, Reinhard (2001) suggested that advertisers consider issues of intent, relevance, context, and pride.

Intent

First, Reinhard (2001) suggested that advertisers ask themselves about the intent of each advertisement. Specifically, advertisers should determine what the advertisement is designed to do. Most advertisements are designed to sell products, build brands, and communicate other types of information. Other advertisements, however, may have a purpose not directly related to the product but may be designed to shock people, to win an award, or to create a controversy. This latter group of advertisements may be stepping on the boundaries of bad taste.

Fashion retailer French Connection has been accused of only trying to shock audiences in its campaign that brands the company as FCUK, which stands for French Connection United Kingdom. Black-and-white advertisements in fashion magazines include the copy, "She says French Connection. He says FCUK" (Figure 6.2). In promoting its first San Francisco store, French Connection created billboards that announced "San Francisco's First FCUK." These boards, as well as taxi-top advertising in New York City, were quickly banned (Chocano, 2001).

Relevance

The relevance question asks how the advertising content is related to the product and to the target. A relevant ad is placed appropriately for its target; an irrelevant ad is not and may be problematic. For example, Toyota's ad agency, Saatchi & Saatchi, recently created a postcard that featured a smiling black man wearing a gold tooth decoration shaped like a Toyota RAV 4 sports utility vehicle (Bean, 2001) (Figure 6.3). Toyota officials

she says french connection.   he says fcuk.

www.frenchconnection.com

Figure 6.2   An advertisement for French Connection United Kingdom reads, "She says French Connection. He says FCUK."

reported that the promotional postcard advertisement was distributed in racks located in nightspots, fitness centers, coffeehouses, and other locations frequented by young, stylish consumers ("Lies About Toyota," 2001) and was intended to build awareness among younger drivers by using an edgy style statement. However, groups including Jesse Jackson's Rainbow/PUSH Coalition complained that the postcard appeared in cafés, restaurants, and bars that were frequented by whites. Rainbow/PUSH suggested that Toyota used the image of a black man to amuse whites (Bean, 2001), and it was thus an inappropriate image. African American writer Warren Brown interviewed young blacks in Toyota's target audience and found that many of them saw nothing wrong with the ad. In fact, some suggested that using a white model in the ad would have been counterproductive to Toyota's strategy because the image of a white male would not be as stylish (Brown, 2001).

Context

Questions of context consider not only what is said in the message but also where the message will appear. The FCUK messages discussed earlier were seen as questionable to present in an outdoor setting, such as a billboard or a taxi top. Obviously, such media reach a wide range of people, including children. However, magazines such as *Allure, Jane, Mademoiselle, Maxim, Nylon*, and *Rolling Stone* carry print ads for FCUK (Chocano,

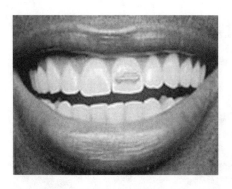

Figure 6.3 This promotional piece from Toyota was offensive to many.

2001). These magazines have a more limited and specific reach than outdoor boards do, and the readership consists of younger adults who may be less offended by such messages. A similar situation occurred when British model Sophie Dahl appeared nude in a print advertisement for Opium perfume (6.4). In England, the print advertisements appeared in magazines and were made into posters that were placed in outdoor locations across the United Kingdom. A self-regulatory group, The Advertising Standards Board, banned the advertisement from posters, yet judged the image appropriate for magazines.

The prevalence of patriotic messages since September 11, 2001, also brings up issues of context. As Keith Reinhard told a *Business Week* reporter, "at a time like this, there's a very fine line between being appropriately patriotic and disgustingly opportunistic" (Brady, 2001). Context issues, such as when and how companies choose to announce their patriotic acts, come into play here. Shortly after September 11, for example, Anheuser-Busch issued a press release stating that police officers and firefighters would receive free admission to Anheuser-Busch theme parks. This was seen as an appropriate message in an appropriate context. In contrast, the Choice Hotels group issued a press release stating that "Choice Hotels Joins Travel Community in Denouncing Terrorist Attacks." Because there was little news value in the announcement and no specific action taken by the company other than denouncing the attacks, this message was seen as opportunistic (Brady, 2001).

Pride

Questions of pride evaluate an individual's own personal feelings about the message that he or she has created. When you look at the message you have created, ask yourself: Would you be proud to sign your name to the ad? To tell people you did the ad? How would you feel about showing the FCUK ad to your parents or grandparents? Are you willing to go to bat for the ad? Your conviction to the message is essential for the message to be made. As an advertiser, you need to take responsibility for your choices.

Choices in Advertising

When advertisers make choices in questionable taste, the messages may (and often do) succeed in creating awareness, generating attention, and gaining publicity for their clients. However, the reason that these messages succeed is not because they are so highly creative but rather because most other advertising messages play by the rules in terms of taste and decency. If every advertiser employed crude innuendo and used imagery in questionable taste, taking the "high road" would be seen as an innovative way to approach an advertising problem (Fletcher, 2001).

The great advertising copywriter Bill Bernbach once said, "all of us who professionally use the mass media are the shapers of society. We can vulgarize society. We can brutalize it. Or we can help lift it onto a higher level" (Van Bakel, 2001, p. 4). Keith Reinhard (2000) echoes these sentiments when he says that advertising should not only be informative and/or entertaining, but it should also remind people of ways to make their lives better. This may cause advertising agencies to make some tough choices; however, to echo Bernbach, "a principle isn't a principle until it costs you money" (Reinhard, 2000).

Figure 6.4   A perfume advertisement featuring a nude Sophie Dahl was banned from outdoor boards yet allowed in targeted magazines.

Summary

In this chapter, we discussed in general terms concerns about stereotyping and taste in advertising messages. We provided ways to think about the effects of such messages on consumers. In the next four chapters, we will examine imagery in advertising directed to and featuring men and women, ethnic groups, elders, and children. Refer back to this chapter when analyzing the arguments and the advertisements presented in later chapters to better understand these issues as they are presented.

7

Cats and Dogs
on Venus and Mars

Gender and Advertising

The emotional, sexual, and psychological stereotyping of females begins when the doctor says: "It's a girl."

—Shirley Chisholm

M en are dogs and women are cats. Women are from Venus and men are from Mars. Writers, filmmakers, psychologists, and advertisers all have used the idea that men and women are different to develop stories, create conflict, and provide persuasive imagery. Not only do advertisers view men and women differently, but men and women also bring different perspectives to advertising. Thus, we can assume that men and women create different meanings from the advertisements they see. Gender roles in our society have changed dramatically since the 1950s, and portrayals of men and women in advertising have been researched since nearly the same time. Researchers have consistently sought to evaluate these roles to examine whether advertising has kept up with societal changes. In this chapter, we examine the different ways men and women view advertising and messages, as well as some of the ways that advertising portrays gender roles today.

The last several decades have seen changes in the role of women in society, both as those who earn money and those who spend money. In 1940, women comprised about 20% of the workforce in the United States. The 1970s saw a wave of women joining the workforce, and working women today represent almost 50% of the total workforce (U.S. Department of Labor, 2000). In addition, the family structure in the United States has changed: Census data indicate that 17.5% of women 40 to 44 years of age in 1995 had not had a child, compared to 10.2% of women aged 40 to 44 in 1976. Smaller proportions of two-parent families and larger numbers of single parents were characteristic of the family structure toward the end of the 20th century (U.S. Department of Labor, 2000).

In addition to their changing roles in the labor force and in the family, women have also increased their power as consumers. Today, women wield incredible buying power: They purchase or influence the purchase of 80% of all consumer goods. Although women have always been the primary purchasers of household products, the 1990s have seen an increase in buying power for women. Numerous products and services that have been considered traditionally male purchases have also come under the purchase authority of women. For example, women are now involved in more than 50% of the purchases of consumer electronics, and women purchase 50% of all cars. Women's influence extends to 80% of all automobile sales. Women buy 50% of all computers purchased, and almost 50% of all stock market investors are women (Popcorn & Marigold, 2000).

Gender and Information Processing

As discussed in Chapter 2, advertisers provide messages and leave the meaning up to consumers to develop. Advertisers are interested in similarities and differences in how men and women receive and evaluate information. One difference involves the actual creation of meaning from a given advertisement. Men look directly at the primary message of a given advertisement (e.g., "buy this beer"). Women not only evaluate the primary message, but they also pick up multiple clues from the message and weave together threads to intuit and infer the inner meaning of the message (e.g., "buy this beer and you will be popular and trendy") (Popcorn & Marigold, 2000).

Once the meaning from an advertisement has been determined, men and women differ in how that meaning is used. These different decision-making processes are related to whether the process is linear or more nonlinear in nature. Men process messages and make decisions more quickly than women do, perhaps because men focus on the primary message of a given advertisement and take in little other information during the process. This is due to the observation that men have a linear thinking and reasoning style, and men tend to have a more task-oriented focus than women have. Women, on the other hand, process the information in an advertisement quickly and from many levels and sources, including music, visuals, voiceover, and text. Women also tend to evaluate and weigh the various sources to process the message and determine what steps to take next. Women's reasoning processes are less task-oriented and more compartmentalized than men's are. Women's decision-making processes are characterized as being incremental reasoning processes, where each piece of information builds on the previous information that is taken in. This nonlinear approach to reasoning allows women to think in terms of interrelated factors, not straight lines. The observation that women evaluate multiple sources supports this reasoning style (Fisher, 1999).

Women and men respond to entirely different stimuli when viewing and evaluating advertising messages (Popcorn & Marigold, 2000). Men respond positively to male imagery, and women respond positively to female imagery. This is why you rarely see hunters in advertisements for products directed to women or bubble baths in advertisements for products directed to men. Interestingly, though, women will use products and respond positively to imagery that they perceive as masculine, although men do not respond positively to images or products that they perceive as feminine (Smith, 1994). Therefore, we occasionally see advertising that features women hiking and camping, but we rarely see men taking a bubble bath.

Women and men also respond differently to the same stimulus. An example of this is athletic imagery: Women rarely think of themselves as athletes unless they are playing a professional sport, whereas men have images of themselves as athletes even if they do not play professionally (Wong, 2001). Therefore, an image of an athlete, regardless of gender, is likely to generate different responses from both men and women.

Gender and Stereotypes

Given that men and women differ in many ways, it should not be surprising that advertisements portray men and women differently. These different portrayals result in intended and unintended effects, which we discuss later in this chapter.

When looking at portrayals and imagery of men and women, it is important to examine a body of advertisements, not just one or two specific advertisements that have imagery that may be stereotypical or in other ways problematic. Stereotypes are created by the continual, extended exposure of consumers to patterns of imagery. It is also important to remember that, as discussed in Chapter 6, there are valid reasons that advertisers use stereotypes. In this chapter, we examine role portrayals of both men and women and provide numerous ads to illustrate our points. Please keep in mind that when examples of advertisements are included, they were selected as representative of advertising trends that appear in society, not just as a "sore thumb" or an aberration from typical messages seen in advertising today.

Role Portrayals

Men and women living in the 21st century lead highly complex lives with multiple societal roles. Men and women are parents, businesspeople, corporate board members, friends, siblings, volunteers, and more. This differs from the *Leave It to Beaver* society of the 1950s, where societal roles were much more specific: Men were the breadwinners, and women were the

Figure 7.1   A traditional mom in a Dodge ad

homemakers. Today, though, society still clings to some of the values of the 1950s. Women, regardless of their employment status outside the home, have more responsibility for maintaining the household and the family's social activities than men have (Popcorn & Marigold, 2000). Indeed, advertising has firmly held on to this traditional portrayal of women as homemakers and uses this imagery to promote all types of products from household goods to computers to automobiles.

In a study of advertisements done in the late 1980s, for example, women were portrayed more often in the home than men were. When women were pictured outside the home, they tended to be portrayed as either consumers (e.g., shopping) or as working in a pink-collar occupation. Women were rarely seen in a professional role such as a businesswoman (Melton & Fowler, 1987). Men, on the other hand, were much more likely to be pictured outside the home and with managerial and professional roles in the workplace. In the 15 years since this study was published, there have been some subtle changes in advertising portrayals of men and women, although traditional imagery continues to be prevalent.

Today, advertising portrayals vary based on the medium in which they appear and, for broadcast media, the times of day when the advertisement is appearing. During the workday, for example, the primary TV audiences are women with children and retired persons. During daytime programming, most of the women in commercials are shown in traditional homemaker roles (the woman pictured in the Dodge ad in Figure 7.1 may not be in the home, but she is clearly a traditional type of mother). Men are rarely seen in the commercials as husbands, professionals, or spokespeople. During prime-time television, when the TV audience is more balanced, women are

Figure 7.2   An equitable portrayal of a woman in a Compaq ad

shown more often in positions of authority and in settings away from the home. During prime-time television, portrayals of men and women are more equitable (Craig, 1992). For example, the individual on the laptop in the Compaq ad (Figure 7.2) can just as easily be a woman as a man; thus, the portrayal is equitable.

Today, we are seeing an increase in portrayals of women and men in ways that neither conform to nor conflict with stereotypical understanding. Several societal changes may have contributed to the growth of such portrayals. First, there are a substantial number of women holding positions at a range of media organizations. Many of these women are working professionally to present a more realistic view of women in the media. Additionally, there are numerous nontraditional publications that have been introduced in the last several decades. Advertisements in women's magazines that may be considered less traditional (e.g., *Working Woman*), when compared to traditional magazines, are more likely to depict employed women in positions of power and responsibility (Ruggiero & Weston, 1985).

Advertisements today are also starting to portray more nontraditional images of men. For example, advertisers such as Roxio and JungSoft have shown men taking care of children and doing housework (Figure 7.3). However, not all of these portrayals can be considered equality portrayals. Some advertisements present images of fathers who are "childish but

Figure 7.3   In this ad for JungSoft, the man in the image seems comfortable in his child care role.

lovable goofballs" (Crain, 2001). One such advertisement is for JC Penney, whose TV ad for its One Day Sale shows different fathers unable to handle their children and wondering out loud where the mothers are (at the One Day Sale, of course). As an advertising trend, this could be problematic if such images are not balanced with other images of men that show them as confident and capable in traditional homemaking situations.

Beauty Stereotypes

When we think of the people who appear in advertisements, we often think of men and women who are perfect physical specimens. They are young, with perfect skin free from acne and nary a wrinkle in sight; they are fit, with a six-pack stomach and no hint of cellulite, and they have full heads of glossy, thick hair. Women tend to be thin, and men tend to have well-developed upper torsos. Two ads for Calvin Klein epitomize this trend (Figures 7.4 and 7.5). Now, we know in our heads that these people are professional models who are paid well to maintain themselves. We also know that advances in technology allow any flaws and imperfections to magically disappear from photographs. However, many view these images as presenting a standard of beauty and fitness that is in many cases impossible to attain, yet attempts are made to attain it anyway by purchasing products.

The cult of beauty is as old as the cult of the male warrior. Think of fairy tales from your youth: Girls and women tend to be portrayed either as good (Snow White, Sleeping Beauty) or bad (the Wicked Witch of the West, Cinderella's stepmother and stepsisters). The good women tend to be young and beautiful, and the bad women are either old or ugly (of course,

Figures 7.4 and 7.5   Calvin Klein ads feature models with beautiful bodies.

examples such as the Snow Queen are exceptions to the rule). Similarly, good men are handsome princes, and bad men are ugly ogres. Both the ugly ogre (who kidnaps the princess) and the handsome prince (who rescues her) desire the beautiful princess. These myths from our childhood continue to resonate with us as adult consumers.

Theories of beauty are culturally constituted, primarily because of common socialization experiences. Thus, individuals in a society possess shared cultural ideals. One of these ideals is that we, as human beings, find specific facial and body configurations pleasing to view (Ashmore & Soloman, 1996). We have associated these pleasing feelings with an overall positive attitude toward beauty, and as a result, we have determined as a culture that beauty is good and preferable to ugliness (Wolszon, 1998).

Since our culture constantly undergoes subtle changes, beauty norms have also changed over time (Solomon & Ashmore, 1992). It has specifically been observed that societal expectations for beauty change with every generation (Jacobson & Mazur, 1995). The standard of voluptuous beauty of Marilyn Monroe in the 1950s changed to the standard of trendy beauty of Twiggy in the 1960s and to supermodels such as Naomi Campbell and Linda Evangelista in the 1980s. Regardless of the "beauty paradigm" currently promoted by society, individuals strive to attain the ideal of beauty that is prevalent in their culture (Englis, Soloman, & Ashmore, 1994).

Today, cultural norms in the United States continue to promote the importance of an individual's physical attractiveness, beginning in infancy and continuing through childhood and adolescence (Martin & Gentry, 1997). For women, beauty has been institutionalized to the point where an entire industry devoted to beauty has been created. Beauty is tied not only to appearance but also to mental health and physical well-being (Brand, 1999). This beauty ideal is an overall "look" that incorporates one's

GET A 10 SMILE

Listen to one of our smiling customers, "I used the Rembrandt Plus' Superior Bleaching Kit and had great results. My teeth are so much whiter."

9 out of 10 people liked the taste, felt it was easy to use and freshened their breath."

• 10 Shades Whiter™
• Safe for Sensitive Teeth
• Helps Prevent Restaining
• Clinically Proven
• Easy to Use

REMBRANDT Plus
"Safe Comfortable Bleaching"

10 SHADES WHITER

PROFESSIONAL-STYLE BLEACHING IN THE CONVENIENCE OF YOUR OWN HOME

For Faster and More Dramatic Results, Visit Your Dentist for Rembrandt One-Hour Whitening

REMBRANDT
CALL 1-800-972-1236

Figure 7.6   The Rembrandt ad sets a goal for anyone who wishes to be beautiful to achieve.

physical features as well as a variety of products or services such as clothing and cosmetics (Englis et al., 1994). Striving to meet the cultural ideal is a key selling message used by many types of advertisers involved in selling beauty-oriented products (Jacobson & Mazur, 1995). The Rembrandt ad, for example, stresses the importance of a "10" smile, suggesting a rating system for beauty in their ad and solving the problem of how the top rating can be obtained (Figure 7.6).

In the United States and in several other cultures, an important part of the beauty ideal today includes a thin body type, and several studies have demonstrated how the female body depicted in all media, including advertising, has become increasingly thin (Turner, Hamilton, Jacobs, Angood, & Dwyer, 1997). Research has indicated that women in advertisements tend to be young, thin, and white (Kuczynski, 1998b). Women who do not fit into this category, such as black and/or older women, are either invisible (Gantz, Gartenberg, & Rainbow, 1980), presented as tokens (Bailey, Harrell, & Anderson, 1993), or are portrayed negatively (Plous & Neptune, 1997). There is a cultural taboo against large female bodies (Wilson & Blackhurst, 1999), and advertisements often present large women as having bad bodies that limit both their wardrobes and their social engagements.

Critics point to women's fashion and beauty magazines as one of the most influential and potentially damaging media channels because they are directly concerned with the cultural ideal of beauty and provide a vehicle where advertisers can easily link their products to the process of trying to attain the beauty (Englis et al., 1994). The types of women portrayed in these magazines, both in advertising and in editorial pages, are parts of the unattainable beauty ideal. The average woman in the United States is 5 feet 4 inches tall and weighs 142 pounds, but the average model is 5 feet 11 inches tall and weighs 115 pounds (Tung, 2002). Models who appear in print advertisements are thinner than 95% of the female population (Wolf, 1991).

Men, too, are subject to cultural ideals of beauty. While the exposure of the male body has historically been off-limits in advertising and other media, the past few decades have shown an increase in the use of the male body to promote products. Beauty standards have been set for men; for example, in terms of facial appearance, men are expected to have square jaws and full heads of hair. Male beauty is also equated with physical strength. Men's bodies in advertisements feature strong torsos, backs, and thighs, and the importance of a "six-pack" has reached almost comic proportions (Figure 7.7).

Figure 7.7   An Altoids ad shows the hyperidealized male torso.

Decorative and Sexual Stereotypes

Closely associated with the idea of a beautiful face and body is the idea of decorative portrayals. When people are portrayed in advertisements, they are either actively involved with the product or service being advertised or passively decorating the advertisement. For example, a model could be seen as having just finished drinking milk (an active portrayal), or the model could be holding the product without interacting with it (a decorative portrayal), such as we see in the milk ad in Figure 7.8. Decorative portrayals show the people in the advertisements as passive and disengaged, whereas active portrayals show the person interacting directly with the

Model behavior.

Want
strong bones?
Your
bones grow
until
about age
35
and the
calcium
in milk helps.
After that,
it helps
keep them
strong.
Which means
milk is
always in
fashion.

got milk?

Figure 7.8   Model Giselle decorates this ad for the Milk Board.

product. Many advertisements featuring beautiful men and women tend to feature them as decorations.

In the previous section, we discussed how portrayals differ by medium. Decorative portrayals tend to occur frequently on weekend television programming, when the primary TV audience is composed of men. Commercials shown during weekend television portray women in a decorative role where they rarely interact with the products being sold. Men are much more active and are portrayed as fun loving, carefree, and single. They tend to interact with the products much more than women do.

The fact that women tend to be portrayed in decorative roles much more often than men suggests that advertisements do not render a realistic depiction of the female gender role (Paff & Lakner, 1997). Specifically, many decorative depictions of women tend to show women in sexual or alluring positions. A sexual depiction is often an explicitly aggressive image of a woman that focuses on her lips, breasts, or groin area. An alluring depiction is less explicit and might feature a woman reclining submissively on a piece of furniture or on the floor or looking at the camera with her lips suggestively parted, as seen in the Hawaiian Tropic ad (Figure 7.9).

Decorative roles are seen as arguably representing society's view of the appropriate place for women in society: taking a passive position (Paff & Lakner, 1997). A recent study of advertisements in *Good Housekeeping* and *Vogue* found that 94% of women in advertisements appeared in so-called decorative roles (i.e., serving no other function than to decorate the product or the magazine page) (Paff & Lakner, 1997). The same study also found many women were shown in roles of dependence or passivity (e.g., leaning on or gazing up to men or reclining on the floor or on furniture).

Sexual and decorative portrayals are used to advertise all types of products and services (Hall, Ijima, & Crum, 1994). Although such images are generally associated with women, in the past decade or so, we have seen an increase in decorative and sexual portrayals of men, particularly in fashion advertising. However, the continued history and presence of women in decorative and sexual roles have generated much more interest and controversy than similar portrayals of men.

When decorative and sexual imagery is used, advertisements often include nonverbal cues as an indication that women lack authority and possess less

Figure 7.9   Alluring women in a Hawaiian Tropic ad

power than men (Simmons, 1986). Probably the most important scholar in the area of nonverbal cues is Erving Goffman, whose book *Gender Advertisements* (1979) explored a range of portrayals of women and men in terms of power. Goffman's findings include that women are generally pictured at a smaller relative size, especially height. Men tend to be pictured as taller than women, putting them in a position of power, authority, and rank (Goffman, 1979) (Figure 7.10). Body language often suggests that women are submissive toward products, such as the woman lying beside her new handbag in the Furla ad (Figure 7.11), whereas men are dominant over products (Figure 7.12).

Women are also seen as more tactile than men; that is, they more often are touching, cradling, and caressing objects. Goffman sees this type of touching as ritualistic, as opposed to more utilitarian aspects of touching

Figure 7.10 A man is dominant over a woman in a Ralph Lauren ad.

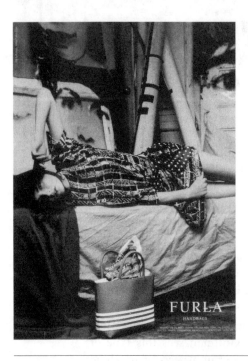

Figures 7.11 and 7.12   A submissive woman is portrayed in the Furla handbag ad. A man
dominates the computer in the Audiovox ad.

such as touch that grasps, manipulates, or holds. Again, this suggests the more passive nature of women in advertising. Similarly, women tend to appear removed from the social situation of the activity pictured in the ads. Often, their gaze is averted (Figure 7.13). Goffman (1979) refers to this as *licensed withdrawal.*

The overarching concern with decorative and sexual portrayals is that the individuals involved in such portrayals may become objects, similar to the objects that the people are trying to sell. With passive portrayals, there is a disconnection between the person and the object and possibly even between people (Kilbourne, 1999). Such feelings may pass on from the advertisement to the world, creating general feelings of disconnectedness among those who see the ad (Kilbourne, 1999).

Figure 7.13 An averted gaze of a model in a Pantene ad

Intended Effects

In the previous chapter, we examined why stereotypes are generally used by the advertising industry. In this discussion of effects, we recap some of the key effects that relate specifically to gender and advertising, as well as provide some additional intended and unintended effects regarding the types of portrayals we have discussed so far in this chapter.

The Stage Is Quickly Set

Advertisers are not alone in using stereotyped imagery. Television programs, magazines, feature films, and other mass-mediated content all provide a somewhat limited vision of men's and women's roles in society that has become familiar to us as consumers. Stereotyped imagery is effective by virtue of its familiarity: Images such as the busy homemaker, the brawny construction worker, and the button-down executive are instantly recognizable. Given that they are working within time and space constraints, advertisers have almost always relied on stereotypes to establish rapport with consumers and move on to more important information about the product or service being advertised. It is efficient for advertising to use gendered stereotypes because the scene becomes immediately set.

Beautiful Things Are Appealing

As social beings, we like to look at beautiful things. Even as babies, we are more attracted to beautiful pictures than to ugly ones. Advertising images capitalize on this idea of liking, as attractive men and women are often used to transfer positive affect from the model to the product (Gulas & McKeage, 2000). Studies show that this "affect transfer" works well. Consumers are more likely to enjoy ads with attractive models than ads with unattractive models (Baker & Churchill, 1977). Attractive models are liked more than unattractive models, and messages using attractive models are evaluated more positively than messages without attractive models (Joseph, 1982). Furthermore, ads with attractive models generate higher levels of recall than ads without attractive models (Chestnut, LaChance, & Lubitz, 1977). This affect transfer also relates to sales: Consumers report increased purchase intentions for the advertised product after seeing ads for the products that feature attractive people (Petroshius & Crocker, 1989).

These predilections can be further explained by a theory called the *match-up hypothesis*, which suggests that attractive persons are highly effective endorsers for products that are used to enhance the consumer's own attractiveness. Effectiveness in this case was measured in terms of both consumer attitude toward the brand as well as their purchase intentions (Till & Busler, 2000). Moreover, attractive endorsers are often considered more appropriate and a better fit than unattractive endorsers, regardless of the product (Till & Busler, 2000).

Role-Product Congruity

The idea that beautiful people can augment the persuasive ability of advertising for beauty-oriented products and services leads to the next intended effect of the use of some gendered stereotypes: *role-product congruity theory*. The role-product congruity theory simply suggests that advertising effectiveness can be increased when appropriate models are used. At first, it was suspected that female models were more effective in promoting feminine products than males, and vice versa (Kanungo & Pang, 1993). This suggests that beautiful women are effective at selling products to make women feel more beautiful. The role-product congruity theory goes beyond that simple suggestion to examine individual gendered role portrayals for different product categories. Research has shown that certain stereotyped portrayals of men and women are appropriate for specific categories of products. For example, women portrayed in employee/consumer roles were seen as appropriate portrayals for products and services in the Business/Travel/Transportation category. Consumers also saw beautiful model roles as appropriate for the Home Products category. However, the beautiful model role was not seen as appropriate in the Business/Travel/ Transportation category. Nor was the employee/consumer role seen as appropriate for the Home Products category (Ferguson, Kreshel, & Tinkham, 1990). This suggests that we as consumers have some idea of acceptable images that relates to the context of the advertisement.

The role-product congruity theory has also been used to examine relationships between images of spokespeople and products. Let us go back to the previous discussion that physically attractive models in advertisements have a positive influence on consumers' attitudes toward beauty-enhancing products (Kahle & Homer, 1985). One explanation for this is *schema theory*, which suggests that memory is a blend of specific memories as well as general abstractions about people, activities, and objects (Gwinner & Eaton, 1999). When considering schema theory in light of role-product congruity, then, we might deduce that messages can become more effective when the products are associated with familiar portrayals of men and women that have been previously implemented in that product category.

The Theory That Sex Sells

We have discussed that advertisers use attractive images to positively connect products to feelings that we already have. Before that connection can take place, the ads must get our attention. Often, sexual imagery is used to break through the ever-growing clutter in the advertising environment. As Twitchell (1996) said, at a minimum, "sex doesn't sell, but it certainly captures attention" (p. 157).

A sexual appeal is a strong psychological appeal, second only to self-preservation. In humans, as in all animals, sexual desire is an instinctive reaction as we search for the perfect mate (Taflinger, 1996). Sexual imagery used in advertising for products like perfume, makeup, and clothing, then, can be explained or rationalized in part by this mating desire in humans: We want to look good to attract a mate and to propagate our species. However, sexual imagery has been shown to have a stronger persuasive ability for men than for women. It may be because men have a different set of criteria for selecting a mate than women do: Men traditionally tend to recognize that a woman who is young, healthy, and beautiful will be a good mate. Therefore, many advertisers use sexual imagery to get a man's attention and then associate buying the product with getting a mate (Taflinger, 1996). These types of messages focus on instinctual or physical types of meaning in messages.

For women, the persuasive power of sexual imagery works on a somewhat different level. A healthy, fit male model will attract the attention of many women and may even create desire for the product (there is a famous Diet Coke campaign with model Lucky Vanous that zeroes in on this appeal). However, women tend to want a little bit more than a healthy specimen for their mates. Women are not only attracted by good looks and physique but also pay attention to the long-term potential of a man—for example, his ability to be a good father and to provide them with money, power, and prestige. All these factors are almost impossible to put into any single advertisement (Taflinger, 1996).

Arguably, then, it is difficult for advertisers to use sex successfully to sell to women. Instead, advertising uses romance to make a sexual connection with women. Romantic images are less blatant and more ambiguous than traditional sexual messages: They provide images of courtship, relationships, and the process of falling in love (Figure 7.14). Sexual imagery in advertisements directed toward women becomes much more intellectual than physical (Taflinger, 1996).

Researchers have also examined whether the use of female role portrayals as sexual objects has an effect on consumers' ability to respond to brand name recall, sales point recall, and buying attitudes (Utt, 1984). In one experiment, for example, researchers found that sex does sell. Subjects who saw an ad for Crystal Coke featuring a female portrayed as a sexual object were more likely to recall the Crystal Coke brand name than those who did not see a sexual portrayal. The first group was also more likely to purchase the product than those who saw a different type of portrayal (e.g., a woman as a homemaker).

Unintended Effects

Given this range of intended effects of using different types of gendered imagery consistently in advertisements, it is not surprising that a range of unintended effects has also been identified and to some extent documented. Many unintended effects are based on an assumption that gender portrayals do not reflect the range of roles that men and women undertake in the world today. Instead, advertisements tend to reflect a more limited representation. Other unintended effects focus on the media's power to create and transmit "cultural meaning" (Ferguson et al., 1990). This power is a more serious concern because advertising is not only providing a limited view of gendered roles, but it is also creating negative portrayals. Such

Figure 7.14 Romantic images in a Holland-American Cruise Line ad

portrayals inaccurately depict men's and women's roles in society and may ultimately influence individuals to believe that the portrayals are accurate. Thus, negative stereotypes are created in a society where the portrayals do not really exist (Ferguson et al., 1990).

Limited Social Roles

If mass media depict only a limited range of roles for men and women, the societal roles that people assume are appropriate for men and women will subsequently be limited. Regarding advertising in particular, it has been suggested that advertising's focus on women in the home may lead to women being excluded from many facets of life outside the home. In particular, a preponderance of female homemaker portrayals may cause both men and women to believe that women are unable to function outside the home without the guidance of men. In addition, advertisements may influence people to believe that women are unable to make decisions or exert power in any type of situation outside the home. The passive role of women in advertisements may suggest that women are dependent on others and unable to actively make decisions on their own. In the long term, passive portrayals in advertising along with the focus on the homemaker role may produce negative perceptions of women's abilities to perform competently in the workplace (Courtney & Whipple, 1983).

Similarly, the limited portrayals of men may result in men believing they are excluded from activities centered around the home. Men may believe that they are not equal partners in child rearing, household maintenance, and other activities This may serve to reinforce the position of women as homemakers, in that certain household tasks can only be successfully accomplished by a woman (Taflinger, 1996).

Value System Focuses on External Beauty

Advertisements that focus on the beauty ideal may send a message that one's looks are the only aspect that is important to the individual and to society. Some critics argue, specifically, that advertisements reinforce a cultural history of determining worth, particularly a woman's worth, by physical appearance (Wilson & Blackhurst, 1999). Fashion magazines, in particular, have been charged with presenting a strict beauty ideal that communicates a specific type of beauty is more highly valued than others (Englis et al., 1994). Advertising and editorial imagery in mass media must both share the blame for this problem.

When individuals are valued for only one part of their selves, their other accomplishments and attributes are trivialized. In our society, for example, some women believe men value them primarily on how they look, and any accomplishments outside of this realm are insignificant. Women can find this offensive and demeaning (Taflinger, 1996).

A value system focused on looks may lead to women developing issues with body image and self-esteem. Numerous studies connect exposure to beautiful, thin models with negative self-esteem among women. Waiflike, thin models (Figure 7.15) appearing in fashion magazines' editorial and advertising pages may make women feel helpless because these models present an image that is impossible to achieve. One research study, for example, showed that college students exposed to fashion magazines had different attitudes toward beauty and self-esteem than women exposed to newsmagazines (Turner et al., 1997). The women who were exposed to fashion magazines felt frustrated about their weight, felt guilty while eating, and were preoccupied with the desire to be thinner. They expressed these feelings more often than the women exposed to newsmagazines.

The consistent portrayal of thin women in all types of mass media, including advertisements, has been seen as playing a part in the cultural phenomenon of body dissatisfaction among women in Western societies (Johnson & Petrie, 1995) and is manifest in studies that relate exposure to attractive, thin models in media to increased amounts of depression and anger (Pinhas, Toner, Ali, Garfinkel, & Stuckless, 1999). Dissatisfaction is also related to decreased ratings of individuals' body image attitudes (Rebek-Wegener, Eickhoff-Schemek, & Kelly-Vance, 1998) and decreased perceptions of self-attractiveness among girls and women (Crouch &

Degelman, 1998). These effects may in turn lead to increased levels of eating disorders (Pinhas et al., 1999), unhealthy dieting (Armstong & Mallory, 1992), smoking (Garner, 1997), and cosmetic surgery among girls and women (Burton & Netemeyer, 1995).

Many fashion magazines are read by girls who are 16 and younger, and many have reported that they frequently see ads that make them feel like they need to diet (Tsu, 2000). Girls in the fifth, sixth, and ninth grade were more critical of their body shapes after looking at magazine advertising than before looking at them (Bass, 1994). Teenage girls who watched television ads using appeals that featured sex, beauty, and youth as selling points were more likely to believe that beauty and popularity

Figure 7.15 Ultrathin model in a Burberry ad

were desirable than girls who watched ads without such appeals (Bass, 1979).

We do not want to downplay the importance and concerns about eating disorders, but some clarification about these disorders is necessary at this point. Although exposure to fashion advertisements has been linked to eating disorders symptomatology, it is important to recognize that such diseases cannot be attributed solely to advertising (Andersen & DiDomenico, 1992). Advertising is part of a larger mass media process providing problematic images to women. In addition, while controlled experiments indicate that such imagery can have some negative effects on women, there is no research that links exposures to advertisements directly to such diseases. Twitchell (1996) explains that diseases like anorexia and bulimia are "multifactoral disorders more attributable to biology, environment and personality than to the appearance of scrawny models in Diet Coke ads" (p. 154).

Figures 7.16 and 7.17   Objectification in two ads: one for Neutrogena and one for Digiverge

Objectification

Objectification is defined as any presentation emphasizing sexually suggestive body parts or not including the head. A focus on body parts results in individuals losing their humanity and becoming objects. In many cases, the body parts highlighted in advertisements suggest that the person becomes a sexual object (Figure 7.16). The process of objectification has been described as demeaning and dehumanizing. Often, objectification occurs at its worst when there is no role-product congruity, such as in the "Nice Rack!" ad shown in Figure 7.17.

Marginalization

The predominance of traditional portrayals of men and women leave little room for portrayals that are nontraditional. This is not only applied to portrayals of individuals but also to portrayals of relationships. In advertising, virtually all sexual or romantic relationships are between a man and a woman. The focus on heterosexual imagery can result in the marginalization of homosexuals. Certain companies such as Coors, Ikea, and Benneton have targeted and portrayed gays and lesbians in advertising, but such portrayals in mainstream, traditional media continue to be rare. Additionally, the imagery in such advertisements does not feature a traditional image of a couple (i.e., two people) but instead will include some type of symbol like clasped hands or the rainbow flags (Chura, 2000). Other times, images of homosexuals are used for comic relief (Mand, 2001). An interesting Web site, the Commercial Closet, further discusses such portrayals and suggests that negative portrayals outnumber positive portrayals of homosexuals in advertising.

Advertising's Responsibilities to Men and Women

In this book, we hope not only to raise issues for you as a current or future advertising professional to be aware of but also to give you ideas of what advertisers can do to improve the industry. Advertising is one industry where one person's efforts and convictions can have an effect on the industry as a whole. With that in mind, here are some strategies and tactics to keep in mind.

Don't Take the Easy Way Out

Advertising plays both a reflecting and a shaping role for men and women (Twitchell, 1996). It is important to recognize advertising's strength in this regard and to use the power of advertising to portray more realistic images of men and women. Stereotypes can quickly set the stage for advertising, but this does not mean that the same types of images must be used repeatedly. Any type of realistic, familiar portrayal can quickly set the stage and aid in the storytelling process. Research has shown that realistic portrayals can have positive results for advertisers and that certain types of imagery, including objectification of women, cause negative responses from consumers (Elliott, Jones, Benfield, & Barlow, 1995). Advertising effectiveness is enhanced when role portrayals are consistent with the role orientation of the receiver (Leigh, Rethans, & Whitney, 1987), so it is important to fully understand the different views of the world held by people in your target audience.

Rethink Your Own Ideas of Beauty

As a shaper of social roles, advertising can do much to affect the cultural beauty ideal that is prevalent in society today. One way to influence the beauty ideal is to produce advertisements featuring women who do not have thin, perfect bodies. For example, less than 1% of all women in advertisements in *Vogue* and *Marie Claire* magazines featured plus-size models

MARINA RINALDI
Sizes 10-22
STYLE
IS NOT
A SIZE...
IT'S AN
ATTITUDE!

Figure 7.18 A Marina Rinaldi ad featuring a plus-size model

(i.e., models who wear size 12 or larger), such as the model featured in the Marina Rinaldi advertisement (Figure 7.18). However, less than 30% of advertisements featured models who were average size (i.e., models who wear size 8 or 10) (Sheehan, 2000).

While the advertising industry avoids using models with larger body types in advertisements, evidence shows that consumers would welcome this imagery. The overwhelming majority of respondents to a *Psychology Today* study wanted models in magazines to represent that natural range of body shapes. The majority of women in this study said they were willing to buy magazines featuring heavier models, even though most believe that clothes look better on thin models (Garner, 1997).

Expand Expectations

Sometimes advertisers make automatic choices without thinking through other options that might be effective. One is the choice of a voice for a voice-over on a television spot. Often, a male voice is featured because it is the default choice. However, agencies should take the time to consider both men's and women's voices for voice-overs. This can add to the perception of women as powerful in our society (e.g., the "voice of reason" or "voice of experience"). In addition, rethink the activity level of girls and women in advertisements, especially in categories where they tend to be portrayed as passive. Show both men and women in a variety of settings, using products, as well as being experts and helping others learn how to use products. In this way, the actual societal roles of both men and women can begin to be presented in advertising.

Celebrate and Criticize

People working at advertising agencies, particularly creative people, love awards. As an industry, then, advertising should look for ways to celebrate positive imagery and bring attention to problematic imagery. One example is the Advertising Women of New York awards that honor ads that portray women in a positive light while chastising other advertisements that they see as problematic. Advertising that has been awarded for positive imagery includes a Gatorade spot featuring Michael Jordan and Mia Hamm. Ads that have been chastised (these awards are called the Ugly Awards) include ads for a variety of companies such as Victoria's Secret, Bally Total Fitness, and Calvin Klein. The Grand Ugly awards have been given to companies like Candy's (for an ad featuring a woman sitting astride a computer monitor with her legs spread) and Herbal Essence's "Organic Experiences" campaign.

Summary

A variety of portrayals of both men and women exist in advertising (and other mass-mediated content) today. Many of the problematic images are the result of the beauty culture in the United States, which is a culture that the advertising industry can choose to support or to effect change. In this chapter, we examined the intended and unintended effects of a range of portrayals and provided "food for thought" for current and future advertisers to consider.

In the next chapter, we will continue our examination of portrayals of people by looking at minorities in advertising.

8

The Melting Pot?

Advertising Portrayals of Asians, African Americans, and Hispanics

It is understanding that gives us an ability to have peace. When we understand the other fellow's viewpoint, and he understands ours, then we can sit down and work out our differences.

—Harry S. Truman

Y ou are probably familiar with the term "melting pot" used as a descriptor of the makeup of the citizenry of the United States. The term melting pot was popularized in a 1908 play titled *The Melting Pot* by British Jewish playwright Israel Zangwill. In the play, Zangwill's idea of a country serving as a melting pot suggested that individuals would melt into a mainstream culture and a diverse population would become homogenized. Today, though, we think of the melting pot as the melting and fusing of different nationalities and ethnic groups to make up the diversity of our country (Herrmann, 1997). This reflects a change not only in Americans' views of immigrant assimilation and integration but also in the definition of an American nation.

If you were to draw a picture of the average American, what would you draw? Most likely, the picture would be strongly influenced by your own worldview. Pictures drawn by people in Biloxi, Mississippi, would probably be very different from those drawn by people living in Seattle, Washington, reflecting the different mix of cultures and people who live in those cities. Advertising also serves as a way to help us define our worldviews and thus our image of the melting pot. For example, a recent advertisement for Gapbody (Gap's lingerie division) (Figure 8.1) reflects a diverse worldview. It features six women: two black women, one Asian, one Middle Eastern woman, a Latina, and one blonde white woman.

Figure 8.1   The Gap ad pictures women from several ethnic groups.

Is the Gap ad a good example of how advertising as a whole views the melting pot that is America today? How does advertising reflect the multicultural landscape? The influence of different minority groups on society has never been stronger than it is today, as our society has seen an increase in the number of Americans who identify themselves as a member of one or more minorities (Wentz, 2001). In this chapter, we examine the growth of minorities in the United States and assess how advertisers both market to these groups and how they portray them.

Minorities in the United States

According to the 2000 U.S. Census, about two thirds (70%) of Americans identify themselves as Caucasian, about 12% identify themselves as African American, a similar percentage identify themselves as Hispanic, and about 4% identify themselves as Asian. Less than 1% of Americans identify themselves as American Indian/Native Alaskan or as Native Hawaiian. About 2% of Americans identify themselves as belonging to more than one racial group.

Growth of Minorities

These statistics do not suggest the influence that minorities have in our society today. Population growth rates of Caucasians compared to minorities' growth rates show that the influence of minorities in America will continue to grow for the next several decades. As a whole, the United States is experiencing a growth rate of 9%, with the Caucasian population only growing at a rate of about 3%. Future population growth in America will come from those groups currently in the minority. The African American population is growing at a rate of 14% per year. The Asian population has experienced a growth rate of about 50% over the past decade and is predicted to double by the year 2020 to represent 8% of the total population (Taylor & Stern, 1997). In the last decade, the number of Hispanics in the United States has grown by 58%. The total minority population of the United States is expected to grow by 10.9% by the year 2020 (Cable Advertising Bureau, 2000).

Given these growth rates, it is not surprising that the ethnic composition of younger people in the United States differs significantly from the ethnic composition of older people. If we look at the 25% of Americans who are currently under the age of 25, about one third of these younger adults are black and Hispanic. In the population as a whole, only about one fourth of Americans are black and Hispanic (Cable Advertising Bureau, 2000).

Minority groups are concentrated in specific places across the United States. Minorities now represent the majority of the population base in both Los Angeles and Miami, and more than 60% of the population in both cities is composed of Hispanics, blacks, and Asians (Wentz, 2001). About half the population of New York City is composed of Hispanics, blacks, and Asians. Blacks tend to live in urban areas: About 50% of African Americans live in the top 15 markets in the United States (Cable Advertising Bureau, 2000). The Asian population is concentrated in five states: 75% of all Asians live in California, Hawaii, New York, Illinois, and Washington.

Spending Power

Minorities have grown not only in numbers but also in their financial impact on society. The Census Bureau reports that the median household income in the United States today is about $43,000. The census group of Asians/Hawaiians/Native Americans has an average household income higher than the U.S. average: $45,904. The median household income for Asian households is almost 20% more than the U.S. average, and almost twice as many Asians have a bachelor's degree compared with the rest of the population (Taylor & Stern, 1997). Caucasian homes have slightly higher median household incomes, about $44,266. The average household income for African Americans is $30,439 and for Hispanics is $33,447. More than 40% of African Americans now consider themselves members of the middle class, and 75% of married black couples own their own homes (Thernstrom & Thernstrom, 1998). Although disparities exist in the household incomes of different ethnic groups, this too will be changing in the future. The average income for whites grew only by about 4% in the past years, while the average incomes for blacks and Hispanics grew by 9%.

Buying power is a measure of household or individual income from all sources minus personal taxes and other tax payments; it is also referred to as disposable or net income. Buying power for Americans in the year 2000 totaled $7 trillion dollars. The Caucasian population represented about 75% of the population and about 80% ($5.6 trillion) of the total buying power. African American consumers had buying power of $572 billion, and Hispanics had buying power of $453 billion. Asian American buying power was $254 billion, and Native American buying power was about $35 billion (Humphreys, 2000). Like population numbers overall, black spending power is growing faster than the national average (Armstrong, 1999), and total minority buying power has almost doubled since 1990 (Cable Advertising Bureau, 2000).

Studies have examined what different ethnic groups spend their money on, and these studies show that there are no differences in per capita spending by ethnic group for a range of categories, including big-ticket items, (e.g., appliances and furniture), and lower-cost items, (e.g., groceries). In a few categories, differences in spending and ownership exist. For example, the percentages owning life insurance policies are similar for whites and blacks: 88% of whites and 85% of blacks have insurance policies. Only about 58% of Hispanics have insurance (Cable Advertising Bureau, 2000). There are slight differences in credit card ownership and usage among ethnic groups, as 63% of whites have credit cards, while only 53% of blacks and 49% of Hispanics do. Credit card usage also differs by group; blacks and Hispanics are less likely than whites to use credit cards for large purchases. Instead, blacks and Hispanics prefer to save their money for big-ticket items.

Minority groups represent greater buying influence than whites in several categories. For example, 55% of Snickers bars are bought by blacks (Wentz, 2001). Blacks also tend to spend more than the average American on personal care items (e.g., soap and shampoo), women's accessories, jewelry, and children's clothing (Bush, Smith, & Martin, 1999). Blacks and Hispanics patronize fast-food restaurants more frequently than whites (Cable Advertising Bureau, 2000). A recent study showed the growth rate for new car buying among blacks is 12 times the rate of whites.

Marketing and Advertising to Minorities

It is clear that minority groups represent important segments to all types of companies that provide goods and services to Americans. However, advertisers' recognition of the importance of the groups is inconsistent. Many advertisers do not specifically target any minority group. Most advertisers that specifically target minority populations identify Hispanics as their primary minority group target, with Asians identified as their second most important target and with blacks, the largest group, as their third priority.

Other groups, such as Native Americans, are rarely targeted, and groups that may be considered Caucasian but do not ethnically identify with Caucasians (e.g., Eastern Europeans and Middle Eastern individuals) are also rarely targeted (Shanahan, 1999).

Advertising Spending

Advertising spending patterns further emphasize advertisers' lack of recognition of minorities. Approximately $280 billion was spent on advertising in 2001. Of this huge budget, $2.1 billion was spent in Hispanic media (e.g., the Univision cable network) and $1.5 billion was spent in black-targeted media (e.g., *Ebony* magazine). Less than $500 million was spent in media targeted specifically to Asians. Of this total spending in advertising, only 1.3% of all advertising dollars was dedicated to targeted ethnic media.

Advertising parity suggests that advertising directed to minority groups should approximately equal the percentage of national income earned by minorities. If the black market represents 3% of the national income, for example, then 3% of all clients' advertising budgets should be targeted to blacks. However, there is not a single national advertiser that devotes at least 3% of its ad budget to the black market (Templeton, 1997).

Media Usage

Some people dismiss these ideas of parity specifically because minorities are likely to be exposed to the same messages that Caucasians are. The nature of a mass medium is to reach the masses, regardless of their ethnic identity. However, studies show that ethnic groups differ somewhat in their media habits. Whites are more likely to read a daily newspaper than blacks and Hispanics. More than half of all whites (54%) are regular newspaper readers, but only about one third of blacks are. The relationship between ethnicity and regular readership of daily newspapers may be due somewhat to the relative socioeconomic status of minorities compared to whites—that is, the higher one's income, the more likely one is to read a paper. However, this observation does not fully explain the difference in readership. African Americans with lower incomes are less likely to read daily newspapers regularly than higher-income African Americans (which fits the socioeconomic model). However, higher-income African Americans are still less likely to regularly read newspapers than higher-income Caucasians ("Media Audiences," 2000). Thus, newspapers seem to lack some specific aspect of content or advertising that would increase their appeal to blacks.

Asians have high newspaper readership, and this may be due to newspapers' inclusion of extensive and specific information that is intrinsically appealing to Asians (Cable Advertising Bureau, 2000). Hispanics represent the highest rate of newspaper reading among any ethnic group. Readership information shows that 71% of Hispanics read a paper daily, with about half of these reading English-language papers, about 40% reading Spanish-language papers, and 10% reading both English and Spanish papers (i.e., reading more than one newspaper). Hispanics spend half an hour a day reading the paper.

There appear to be greater commonalities among ethnic groups in television viewing than in newspaper reading. You have probably noticed that some TV networks feature programs with multicultural casts (e.g., the popular shows *ER*, *Law and Order*, and *CSI*). Other networks, such as UPN and the WB, attempt to appeal specifically to blacks, reflected in high ratings for black viewers in programs such as *The Steve Harvey Show* (CNN, 1999). If you examined the most-watched series for both blacks and whites, the lists would be similar: Programs like *ER*, *60 Minutes*, *Monday Night Football*, and *NYPD Blue* are watched by equal proportions of blacks and whites.

Blacks spend 40% more time each week watching television than the general population, and shows featuring black families are watched by blacks more than other ethnic groups (Cable Advertising Bureau, 2000). Individuals in black homes watch about 4 hours of television each day. In an average week, the average black household watches 14 hours of prime-time television, 11 hours of daytime television, and 7 hours of late-night television (Nielsen Media Research, 2000). Local TV news has viewing levels that are fairly representative of ethnic groups in the local market, although African Americans are less likely than Caucasians to watch world and national TV news. These differences in TV news viewing levels are not as pronounced as they are for daily newspaper readership.

Hispanic households also watch about 4 hours of television each day, with half of the time spent watching English-language programs and half of the time watching Spanish-language programs. Hispanics watch more TV than average in the prime-time and daytime hours: They watch about 17 hours each week in prime time and 10 hours in daytime. Hispanics watch much less late-night television than average.

There is minimal information on the television habits of other ethnic groups, probably because they represent a small proportion of the population and it is difficult to get reliable ratings statistics from such small groups. It has been suggested, though, that Asians are similar to Hispanics in that they watch programs in both English and their native language. However, there are fewer Asian-language options available in the broadcast media than Hispanic options. The average Asian adult watches about 6 hours of native-language television each week (Mogelonsky, 1998).

Blacks and Hispanics listen to the radio often and spend significant amounts of time listening to ethnic stations. Blacks spend 16% more time listening to the radio than whites do (Armstrong, 1999). The majority of blacks listen to radio stations with an "urban" format (Cable Advertising

Bureau, 2000). Hispanics listen to the radio about 4 hours a day and, like their television viewing, this time is split equally between English- and Spanish-language radio programming.

Advertising Attitudes

It is very difficult to generalize as to how different groups approach advertising because there is a wide range of approaches and attitudes toward all types of mediated communications in our society. However, research has examined the roles of advertising and brands for different groups in society, including ethnic groups. Overall, for example, blacks are more positively disposed toward advertising than whites are (Bush et al., 1999). Blacks also appear to have more positive feelings toward brands in general than other groups: Blacks are willing to pay more for brands than other groups are, and they are more loyal to brands than the average consumer (Cable Advertising Bureau, 2000). Asians also highly value brands and make purchase decisions based on both the value associated with the brand and the reputation and history of companies that own brands—information that can come from brand images (Cable Advertising Bureau, 2000).

There are also differences in ethnic groups' perceptions of advertising appeals and strategies used by advertisers. For example, blacks tend to pay more attention to commercials run in television shows with black casts than they do to commercials in television programs with white casts. For Hispanics, commercials in Spanish are more effective at increasing brand awareness than English-language commercials (Cable Advertising Bureau, 2000). These findings suggest that advertisers are incorrect in their perceptions that targeting whites will effectively reach minorities.

Recently, several advertisers have created their own magazines to appeal to the specific needs and attitudes of minorities, particularly Hispanics. Procter & Gamble, a company that manufactures a range of household and personal care products, now publishes a magazine called *Avanzando con Tu Familia (Moving Ahead With Your Family)*. This magazine features household advice as well as advertising for Procter & Gamble brands, all in Spanish. Sears has also created a quarterly magazine called *Nuestra Gente (Our People)* (Figure 8.2). This magazine features articles about Hispanic celebrities and advertisements for Sears fashions in Spanish. With such magazines, advertisers can address specific ethnic needs and provide messages about products that solve specific ethnic problems.

Portrayals of Ethnic Groups

Does advertising present an accurate worldview in terms of the melting pot of American society? We now examine portrayals of ethnic groups in

Figure 8.2   The magazine *Nuestra Gente* is published by Sears.

advertising, specifically from the following perspectives: How frequently do minorities appear in commercials? What types of commercials do minorities appear in? In what roles are they portrayed? The intended and unintended effects of such portrayals are then examined.

Frequency of Representation

Recall the discussion of advertising parity earlier in this chapter that suggested that parity was achieved when spending for minority group ads equaled the group's spending power. Frequency of representation is a similar concept, which looks at the number of minority individuals in advertisements as a proportion of all people shown in advertisements. It suggests that for portrayals to be at parity, minority representation in advertisements should approximate the minority's proportion in the population (Taylor & Stern, 1997).

Any discussion of the frequency of portrayals of minority groups in advertising must begin with the findings that Caucasians are the dominant group portrayed in all types of advertising. For example, a recent study of the portrayals of ethnic groups found that Caucasians appeared in almost all of the television commercials studied. African Americans appeared in about 33% of all television advertisements, Hispanics appeared in about 10%, and Asians appeared in about 8% (Taylor & Stern, 1997).

Looking specifically at ethnic group prominence in the commercials, the study found that minorities only occasionally appear as the sole or the primary character in most television commercials today. Caucasians played major roles in 90% of the spots, regardless of gender. African Americans appeared in major roles in half of the commercials, with women playing more major roles than men. Hispanics played major roles in about half of the commercials they were in, and male and female major role portrayals were equivalent. Asian models played major roles in about half of the commercials in which they appeared, although very few Asian women had major roles in commercials (Taylor & Stern, 1997).

A different study showed that the number of blacks in commercials has been increasing over the past decade (Bush et al., 1999). Blacks are more likely to appear in integrated advertisements (e.g., along with people representing other ethnic groups). When they appear, they tend to be in only minor or background roles and are rarely the sole character in an advertisement (Green, 1999).

A third study reinforced the lack of blacks as sole characters in advertisements. This study looked at ethnic portrayals in different product categories and provided the following statistics on television commercials:

- Of the 105 commercials for autos or trucks that showed only one race, the percentage all-Caucasian: 100%.
- Of the 74 commercials for perfumes that showed only one race, the percentage all-Caucasian: 98%.
- Of the 47 commercials for jewelry or cosmetics that showed only one race, the percentage all-Caucasian: 100% (Entman & Rojecki, 2000).

Think about these statistics in light of our earlier discussion that blacks tend to spend higher than average amounts on jewelry and personal care products and have growth rates for new car purchasing far larger than whites. The lack of black representation in major roles in commercials may suggest that many advertisers lack foresight and understanding of ethnic targets.

The Magazine Publishers of America (MPA) monitors placement of minorities in magazine editorial and advertising content. Their most recent study analyzed publications with a cover date of August 2001 and found that Asians, Hispanics, and African Americans comprised only 19% of images in advertisements featuring images of people. In 1999, the study found that 29% of images in advertisements featured these minority groups; thus, the presence of minorities has decreased by about one third in a 2-year period (Magazine Publishers of America, 2001). The study showed, however, that African Americans were presented in advertisements about equally to their population: They appeared in 12.4% of ads and represented 12.3% of the U.S. population. Asians had a much higher appearance in magazines compared to their presence in the population: They appeared in 6% of ads featuring people, and they represented about 4% of the population. Hispanics, though, appeared in only 2% of ads, which is much lower than their population penetration would suggest that they appear (Magazine Publishers of America, 2001). However, the study reported that there was some difficulty in consistently identifying the presence of Hispanics in print advertising.

The same study indicated that magazines featuring the greatest percentage of advertisements containing minorities included *Fortune*, *Better Homes and Gardens*, *Redbook*, and *People*. Ads that had limited numbers of minorities in advertisements included the newsweeklies (*Time*, *Newsweek*, and *U.S. News and World Report*), as well as *Esquire* and *Sports Illustrated* (Magazine Publishers of America, 2001).

When you look at media directed specifically to minorities, the entire picture changes. In media targeted to blacks, for example, black models are often seen: 80% of the people in ads in *Essence* magazine are black. In the Hispanic-targeted magazine *Latina*, about half the people in ads appear to be Hispanic. In the Asian magazine *A*, all of the advertisements featured Asian women (Magazine Publishers of America, 2001).

Figure 8.3   Many ads that feature a minority character also feature a Caucasian one, as evidenced by this Nice 'n Easy ad.

Although these three ethnic groups are the ones primarily discussed in academic research and the media, it is important to recognize the other minority groups in the United States and the fact that they are invisible in both research studies and in advertising. Most notably, Native Americans account for 2% of the U.S. population and are almost never seen in advertisements or in any other mass media. This lack of attention is discussed later in this chapter.

Types of Products

Minorities tend to appear in advertisements in specific product categories. Blacks, for example, appear frequently in ads for health and beauty products (although not as the sole person in the advertisement, as discussed earlier). Advertisements in the health and beauty category, in fact, use the greatest mix of multicultural models (one example is the Nice 'n Easy ad in Figure 8.3). Black models are also overrepresented in advertisements for liquor, wine, and beer and underrepresented in advertisements for clothing (Jacobson & Mazur, 1995). Another study found that blacks appeared frequently in commercials for food and beverages, as well as for financial products (Figure 8.4) and cars, but rarely appeared in advertisements for over-the-counter drugs (Taylor & Stern, 1997).

Asians appear often in print advertisements for products and services related to science and technology, such as computers (Magazine Publishers of America, 2001) (Figure 8.5). On television, they are seen in advertisements for both cosmetics and retail stores, yet are rarely seen in advertisements for food and beverages, over-the-counter drugs, and automobiles (Taylor & Stern, 1997). Hispanics appear in advertisements for the greatest range of products, including automotive, entertainment, and clothing. Hispanics also appeared in commercials for telecommunications companies (e.g., for long-distance services), as well as in advertisements for banking and finance. Caucasians, not surprisingly, appeared consistently in advertisements for all these products (Taylor & Stern, 1997).

©Wachovia Corporation

$800,000 IN CAPITAL GAINS
÷ 4 SHELTERED INVESTMENTS
+ WACHOVIA
─────────────────
= SOLVED

You've invested wisely. Now it's time to enjoy your earnings. One small problem–taxes. Wachovia can present you with new choices, including tax-advantaged wealth management options designed to make sure you keep as much as you deserve. Problem solved.

WHAT WEALTH MANAGEMENT PROBLEMS DO YOU NEED SOLVED?

LET'S GET STARTED?

WACHOVIA

Figure 8.4   Financial products such as those offered by Wachovia are one of the few categories in which blacks are often featured.

Products targeted to teens, such as clothing, makeup, accessories, candy, snacks, and fast food, often feature minority teens in their advertising messages (Figures 8.6 and 8.7). This may be due to perceptions that so-called "ethnic" cultures are trendy and cutting edge, whereas Caucasian culture is traditional and boring. This trendy aspect can appeal to both minority teens and to Caucasian teens. For example, brands like Nike and Tommy Hilfiger were purchased initially by young black men, who integrated the looks into rap culture (Klein, 1999). As that type of culture increased in popularity among all teens, not only because of its trendy style but also because of its rebellious nature, Nike and Tommy Hilfiger were included in the wave of popularity. Similarly, Hispanics in Los Angeles began the trend of wearing shower sandals in the late 1980s. Shoe manufacturer Converse marketed the sandals to kids outside Los

The smiles around the conference room table have yet to fade when reality starts to sink in: The deal has just been inked, but success now depends on your ability to figure out how to combine environments, integrate old systems with new ones, make disparate hardware and software work together. And while you're at it, make sure the whole infrastructure stays up and running.

One thing's for certain, though. You can't just throw more money at the problem. In today's marketplace, you have to throw more intelligence at it. And that means finding someone to work with you who understands that the problem you're facing comes with its own unique set of timing, budget and technology constraints.

To that end, we offer up the breadth of experience that comes with HP Services: 30,000 professionals in 120 countries who prefer to solve problems more with their heads than just with a purchase order. Solutions based on your particular business needs—whether they require consulting, financing, education, support or even total outsourcing expertise.

We've helped thousands of businesses with virtually every aspect of their IT environments. From designing and maintaining powerful, always-on infrastructures to implementing smoother, large-scale systems migrations and integrations to supporting multi-vendor environments. All without forcing them into restrictive niches or long, expensive engagement cycles.

HP infrastructure solutions—servers, software, storage, services and beyond—are engineered for the real world of business. Because the last time we checked, that's where we all work. Call 1.800.HPASKME, ext. 246. Or visit hp.com/go/infrastructure.

Infrastructure: it starts with you.

Figure 8.5   Asians are often featured in advertisements for high-tech products, such as this HP ad.

Angeles as part of the cutting-edge Latino culture. Malcolm Gladwell refers to such diffusion of trends into the population as a democratization of an idea (Rushkoff, 2000). Eventually, what is seen as cool in teen culture may also diffuse into adult culture, although by then the trend will no longer be seen as cool by teens.

Types of Role Portrayals

As we have seen so far, the advertising worldview of minority groups is somewhat different from the worldview of Caucasians. When examining the types of roles portrayed by minorities in advertising, it appears that the range of portrayals is somewhat limited. Therefore, minority portrayals in advertising are not necessarily evocative of the range of roles minorities play in our society.

Blacks are often portrayed as athletes, entertainers, and as reliant on others in society (Figure 8.8) Throughout the first half of the 20th century, advertisements featured blacks as domestic servants (e.g., Aunt Jemima and Uncle Ben). While some of these advertising portrayals linger on, in general they have been replaced by other portrayals suggesting in a less explicit way that blacks are dependent on others. Blacks are often seen in advertisements as being in need and assisted by others: Any commercial for a cash-advance service, for example, is likely to feature blacks needing a loan and whites behind the counter. In addition, blacks are often pictured as caregivers for children. This type of portrayal could be seen as an extension of the "domestic servant" role (Humphrey & Schuman, 1984).

Toward the latter part of the 20th century, blacks began to be featured in advertisements predominantly as sports figures and entertainment personalities. These portrayals have increased to the point today that this role tends to be overrepresented in advertisements when compared to other minorities and to whites. Famous black athletes sell a range of products from cars (Tiger Woods for Buick) to shoes (Kobe Bryant for Adidas and Nike) to underwear (Michael Jordan for Hanes)

Figure 8.6 Minorities are portrayed in an ad for Fruitopia directed toward teens.

to fast food (Shaquille O'Neal for Burger King). Entertainers such as Queen Latifah are featured in cosmetics advertising (Figure 8.9).

Equally limited is the range of portrayals for Hispanics. Advertising presents four common Hispanic stereotypes: bandit, lover, spitfire, and sweet señorita (Figure 8.10 shows the spitfire image in an OPI ad). These roles are also gendered: Men appear as the bandit or the Latin lover (e.g., Ricky Martin in Pepsi's Joy of Cola campaign), and women appear as the Latina spitfire (e.g., pop star Shakira in spots for Pepsi's Joy of Cola) or the sweet señorita (Artze, 2000).

The bandit image is particularly offensive to the Hispanic population. This image was created for Frito-Lay, and similar bandits were used by a number of other companies, including Granny Goose potato chips and Elgin watches (Noriega, 1997). The bandit stereotype focuses on an image of a dirty and unlawful Hispanic spokesperson and obviously would not be appreciated by many Hispanics. Multiple Hispanic groups, such as the Mexican-American Anti Defamation Committee, fought a long and

FIGHTS BREAKOUTS
WHILE YOU WASH

FIGHTS BREAKOUTS
AFTER YOU WASH

The cleanser that leaves invisible acne medicine in your pores

Figure 8.7   This ad for Johnson & Johnson Clean and Clear includes both a Caucasian and a Hispanic teenager.

eventually successful battle to prevent Frito-Lay from using the Frito Bandito character (Nuiry, 1996).

Asian stereotypes are limited to the exotic character, the hard worker, or the model minority. The exotic image features portrayals of Asian women as dragon ladies or China dolls, women at opposite ends of the spectrum. Dragon ladies are women who are inherently scheming, untrustworthy, and backstabbing. China dolls are docile and delicate women subservient to men. The Japanese geisha can fall into the China doll category. Other exotic imagery includes stereotypes of Asians as martial arts fighters, such as the Mountain Dew spot that is a takeoff on the movie *Crouching Tiger Hidden Dragon*. Another example of the exotic image is seen in the milk ads in Figure 8.11.

The hardworking Asian portrayal is seen in images such as the Korean grocer (working long hours), Japanese businessman, and TV anchorwoman. In some ways, the hardworking Asian portrayal is related to pictures of Asians as the model minority: These Asians get good grades, are good corporate citizens, do not rock boats, and are hard workers. In some cases, this model minority portrayal presents Asians as flawless to the point of being robbed of humanity. Associated with this hardworking image is a lack of portrayals of Asians in family settings (Taylor & Stern, 1997).

Intended Effects

Minorities appear in advertising messages but in a limited range of portrayals and for a limited range of product categories. At this point, you might be asking yourself: What are advertisers thinking? How can they ignore such an important segment of the population? However, as you might suspect, advertisers' choices have intended and unintended effects.

Assimilation and Acculturation

Assimilation is the action of making or becoming like something else; acculturation is the adoption of an alien culture. Both terms present the same phenomenon from different points of view (assimilation from the point of view of the dominant culture; acculturation from the point of view of the minority culture). Advertisers may believe that, when targeting some consumers with messages

Figure 8.8   Black entertainers featured in advertisements for handbags (Dooney and Burke)

for certain products or services, minority groups have assimilated into Caucasian culture to the point that acculturation has occurred. Consequently, images and concepts become equally appealing to Caucasians, African Americans, Asians, and Hispanics. An example of this is the portrayal of the good mom discussed in an earlier chapter. Arguably, the concept of a good mom transfers across cultures, and thus showing a white good mom may resonate as strongly with minority women as it does with white women.

Connecting With What Is "Cool"

On the other hand, in some cases, using minorities in advertising is more appealing than using Caucasians. Using minority teens in advertisements for teen-oriented products like electronics, apparel, and snacks appeals to a range of teens in the United States. As a whole, teenagers are highly

Figure 8.9 Actress Queen Latifah is featured with singer Faith Hill in an ad for Cover Girl cosmetics.

influenced by the cutting-edge trends of minorities (Chura, 2001). Black culture, in particular, has always been associated with what is cool. For example, music styles from jazz to blues to rock 'n' roll to hip-hop have had a strong black influence (Klein, 1999). Asian culture is seen as advanced in technology, which may also appeal to teens, who tend to be the earliest adopters of technical products.

Setting the Stage

As discussed in Chapter 6, advertisers have specific reasons for using stereotypes. Advertisers continue to use stereotyped imagery because it is embedded in communication shorthand and tends to set the stage quickly for advertising messages.

Unintended Effects

Marginalization and Invisibility

Overall, minorities tend to be underrepresented in advertising. In addition, it is clear from the statistics presented earlier in this chapter that, although some minorities tend to be somewhat fairly represented, certain minority groups may not be represented at all. For example, the advertising community has largely neglected the black middle class. Middle-class black families rarely appear in advertising messages.

Another example of the industry's underrepresentation is the fact that advertising tends to focus on minority groups only on specific occasions. For example, advertising directed to the black community has been criticized because it runs mainly in February, which is Black History Month. This suggests that blacks are only customers once a year (Franklin, 2000; Templeton, 1997). Additionally, the Hispanic community is often featured in advertising during the first part of May (during the Cinco de Mayo celebration) and ignored throughout the rest of the year.

This invisibility of minorities in advertising may have several effects. Invisibility may result in holding minorities back from opportunities. The messages may suggest that minorities should refrain from trying to become visible in society and that it is better to stay in their place and not try to improve themselves or take advantage of the American Dream. Minorities become ostracized from the mainstream culture.

Figure 8.10 OPI Nail Lacquer features the "spitfire" in their ads.

When minority groups are not seen as the central focus of the message, they then become cast as cultural outsiders. This may slow down the group's assimilation into the host culture and can be particularly problematic for Asians and Hispanic immigrants to the United States because many in these groups wish to assimilate quickly and easily (Taylor & Stern, 1997). In particular, the exclusions of Native Americans and Asian women from advertising will make them feel neglected by advertisers, creating a silent minority that is further ostracized from the mainstream (Taylor & Stern, 1997).

The limited range of societal roles also communicates what could be seen as society's priorities for specific groups. For example, if African Americans see only athletes and entertainers as role models, they may believe that these are the only types of jobs that are valued. They may not consider other career goals and only focus on goals presented to them in the media, which they may not be able to attain.

Figure 8.11 Exotic images in milk ads

Marginalization and invisibility of minorities can also negatively affect the overall worldview that members of ethnic groups have of other groups. For example, whites in America are likely to misinterpret some basic information about minorities, such as the size of the groups (many whites believe that minority populations are smaller than they really are). Both blacks and whites exaggerate the percentage of blacks living in the inner city because most media portray blacks living there. In reality, blacks who consider themselves to be middle class outnumber those with incomes below the poverty line by a wide margin (Thernstrom & Thernstrom, 1998).

False Perceptions of Diversity

"One of the dangers of marketing schemas and demographic sketches is that they often reduce complex, multifaceted audiences to stereotypical simplifications that lack the original group's rich diversity" (Gobé, 2001, p. 34). Another unintended effect is that the advertising industry rarely recognizes subcultures or subgroups that exist within each minority group. For example, there are six major Asian subgroups: Chinese Americans, Japanese Americans, Filipino Americans, Korean Americans, Vietnamese Americans, and Indian Americans. Hispanic subgroups include Mexicans, Puerto Ricans, and more. By treating all members of a minority the same, the culture's wealth of diversity is ignored.

Fetishization

Fetishization is the process of making one feature stand for a whole person. It is similar to the concept of objectification discussed in Chapter 7, which is treating a person as a sexual or other kind of object that is defined more by your own needs or ideas than by the person him- or herself. Using black culture in advertisements to whites and other groups fetishizes black style. In turn, blacks begin fetishization of white wealth (Klein, 1999). That is, whites develop an exemplum of blacks as stylish to the exclusion of any other portrayal. Blacks in turn think of whites only as wealthy people who are hopelessly uncool and only have a desire to be cool. Again, another exemplum is developed. Any such limited viewpoint can be highly problematic and possibly dangerous.

Some critics argue that fetishization can reflect and perpetuate racism in our society. Specifically, the roles and images that are portrayed in advertisements and other mass media reinforce racial subordination. By creating an exemplum that turns the minority group into objects rather than people, one group develops negative attitudes toward another group (Noriega, 1997). This is an example of expectancy theory, discussed in Chapter 6, at its worst.

Advertising, Minorities, and the Future

What does the future hold for minorities in advertising? Before we answer this question, we must first consider why some advertisers continue to use stereotypes of minorities in their advertising to this day. Many possible explanations exist. Some argue that advertising agencies' limited worldview is a result of an industry that is run by a homogeneous group of white men who do not understand or even try to understand minorities and minority culture. But this may be too simplistic an explanation, given the wide range of advertising agencies working today. What is probably more realistic is that advertisers and marketers have come to realize the importance of minorities (both in terms of targeting and in terms of purchasing influence) but have not yet figured out how to allocate marketing funds in meaningful ways to minority targets.

Advertising budgets rarely contain funds specifically earmarked for minority targeting. Advertisers have attributed this to the difficulty of determining the percentages of sales that come from minority groups; thus, determining appropriate parity levels is almost impossible ("Face Reality of New Demo," 2001). Moreover, although there are several agencies that develop messages specifically for minorities, such messages may not always be successful in communicating to minorities. Often, these multicultural agencies are following strategies set out by mainstream agencies that plan and execute messages for the white majority target. These strategies might or might not resonate with members of minority targets ("Face Reality of New Demo," 2001).

With this explanation of the challenges facing advertising agencies in terms of minority markets, let us now examine some of the current changes in the advertising landscape that we have seen. Large conglomerate agencies have recently been purchasing smaller multicultural agencies and have integrated them into the mainstream agencies. Agency giant Ogilvy and Mather, for example, recently bought the Hispanic agency Latin Works. Working with the mainstream creative group, Latin Works developed a Miller Lite campaign for the Hispanic market that ran nationally. This campaign was seen as highly successful in part because Latin Works participated with the mainstream agency in all facets of the campaign, including strategic development, instead of implementing a strategy they did not develop.

Such a team effort is seen as important for the success of minority advertising because it is a challenge to develop effective yet not offensive culturally based marketing communication (Armstrong, 1999). To create messages that do not perpetuate negative stereotypes of minorities and that work to develop more contemporary portrayals of all persons in the United States, there are several points to keep in mind.

Put a Range of People in Ads

People like to see images of people like themselves in advertising. This does not mean, however, that Caucasians only like to see Caucasians in commercial messages. Caucasian consumers respond just as favorably to ads featuring minority models as to ads featuring Caucasian models (Green, 1999). Using minorities more frequently in advertisements is a first step to making minorities more visible and to having the opportunity to provide a range of images of minorities in the media. In addition, research has shown that using minorities in advertisements can increase sales to minority groups without negatively affecting sales to Caucasians (Duvert & Foster, 1999).

From a long-term perspective, increasing the number of minorities in advertisements may help consumers change their worldviews regarding minorities. Accommodation theory suggests that as person A becomes more similar to person B, the likelihood that person B will favorably evaluate person A increases (Green, 1999). So, when persons of one race see that there are some people in another race that have wants and needs similar to theirs, they will begin to broaden their own picture of what people of that race are like.

Learn About Lives Other Than Your Own

In addition to increasing the visibility of minorities, advertisers need to present positive images of multicultural life. To do this, they need to understand more about multicultural life and experience it for themselves. Advertisers need to recognize the importance of the culture in the community by getting involved from the bottom up, not from the top down, in recognizing the rich cultural diversity of their markets (Shanahan, 1999).

Advertisers need to present a variety of cultures in their messages, but they must be sensitive enough not to bleed one culture into another during the creation of the messages. One approach to marketing to minorities is premised on the idea that communications are most effective when their various elements (e.g., how the message is delivered, the content of the message, and the values and symbols inherent in the message) refer to the specific culture (Armstrong, 1999). Having different types of cultural symbolism in a single message, then, may be confusing, alienating, and damaging to the brand.

Similarly, advertisers should recognize that some concepts and images work better for multicultural advertising than others do. Focusing on product attributes may not be the best strategy, as all attributes may not be equally relevant to different minority groups. Instead, consider using emotional appeals that resonate throughout different groups.

Recently, some advertisers have developed a process known as *blurring*, which is a mixing and blending of racial and ethnic traits that allows advertisers to tap into messages that resonate across traditional ethnic boundaries (Wentz, 2001). Snapple's brand Mistic, which is targeted to urban populations of African Americans and Hispanics, uses the tag line "Go Bold." This sentiment was seen as representing an important urban cultural value: bold self-expression. This is a departure from the advertising for other beverages, which target minorities using cultural icons (e.g., Sprite's use of Kobe Bryant and Pepsi's use of Rick Martin). The tag line for Mistic resonated with urban youth to a great extent: Mistic's sales rose by almost 30% after the campaign began.

Make Multicultural Advertising a Priority

Paying lip service to the importance of minorities today is not enough. Clifford Franklin, in a criticism of the preponderance of advertisements about blacks during Black History Month and the dearth of advertising during the rest of the year, challenged agencies to question their clients and bring the issue of minority advertising into the forefront. He wrote,

> But we are all supposed to be stewards of the marketing budgets that we control, and we have a fiduciary responsibility to educate our clients on whether money is being spent to garner results. . . . we also have a responsibility to the African-American community to question the sincerity of the companies we represent. (Franklin, 2000, p. 62)

Be Accountable

Agencies need to measure and report on their efforts. By doing so, they begin to develop a history that suggests ways to better target resources and identify what works and what does not. Additionally, the industry needs to be accountable, and sharing success stories is one way to do so (American Advertising Foundation and American Advertising Federation (2003).

Summary

In this chapter, we examined minority groups in the United States and the discrepancies between their economic importance and their portrayals in advertising messages. Trend data suggest that the influence of minorities in our society will only continue to increase; thus, it is imperative for advertising professionals to evaluate their practices and consider ways to include a diverse range of minority portrayals in their messages.

In the next chapter, we will examine another group that rarely appears in advertising: older adults. Like minorities, exclusion of this group can cause marginalization of individuals in the group. Exclusion can also strongly influence the worldview that younger people have of aging.

9

Older and Better?

Elders and Advertising

At that moment, I realized that from the standpoint of advertising and corporate America, I was a dead man walking.

—Jerry Della Femina, on his 50th birthday

Did you know that the year 1999 was the International Year of Older Persons? The United Nations sanctioned this celebration, a focal point of which was a proclamation that highlighted a UN principle stating that older people around the world should be treated fairly regardless of age, gender, racial or ethnic background, disability, or other status. The principle also stated that older people should be valued independently of their economic contribution to society (Carrigan & Szmigin, 2000).

How do you think the United Nations would feel about a recent advertisement for St. Ives Coenzyme Q10 Wrinkle Corrector (Figure 9.1)? This ad does not feature any beautiful young models; in fact, there are no people in the ad at all. The headline reads "Clinically Proven Time Machine," and the subhead asks, "how many years younger will you look?" In 11 little words, the advertisement clearly suggests that becoming old is bad, it is expected that we will be unhappy to age, and we will want to look younger. Even the name of the product, a "Wrinkle Corrector," suggests that there is something incorrect about aging and developing wrinkly skin. The ad quickly positions being young as desirable and being old as unthinkable. This stands out in stark contrast to the goals of the International Year of Older Persons celebration.

In this chapter, we examine the youth bias in advertising and the current state of elders in advertising. Specifically, we examine how often older people appear in advertisements, for what types of products, and in what

Figure 9.1   Coenzyme Q10 advertises itself to be a "clinically proven time machine."

types of roles. This discussion, though, must be considered in light of the major demographic changes occurring in the United States.

The Third Age in American Culture

Some claim the most important demographic for advertisers and marketers to consider is that of age. Whether a teen, a young adult, a thirty-something, or someone entering the so-called "third age" (the age after being a child and raising a child), the age of an individual will not only be a key determinant of what consumers want and need to buy but also of whether consumers have the money to afford the purchase (Clark, 1988). Using simple logic, you might then expect that older people would be a desirable target for marketers. For one reason, many older adults have money to buy what they want: They are either at the top of their earning power or living comfortably on their retirement incomes. They have more time to consider purchases than consumers with young children do. Finally, virtually all older adults have the ability to be exposed to many different types of media to learn about a range of products and services. In Europe, many products and services are directed toward older adults, who are portrayed in European advertising as active and fun-loving people (Clark, 1988).

However, American culture has been criticized as having a blatant disregard and disrespect for older people (Tupper, 1995). Such attitudes have been influenced by a number of factors such as:

• Mass immigration. Historically, immigration from other countries to the United States is done by young people who leave the elderly behind. This lack of a tie with older adults may contribute to general disregard for older people.

• Cultural values. The United States was founded on principles of individualism, independence, and autonomy. As people age, they may have to give up some of these valuable freedoms and therefore may not feel part of society.

• Increased mobility. As children grow up and move away from their parents, family ties can often be loosened. As with mass immigration, the value of the wisdom of the older generations becomes less important to society.

• Medical advances. The incidence of younger people dying due to disease has decreased dramatically. Unlike other times in history, death is now associated primarily with old age.

Along with these specific factors is an overall devaluation of tradition in society, as new technology demands constant change and looking for the latest thing as opposed to valuing the past. In light of all these factors, it is now difficult in our society to think about old age as a valued and contributory phase of life (Butler, Lewis, & Sunderland, 1991, p. 30).

Older people are generally absent from our mass media. Older people in the United States do not have their own TV shows, they are not singing songs you hear in the top 40, and they rarely appear in television commercials for products other than health-oriented items. When they do appear in commercials for mass marketed products, older people are often stereotyped and mocked. Who has not parodied commercial lines such as "I've fallen and I can't get up" and "where's the beef?". Elderly populations suffer from negative stereotyping more than any other identifiable social group (Dali, 1988).

What exactly is old age? Researchers report three types of age: chronological, biological, and psychological. Chronological age is the age that the calendar says you are—the age on your driver's license. As you know, this is a poor indication of what a person is really like: You may know very mature 10-year-olds and highly immature 19-year-olds. Biological age is the age of your body; it is a result of how well an individual takes care of him- or herself. Biological age is influenced by an individual's diet, his or her level of exercise, if he or she smokes and drinks, if he or she worships the sun, and other lifestyle factors. Psychological age is influenced by an individual's experience, wisdom, and confidence (Leinweber, 2001). For example, a 50-year-old with a child graduating from college will have a different psychological age than a 50-year-old with a child in elementary school because the two parents have likely had highly different life experiences.

It is important for advertisers to consider all three types of age when thinking about older adults as consumers and to avoid generalizing based on biological age alone. For example, studies show that individuals over the age of 60 tend to view themselves as 15 years younger (Polyak, 2000). Given today's advances in medicine, old age increasingly becomes a relative term: Individuals who live to be 65 can expect to live on average to age 83 (Polyak, 2000). In fact, many Americans define the beginning of old age as the decline in mental functioning or physical ability; only 14% said that it began when they reached a specific age (Gardyn, 2000).

Today in the United States, we are experiencing a dramatic population shift that will strongly influence how advertisers and marketers look at, communicate with, and develop messages for elders. The baby boomers, that huge bubble of citizens born post–World War II, are entering their third age and are becoming part of the demographic group that traditionally has been ignored by advertisers. Although we are not sure how advertisers and marketers will react, it is likely that changes in the status quo will occur.

The Youth Bias in American Advertising _____

Much of American advertising reflects the overall youth bias in Western, and specifically American, culture. The people who appear in American ads tend to be young and attractive, and they tend to have perfect bodies (Bradley & Longino, 2001). The youth culture stresses the importance of an individual's physical appearance to his or her self-concept. Since most advertising today is directed to people under the age of 40, it is not surprising that advertisements reinforce the youth bias. However, as people age, the importance of physical appearance to one's self-concept generally diminishes. Instead, one's self-concept becomes based on values such as achievement, comfort, and security (Bradley & Longino, 2001). Thus, many advertising messages seen today by older Americans have little meaning for them. Interestingly, though, the next generation of older adults, aging baby boomers, was a primary force in the development of the youth bias in advertising.

A Historical Perspective

How has the youth bias been inculcated into our culture? It may have started with flappers, a group of young people from well-off families who spent a lot of time in the 1920s enjoying social life. Flappers were seen as trendsetters in society, and advertising targeted the flappers to position their products among a highly visible proportion of the population. Additionally, flappers lived what seemed to be a glamorous, carefree life: a life that many might aspire to.

As flappers grew older, a consumer pattern was created: Younger people spent a lot of time trying to find the newest, trendiest products and then they would settle down in their 20s and 30s and buy homes, furniture, and appliances (Lee, 1997). Once that set of spending patterns was fixed, the household members moved on to purchasing babies' and children's clothing, saving for college education, and planning for retirement. By the time they reached middle age, they had bought all that they needed to buy (Lee, 1997). Thus, the flappers of the 1920s become the older adults of the 1950s and had settled down into a life that was fairly complete in terms of their consumer purchases.

This cycle is changing with the aging of the baby boomers. The baby boom population is made up of Americans who were born between 1946 and 1964; today, in 2002, baby boomers range from 38 to 56 years old. When baby boomers first came into their own in the 1970s, a number of products and campaigns were targeted to the boomers. Not only was the boom large in terms of sheer numbers, but baby boomers also tended to be one of the most affluent segments in history, and they were not conservative in their spending habits. Throughout the 1980s and the 1990s, baby boomers were primary targets first for youth-oriented products like soda and fast food, then new homes and cars, followed by all types of parenting products.

Every 7 seconds, a baby boomer turns 50. By the end of this decade, the vast majority of baby boomers will be older than 50. Today, right now, there are more people over 65 years old than there are teenagers in the United States. This once-desirable boomer population is losing some of its luster among advertisers, particularly due to the youth bias in advertising. This is most clearly seen in the types of media available to reach Americans today, as well as the advertising rates associated with different programs and vehicles.

Skewing Younger and Costing More

Advertisers will pay more to reach younger people than to reach older people. The youth bias is manifest in programming decisions, where programs that appeal to older demographic groups are often canceled and replaced with programs that allow TV stations to draw more younger viewers. For example, 4 million young people watch the WB Network's show *Dawson's Creek*. The WB Network charges about $100,000 for a 30-second spot on the show. The CBS show *60 Minutes* brings in almost four times as many viewers as *Dawson's Creek*, but CBS charges almost the same amount for the *60 Minutes* spot as the WB charges for the *Dawson's Creek* spot (Surowiecki, 2002). Why would an advertiser pay the same amount to reach only 25% as many people? For advertisers, the answer is simple: The viewers of *Dawson's Creek* are more desirable to advertisers than the viewers of *60 Minutes*. The viewership base of *60 Minutes* is older adults; most of the viewers are over the age of 50. In comparison, most of the viewers of *Dawson's Creek* are under the age of 25. The cost comparison of *Dawson's Creek* and *60 Minutes* is not an anomaly; in general, the cost to reach 1000 younger people is three times that of reaching 1000 older people. This premium is due in part to the desirability of younger viewers from a targeting perspective and in part because younger viewers watch less television than their elders (Ahrens, 2002).

Recently, the ABC network wanted to replace Ted Koppel and his late-night news program, *Nightline*, with CBS star David Letterman's *Late Show*. Although *Nightline* consistently drew higher ratings than *Late Show*, Letterman attracted significantly more young viewers than Koppel (Ahrens, 2002). ABC was eager to tap into these viewers, since David Letterman's edginess is viewed as a more complementary environment for younger-skewing (and high-spending) brands such as beer and cars. It was estimated that replacing Koppel with Letterman would have greatly increased revenues at ABC. In the end, David Letterman chose to stay at CBS, and ABC is evaluating their next step in late-night programming.

The youth bias perpetuates through the advertising industry because the advertising industry itself is a young business. The average age of an individual working in an ad agency in the United States is 31 (Carrigan & Szmigin, 2000), and there are few people working at ad agencies who are over the age of 40 (Lee, 1997). Although some advertising professionals in their 20s and 30s understand and appreciate older generations, most young staffers are fixated on advertising that's "hip, cool, impressive to their peers, and award-winning" (Lee, 1997, p. 48). This has been dubbed the "internal audience" problem at advertising agencies (Surowiecki, 2002): How do you get young people interested and excited about advertising to older adults? Addressing this internal audience problem means changing agency culture, which could be difficult, or that clients hire special interest agencies that focus solely on older target audiences.

Elders in Advertising

Criticisms of how the advertising industry views elders focus on the frequency of portrayals, the range of portrayals presented, and the tone in which the portrayals air.

Frequency of Portrayals

Older adults are rarely seen in any type of mass media, including advertising. The mass media emphasis on youth and beauty is one reason older adults are ignored. Studies done during the 1970s and 1980s show that less than 5% of commercials feature any elder characters at all (Francher, 1973; Gerbner, Gross, Morgan, & Signorielli, 1981; Swayne & Grego, 1987). A more recent study showed that while 12.6% of the U.S. population was aged 65 and older, only about 8% of the characters in prime-time commercials were seen as that old (Tupper, 1995).

Females far outnumber males in the population of older adults: A male–female ratio of 63:100 exists for adults aged 65 and older, and the ratio is 46:100 for adults 85 and older. On television commercials, though, the ratio of older men to older women is 133:100. In magazine advertising, the story is much the same. In a study of seven popular magazines and more than 6000 print advertisements, older adults were seen in about 3% of the ads, and only about 25% of all portrayals of older adults were female (Gantz, Gartenberg, & Rainbow, 1980). The only category displaying portrayals of older adults equivalent to the population were in magazines aimed at the older market, such as *Modern Maturity* (Kvasnicka, Beymer, & Perloff, 1982). The situation is worse for elders who belong to minorities: African American, Hispanic, and Asian elders are rarely, if ever, seen in advertisements. One study indicated that less than 1% of all television commercials airing over an 8-week period featured older minority characters (Tupper, 1995).

Role Portrayals of Elders

Role portrayals of elders are often tied directly into the products that sponsor the advertising in which they appear. The primary categories where older adults appear are financial services, food, and health. Each of these brings about a different set of portrayals.

Elders are most often portrayed as retired or as persons planning for retirement, which is reflected in the frequency of their portrayals in advertisements for financial services (Figure 9.2). Retirement can be pictured as a time of inactivity and occasionally of withdrawal (Gardner, 2000). Elders tend not to be seen in the workplace or out with large groups of people but are seen at home thinking about the immediate future and their

RETIREMENT.
IT'S A LOT MORE ENJOYABLE WHEN LINCOLN'S WORKING WITH YOU.

At Lincoln Financial Group, we provide a broad range of financial solutions
to help you enjoy the work of a lifetime. Our retirement transition ideas
and our estate planning solutions can help make sure you're on target
for today as well as the future. See your financial advisor or call
1-877-ASK LINCOLN. *www.LFG.com*

Lincoln
Financial Group®
Clear solutions in a complex world®

Figure 9.2   Elders are often pictured in ads discussing
retirement.

financial needs (Figure 9.3). Often, such portrayals may generate a sense of uneasiness, as viewers compare themselves to the older adults in the ad. For example, viewers of an ad may ask themselves: Am I doing better than them?

In advertisements for food products, elders are often seen as the doting grandparents or as empty nesters. Again, they are seen primarily in the home and not out in the community or workplace. Many older adults appear in advertisements focusing on health and health concerns in particular (Figure 9.4). When older adults are seen as vital, they rarely participate in physically strenuous activities. Instead, they are seen as avid gardeners or riding a golf cart (Adler, 1996).

Advertising Stereotypes

When looking not only at the types of products that older adults advertise but also at the other characteristics of older adults in advertising, some specific stereotypes appear.

The "Happy Couple on a Beach" Stereotype

Ads featuring elders often show them dressed in L. L. Bean khakis, walking in natural outdoor settings in a perfect, calm, and tranquil environment, such as the couple in the TripleFlex ad in Figure 9.5. This stereotype suggests a lack of sophistication in the people developing the advertising and results in messages that treat all members of the elder population in the same way (Chaplin, 1999). Of course, you will be able to find elders who like to walk on the beach or enjoy the peaceful outdoors. However, such images of older adults are not balanced by portrayals of them in the workplace, volunteering in the community, playing sports, and shopping. Thus, the problem becomes not where we see older adults but where we do not see them. The presentation of a third-age lifestyle is limiting to elders and to those of us who may not be elders but interact with them regularly. In addition, many elders dislike this type of imagery because even though it is idyllic, it is seen by many older adults as sanitized, homogenized, dated, and lacking in any sort of hipness or edginess (Chaplin, 1999).

Crotchety Neighbor

Elders are seen as having different attitudes from youth and are often seen as more "set in their ways" than other groups (Figure 9.6). Older adults tend to be portrayed as less fair and less

Figure 9.3   Elders are seen at home worrying about their futures.

rational than younger adults are (Gerbner et al., 1981). This stubborn attitude directly reflects the industry's view of older adults as people who are not open to new ideas and are fanatically loyal to their brands; therefore, advertisers should not bother marketing to them (Dychtwald, 1988, p. 290).

Ill Elders

The AARP (formerly, the American Association of Retired Persons) has found that many ads characterize old people as sick, feeble, infirm, deaf, confused, or perhaps even socially isolated (Figure 9.7). Of course, many such portrayals suggest that the situation can be addressed by the purchase of a product. Such images were reinforced in the media by the controversial ballot counting in Florida during the 2000 presidential election. Many reporters covering the election controversy blamed the large population of

Figure 9.4   This ad for Tylenol Arthritis shows an elder's hand alongside that of a child.

elders for much of the confusion: Older voters were shown as lacking the intelligence to understand the voting procedure (Gardner, 2000).

Intended Effects

Advertisers' limited vision of older adults may reflect the youth bias in the advertising industry today, but there are also intended effects to the choices made by advertisers regarding portrayals of older adults.

Figure 9.5 This TripleFlex ad shows a happy couple not on a beach but in the woods.

High Level of Media Exposure

Older adults' media habits differ from those of younger adults. Specifically, older adults tend to be heavier users of all media than any other age group. For example, while 42% of the general population read a newspaper daily, 71% of elders do. In addition, persons 75 years and older watch more than 5 hours of television daily, again more than any other demographic group (Polyak, 2000). Given their media habits, older adults

Few things come with a money-back guarantee.

So tasty, we know you're going to love them. And if you don't, we'll give you your money back. Guaranteed.
THEY'RE THAT GOOD.™

Figure 9.6   The elder in the Pastry Swirls ad is set in her ways.

will naturally be exposed to information about a wide range of products and services. They probably receive the fullest media worldview of any target market. Thus, the intended effect of most advertising campaigns is to reach less accessible targets; advertising messages and media placement are more effective if they concentrate on young people.

Older Adults Are Brand Loyal

As previously mentioned, there is a feeling among advertisers that older adults are no longer discriminating buyers. Older adults are seen either as brand loyal to a fault or as indiscriminant consumers who will buy anything they see on home shopping cable programs (Della Femina, 1997). Older adults may be more brand loyal than other groups because brand loyalty simplifies the purchasing process. This mirrors other actions taken by elders to simplify their lives (e.g., moving into smaller homes) (Lipke, 2000b). In addition, older adults grew up with fewer brand choices than younger adults did, so they are not as accustomed to switching brands as younger adults.

Advertising's effects on older consumers, then, would be minimal because advertising would only serve to remind brand loyal consumers of their existing brand loyalty. Simply hearing the brand's name would remind them of their brand loyalty. However, elders' brand loyalty is currently being called into question. Recent studies have shown that brand loyalty is on the decline among all age groups, including elders (Lipke, 2000b). Simple name recognition may no longer be enough to retain current levels of brand loyalty.

Figure 9.7   The elder in this ad is not able to spend as much time as he would like with his grandson due to chemotherapy treatments.

Older Adults
Have an Affinity Toward Youth

   Age is crucial to brand perceptions: It is instinctive for consumers to discern which products are targeted to older people and which to younger

IN ONE WEEK, TAKE YEARS OFF YOUR EYES.
Visibly Firm Eye Cream with Active Copper.™

> Copper, a collagen-building mineral, found naturally in your body, is essential for firm skin.
> Neutrogena's Active Copper™ technology gently replenishes copper.

Within one week, clinically proven to:
Firm skin around the eyes ✓
Reduce puffiness ✓
Improve skin's elasticity ✓
Smooth the appearance of fine lines ✓

Neutrogena®
Visibly Firm eye cream

Neutrogena

Figure 9.8   This model probably isn't old enough to need the product being advertised.

people. Older people are likely to purchase products marketed to younger consumers, but younger people will not purchase products directed to older adults (Della Femina, 1997). Indeed, once a product is marketed to older people, it is nearly impossible to market it to younger people (Carrigan & Szmigin, 2000).

As previously discussed, once people pass the age of 60, they tend to view themselves as 15 years younger than they really are. In general, older adults tend to perceive themselves as 75% to 80% of their chronological age. Therefore, using models 10 to 15 years younger than the target is the norm in advertising today (Bradley & Longino, 2001). The rationale is that if an older adult's calendar age is not central in defining the older adult's self-perception, there is little value in using models that match an individual's calendar age in advertising.

Role-Product Congruity

The idea of role-model congruity was discussed in Chapter 7. Basically, this theory suggests that advertising effectiveness can be increased when models appropriate for the products are used. Therefore, older models should be effective for age-neutral products, whereas younger models should be effective when the product is related to the consumer's self-image. This is why younger women are used as models in products that they apparently have no real use for, such as antiwrinkle creams and lotions (Bradley & Longino, 2001) (Figure 9.8).

Unintended Effects

The choices made by marketers and their agencies result in unintended effects toward the target audience and others in society.

Older Adults Are Invisible

The lack of presence of elders in advertising could have the effect of making them invisible in all aspects of society. This may be especially problematic for elderly women, who are featured much less often than elderly men in advertising, misrepresenting their presence in society (Tupper, 1995). If elders are not seen in our society, others may not consider them important in societal processes (e.g., elections) or in the workplace, where age discrimination could be apparent. Arguably, reinforcement of the invisibility of elders can cause harm to older people's opportunity for treatment equal to that of younger adults (Gardner, 2000).

Older Adults Are Offended

When elders are seen, they are often pictured in stereotyped images or situations. Elders themselves report that they are dissatisfied with the marketing efforts and are offended by some of the portrayals that they see (Bradley & Longino, 2001). Many advertisements feature stereotypes that rarely resonate with elders.

A particularly offensive image of elders features the stereotype that elders are infirm, walk with canes, are taking medicine constantly, and have general problems functioning in the world physically. Elders are highly concerned with advertising's emphasis on their medical conditions (Leinweber, 2001). The apparent lack of authenticity of images that picture elders as old-fashioned and separated from the mainstream suggests to older consumers that the advertisers have no idea who they are or what they need. The general concerns with such offending imagery may result in elders boycotting some products (Festervand & Lumpkin, 1985).

Older Adults Are Devalued

Repeated exposure to commercials that carry a negative subtext may lead to the overall devaluation of elders by others in society. Negative stereotyping circumscribes elders' potential by placing emphasis on unproductive and unsuccessful elders. This may create a self-fulfilling prophecy in which the capacities and experiences of elders are limited (Vasil & Wass, 1990). By showing elders as feeble, absent-minded, stubborn, or helpless, subtle effects may accumulate and add to the estranged social conditions many older Americans face today (Tupper, 1995). The emphasis on dependence of elders, either on younger caregivers or on prescription medications, may only serve to reinforce this devaluation of elders.

Creating Negative Expectations About Aging Among Younger People

As we have mentioned several times throughout this book, the media influence our worldviews. Thus, how the media portray older adults is not only damaging to the older adults themselves but also to younger people. Negative stereotyping and ageism create negative expectations, fear, and dread of aging among younger adults (Vasil & Wass, 1990).

The Future and the Coming Demographic Shift

Who are elders? How do we define them in the population? As we mentioned earlier in this chapter, there are three types of age: calendar, physical, and psychological. Although calendar age is a poor measure of how an individual sees him- or herself, it is the one measure that advertisers use primarily to define basic groups. In addition, by that definition alone, the face of older adults is morphing in front of our eyes.

The population in the United States is growing older, mostly due to the aging of the baby boomers, which is causing an explosion of Americans at the 50-year-old-plus range. The sheer size of this group has empowered baby boomers like no other generation (Gobé, 2001). As a group, boomers are unlikely to approach the aging process in the same way their parents and grandparents did. This new approach has been described as reaching a "youthful maturity" (Gobé, 2001, p. 4). The approach is due in part to the fact that baby boomers are healthier, better off financially, and more active than any previous mature group.

As boomers reach the age of 50, some think about retirement, but many others have different things on their minds. As they get older, baby boomers are going back to school, changing jobs, getting divorced or remarried, and perhaps starting a second family. They want to be recognized as individuals with a lot to contribute to society, not as a group on the verge of becoming a burden to society. This change in the older adult mind-set has already stimulated one influential organization of elders to change their name from the American Association of Retired Persons to the AARP. One must be 50 years old to join the AARP. This name change is the result of a recognition that its core group of future members, baby boomers, are not retired and have few thoughts of retirement (Koezler, 2000). The organization found that boomers thought the AARP was primarily for persons much older than they were, and enrollment in the AARP was starting to decline. The organization retooled not only their name but created a new publication called *My Generation* to work in tandem with their large circulation *Modern Maturity* to appeal to this younger group of older adults. Although *My Generation* was not successful, the AARP continues to look for ways to attract people to the organization.

As previously mentioned, baby boomers have an incredible concentration of wealth and power. Nearly half of all baby boomers report that their personal financial situation is "good" or "excellent." This is the first group in recent history that will not rely on Social Security or limited pensions for their retirement income, and they are expected to benefit from the largest transfer of inherited wealth in history as their parents die (Kantrowitz, King, Downey, & Scott, 2000). As you might imagine, these individuals have a large economic influence. Of all age groups, total household income is highest for those with households headed by someone aged 45 to 54. While households headed by persons 55 to 64 have slightly lower incomes than the 45 to 54 age group, they also have smaller households (since any children are likely to have moved out), resulting in more buying power per person in the household (Lee, 1997). Traditionally, household income decreases as individuals get older, but this may not be the case in the near future. Not only will individuals be drawing from privately funded retirement plans, but they will often continue to work. Today, 25% of seniors aged 65 to 72 still work full time, and many more have part-time jobs (Adler, 1996). Of the baby boomers who are reaching retirement age, about 80% plan to work at least part time during their retirement years (Koezler, 2000).

In terms of purchases, the change in lifestyle may instigate a range of new purchase opportunities and experiences for older adults. People between the ages of 35 and 64 account for about two thirds of total consumer spending (Surowiecki, 2002). Recent studies have shown that between the ages 35 and 54, an individual's brand preferences become "disestablished"; that is, older people abandon favorite brands and try new brands (Surowiecki, 2002). This is possibly because of changes in brand formulation or in the individual's body or lifestyle, but the myth of the "unadventurous elder" may be proven untrue.

As the number of boomers passing the 50-year mark increases, many will become empty nesters who may buy new and more expensive furniture to replace the couch that has the soda stains. They may also consider purchasing a sports or luxury car, since they no longer have to pay a premium for their children's automobile insurance (Lee, 1997). Premium brands like Lexus would not exist without the older population group (Surowiecki, 2002). Mercedes is also appealing to the older generation, featuring images that emphasize the history and provenance of the brand (Johnston-Jones, 2001).

New market niches are also being developed with the baby boomers in mind. Cosmetics companies are targeting consumers with products like

Figure 9.9 S. C. Johnson chairman and spokesperson Sam Johnson

Grey Chic hair coloring for older women (Singh, 2000). Older adults are the fastest growing group of online users, and numerous Web sites such as Third Age (www.thirdage.com) promote shopping and other online activities to elders. Online, popular sites like eBay appeal to as many older people as younger ones (McLuhan, 2000).

We are also beginning to see a shift in how advertisers and marketers are seeing elders. Advertisers are beginning to notice that there is a difference between showing elders in ads and really engaging with them as a target (Johnston-Jones, 2001). Ad agencies like J. Walter Thompson have special units designing messages especially for older consumers. Recently, older people have been used in advertising to promote the authenticity of the company. Sam Johnson pitches for the S. C. Johnson Company, and Columbia Sportswear chairwoman Gert Boyle tests products on her son (Figures 9.9 and 9.10). Older people have been used in ads for Compaq computers and Clinique cosmetics, achieving positive reactions from all age groups, contrary to previous beliefs about alienating younger persons by advertising to older persons (Carrigan & Szmigin, 2000).

Considerations in Advertising to Elders

Advertisers should immediately begin to rethink their approach to targeting elders in advertising. Advertising can play a major role in the socialization of older adults and in influencing how younger audiences view older persons. Additionally, the burgeoning population of baby boomers makes it imperative for agencies to reevaluate how they use older adults in their advertisements.

Figure 9.10 Columbia Sportswear chairwoman and spokesperson Gert Boyle

Utilize Key Values

Advertisers must understand and feature the values of older people in advertisements. Elders strongly value autonomy, social connectedness, altruism, personal growth, and revitalization (Bradley & Longino, 2001, p. 20). Advertisers should select imagery that promotes appropriate values for advertised products and services. In addition, studies show that healthy elders will develop their self-identity not only from what they have accomplished in the past but from what they plan to accomplish in the future. Understanding this perspective should provide a richer pool of strategic ideas for advertisers.

Give Elders Something to Do

Advertisers should look to feature active older spokespersons in advertisements for a range of products and services, not just in ads for products targeted to elders. By featuring older adults in commercials for younger viewers, a more positive view of the aging process may develop.

Recognize a Range of Elders

Advertisers must also recognize that there are many subgroups in the entire population of 50 and older consumers. In this group, some elders are still working, some may have kids in elementary school, and others have kids in college. Some are retired, some are in the process of retiring, and others are not even thinking about it. A woman in her 40s, for example, might be a mother of young kids, a grandmother, on her second marriage, or recently divorced.

Additionally, baby boomers represent a range of life influences. Older boomers reached adolescence during the Vietnam War, and as young adults, they realized that they did not have to buy into the roles and structures established by the older generation of their time. These older boomers were also influenced by struggles for civil rights and women's rights (Morton, 2001) and during their youth became spiritually adventurous and socially active.

Younger boomers were influenced by Reaganomics, "just say no," and emerging technology. They experienced instant wealth and were the first yuppies and part of the "Me" generation, where persons and ideas that were not immediately useful or pertinent to their lives were seen as unnecessary. Younger boomers are more conservative than older boomers. Older boomers believe they can make a difference in society, whereas younger boomers believe they can make a difference in themselves (Morton, 2001).

Take Away Burdens

Advertising messages should empower older adults, not make them feel like burdens on society. Advertising should inform older adults about how the product or service will enhance their lives, address a problem, or help them achieve an objective. Older adults, like younger adults, should be seen as positive forces in society.

Consider Elder Eyes

Tactically, advertisers should rethink text and color issues for both broadcast and print advertisements. For example, a simple decision like font size should be closely considered to accommodate sight problems among people over the age of 40. Also, rethink color contrasts and test such contrasts to make sure they are apparent to older adults (Underhill, 1999).

Reconsider the Youth Bias

Finally, the industry needs to address the stereotype that advertising work is strictly for the under 35 crowd. (Moore, 2001) Advertising needs constant infusions of the new into the work, but it also needs maturity. Without both, agencies may not be able to sustain the quality of work needed to be successful (Moore, 2001).

_____ **Summary**

Advertisers have neglected elders in advertising messages: Elders are either ignored or are presented as disconnected from society as a whole. However, as baby boomers age, they present an opportunity for advertisers to reconnect with a group with the financial power to make or break brands. Advertisers should consider reconnecting with elders and understanding more about their lifestyles to create messages that best resonate with this group.

In the next chapter, we will go to the other end of the age spectrum and consider advertising directed to children.

10

Getting
Older Younger

Children and Advertising

The test of the morality of a society is what it does for its children.

—Dietrich Bonhoeffer

In the United States, we treasure children. They are our legacies and our hopes for tomorrow. They are also part of our connections to the past. Although we value children and the institution of childhood, it is a cliché in our society today that children are different now from in the past: Children grow up faster and mature earlier than in any other generation. As a result, children of all ages are prized as consumers, perhaps now more than ever.

Today in the United States, the U.S. Census Bureau estimates that there are more than 70 million individuals under the age of 18. About one third of this group is 5 years old or younger, another third is between the ages of 6 and 11, and the final third is between the ages of 12 and 18. These groups are projected to grow by about 10% in the next 20 years. About two thirds of these individuals are white, another 15% are Hispanic, 15% are black, and the balance are Asian, Pacific Islander, or Native American. In the next 20 years, the percentage of whites in the population is expected to decline to about 50%, with increases seen in Hispanic and Asian proportions (U.S. Census Bureau, 1999).

Children are a huge and growing market for advertisers and marketers. Of course, teenagers have always been targeted with advertising messages, given that they have access to automobiles to go to the mall, and many teens have after-school jobs that provide them with some disposable income. However, younger children, such as those between the ages of 4 and 12, are becoming increasingly attractive to marketers because they have their own significant sources of income (e.g., through allowances and gifts). In the year 2000, children aged 4 to 12 spent more than $29 billion of their own money on a range of products, including clothes, candy, toys, and CDs (McDonald & Lavelle, 2001).

Children as Consumers

In the past, the advertising industry considered children as "consumers in training." Today, though, the training ends early, and children become valued as consumers in their own right. Children have become more important as advertising targets for several reasons.

The Nag Factor, or the Direct Influence of Children. Children exert considerable influence on their parents' purchase decisions. The growth in the number of single parents in the United States, as well as the increase in dual wage earner households, means that children are taking responsibility for more purchase decisions than before. The nag factor suggests that children are often very important partners with their parents in making purchase decisions for a range of products and that they are also involved in the decisions at an earlier age. In the year 2000, for example, children had a direct influence on an estimated $290 billion in family spending. Children were involved in about half of purchases of sports utility vehicles (SUVs) and minivans. The nag factor has an impact on many marketing decisions, as messages must appeal not only to the primary purchaser but also to his or her child or children. For example, Ford's Windstar minivan featured a promotion tying into the popular children's cartoon *Blue's Clues.* Other minivan manufacturers feature characters popular with children in their advertising messages not only to promote video systems in their minivans but also to attract children's attention to the message (Figure 10.1).

The Guilt Factor, or the Direct Influence of Children's Spending. The growth in the number of single-parent households and of households where both parents work has led children to become important influencers in the purchasing process and has also created a more affluent base of younger individuals. Time pressures on the parents in such households can result in parents assuaging their own guilt by giving their children spending money. Today, then, children control larger amounts of money than children of any other generation.

The Closed Gap Factor, or the Peter Pan Syndrome. Many of today's generation of children have baby boomer parents. As we discussed in the previous chapter, baby boomers have traditionally been known as having a huge influence on society, and when it comes to raising children, they are no exception. Baby boomer parents do not want to be perceived as boring to their children; that is, they do not want their children to view them the way that the boomers viewed their own parents. Marketers have capitalized on this trend by creating shopping experiences in which the whole family can participate. In this way, children should feel that their parents are not outdated but are in tune with the same things children are. Marketers are putting more emphasis on finding out what kinds of products and experiences are appealing both to parents and to children (Gibbs et al., 2001). An example is the concept of the Old Navy store. A typical Old Navy has special sections devoted to children and adults that are tied in by thematic presentations in the in-store displays and in the clothing styles. Even their ads feature imagery that appeals to parents (old sitcom stars), teens (models dressed in trendy fashion), and younger children (the Old Navy dog).

Figure 10.1 This minivan ad featured characters and images from *E.T.: The Extra-Terrestrial.*

The Technology Factor. Children are the "information gateways" for their parents due to their higher levels of experience and interactions with computers (McDonald & Lavelle, 2001). Children are often the computer consultants for the whole family and have great impact on purchase decisions in that area. Children also help parents feel comfortable with the Internet and can provide coaching that may influence online searches and purchases.

The Future Factor. Of course, children will have future spending power and also are often "clean slates" when it comes to brands and affiliated brand imagery. Marketers and advertisers believe they need to generate brand loyalty among young children so that as children grow up and reach their full capacity to consume, they will already have brand preferences firmly in place.

Children and Brands

Today's children are becoming brand savvy at an earlier age than ever before. Children today are developing brand preferences not only for products and services that are traditionally associated with children (e.g., fast-food restaurants, candy, and toys) but also for those that are not. For example, over one third of children aged 9 to 11 had specific likes and dislikes for hotels (McDonald & Lavelle, 2001). Children as young as 5 ask for products by brand name (Alexander & Dichter, 2002). This is not surprising, given the estimate that more than $2 billion of advertising funds each year are directed specifically to children.

The relationship of children to the branding process is problematic to some critics. A recent article in *Time* magazine said that advertising creates "cravings that are hard to ignore but impossible to satisfy" (Gibbs et al., 2001 p. 41). Indeed, there is evidence that advertising and other branding messages contribute to the development of a consumer culture among many children. For example, two thirds of parents say their children define their self-worth in terms of possessions, and half of parents say their children prefer the mall to other activities such as hiking or being somewhere with the family (Gibbs et al., 2001). In addition, a majority of parents have bought a product that they disapproved of because their children said they needed the product to fit in with their friends (Gibbs et al., 2001). Critics are also concerned that children learn at an early age that problems can be solved and happiness can be attained by buying things. Thus, they are developing a consumer-based value system that does not recognize the value of any nonconsumer activities in life.

This criticism can be balanced by taking a step back and examining the lifestyles of youth in America today. A closer look at today's teenagers, who have grown up in a highly brand- and advertising-intensive media environment, shows that many of the concerns of critics are possibly unfounded. Today's teens are twice as likely to do volunteer work as teens 20 years ago. Teens are drinking less alcohol than teens 10 years ago, and teen pregnancy and abortion rates have also declined (Gibbs et al., 2001). Additionally, children and teenagers are closely in tune to their parents' economic situations and are as affected by economic circumstances as their parents are. A recent study showed that spending among children has dropped and that 12% of children said their allowance had recently been cut (Gibbs et al., 2001).

Children as Vulnerable Consumers

Regardless of whether children are affected by consumerism or not, advertisers should understand that children are a vulnerable population because they lack the sophistication and experience of adults. Specifically, children are considered a vulnerable population for several reasons.

Limited Information Sources

Children have more limited sources of information than adults. This is especially true for children who cannot yet read and receive much of their information from a single source, television (Schudson, 1984). Most of the programming on television, other than children's television programs, is uninteresting or not understandable to children. Television commercials, though, have focused story lines, fun music and fast action, and replicate traditional children's television more than any other type of program. This suggests that children will pay attention to commercials, even if they are not paying close attention to the programs in which they appear. Commercials, then, have the potential to be one of the most highly persuasive messages that children see.

Limited Personal Experience

Children have limited personal experience with consumer products (Schudson, 1984). Because of this, children (younger children in particular) are relatively trusting of advertisements. In fact, they view television more like a word of mouth medium than a mass media channel (Adler et al., 1980). Word of mouth is seen as a highly credible form of communication. Television advertising, then, becomes a highly persuasive technique to reach children.

Limited Context for Claims

Finally, children have little context to examine and evaluate specific claims made in advertising messages. Therefore, they cannot evaluate the actual value of the messages directed to them. For example, children may hear advertisements promoting products in terms of their price, but they have little context to evaluate whether the price is appropriate, given the value of the product and/or their own family's disposable income. Children also do not compare prices to other products, and unlike adults, they do not possess reference sets of prices for different product categories (Schudson, 1984).

Children, Advertising, and the Learning Process

Now that we have acknowledged children as a vulnerable population, let us step back for a moment and examine some of the psychological processes that influence how children learn. This information helps provide a context so we can better understand the influence of advertising on children today.

Social Learning Theory

One way of understanding how children learn is Albert Bandura's social learning theory (Unger & Crawford, 1992). Social learning theory suggests that a child's behavior is not biologically determined or inevitable but instead is a result of day-to-day interactions between the developing child and his or her environment. That is, what a child sees often becomes what a child believes to be the truth. Day-to-day interactions include activities such as a child observing other children and adults both at home and outside the home, a child receiving a reward for an appropriate behavior, a child receiving a punishment for misbehaving, a child imitating parents' or teachers' attitudes and behaviors, a child interacting socially with friends, and a child imitating attitudes and behaviors seen in mass-mediated content such as television.

Television brings readily observable models into a child's home (Smith, 1994) and becomes of particular concern for several reasons. Children in the United States watch a lot of television: The average child watches about 3 to 4 hours of TV a day for a total of 28 hours each week (Center for Media Education, 1997). Watching TV is the top after-school activity for 6- to 17-year-olds. In some ways, television becomes what is known as a "proxy peer" because most children watch TV for more time than they play with other children. They also spend more time watching TV than they spend in the classroom: Each year, most children spend about 1500 hours in front of the TV and 900 hours in the classroom (Center for Media Education, 1997).

The content of the television children watch is, of course, composed of both programming and commercials. Children see at least 1 hour of commercials for every 5 hours of programs they watch on commercial TV. The average child sees more than 20,000 commercials each year so that by the time a child turns age 21, he or she will have seen approximately 1 million TV commercials. In a poll of 351 parents, 71% said their children were exposed to too much advertising, while only about 25% said they were exposed to just the right amount (Gibbs et al., 2001).

Television as Curriculum

Many have noted the high level of influence that television can have on children. Neil Postman (1985) said that television is a curriculum: a "specially constructed information system whose purpose is to influence, teach, train or cultivate the mind and character of youth" (p. 145). Television presents information about the world that helps children develop their own worldviews. In addition, television can be a vehicle of socialization, a source from which children acquire knowledge about all types of social behaviors, including gender roles and expectations. Bandura's social learning theory suggests that since children accept what is "real" from television, the continual exposure to advertising and other mass-mediated messages

Figure 10.2 Example of a banner ad

will create and/or moderate the concepts children develop about the real world. Children will also develop ideas as to what types of behaviors are appropriate and inappropriate from what they see on television.

Television has traditionally been seen as the primary medium children use, but the Internet is growing both in popularity and influence. The Kaiser Family Foundation has estimated that every American child is exposed to 40 hours a week of commercial messages from TV, billboards, computers and the Internet, and other media (McDonald & Lavelle, 2001). Of children between the ages of 5 and 17 (a total of 48 million children), 90% now use computers. Although more than 50% of the U.S. population as a whole uses the Internet regularly, 75% of 14- to 17-year-olds and 65% of 10- to 13-year-olds use the Internet (National Telecommunications and Information Administration, 2002). While children use the Internet for many reasons, it is highly valued by younger people as a communications tool. A study by AOL found that many teens prefer communicating via the Internet to communicating via telephone (Pastore, 2002).

The Internet has increased the opportunities for marketers and advertisers to target children. Today, more than two thirds of Internet sites designed for children and for teens use advertising as their primary revenue stream (Neuborne, 2001a). Advertising on Internet sites directed to children and teens encompasses a wide range of tactics. Banner ads and buttons are often used (Figure 10.2). Advertisers and marketers also associate brands with online games (e.g., brands can be game pieces or hidden treasure prizes in interactive games) and provide downloadable e-mail postcards and digital cards (for children to collect or send to their friends) (Figure 10.3). They have also established children-only chat rooms and news groups (where marketers log on to ask children about products and services and promote their own offerings).

_____ Regulation of Advertising Directed to Children

Given the concerns about what children see, hear, and learn from the mass media, both government and self-regulatory functions monitor and regulate

Figure 10.3 Promotions attract kids to web sites.

children's media, including commercials. The regulatory area is governed under the Children's Television Act (CTA), and the self-regulatory agent, the Children's Advertising Review Unit (CARU), is part of the Better Business Bureau.

Children's Television Act

Congress passed the Children's Television Act (CTA) in 1990. At that time, Saturday morning television was regarded as junk food for the mind, as many children's shows were product oriented and action oriented (remember the *Teenage Mutant Ninja Turtles*?). There was little programming on the air that was considered educational or seen as providing any other type of benefit to children. The CTA was designed to compel the broadcast television industry to go beyond serving only children's entertainment needs and to demonstrate in specific terms how they were serving the educational and informational needs of children. Additionally, networks and stations were required to dedicate a minimum of 3 hours each week to educational programming. The CTA also limited commercial time on children's television programming to 10.5 minutes per hour on weekdays and 12 minutes per hour on weekends.

Many critics do not believe that the programming goals of the CTA have been met. For example, some stations reported that they aired the TV show *The Jetsons* as part of their educational programming because it teaches children what life will be like in the 21st century. Others complained that educational programming appeared late at night, when children were not likely to see the programs. However, it has been recognized that certain aspects of the CTA have been fully adopted, specifically the limited commercial time regulation (Center for Media Education, 2002). More recently, the Federal Communications Commission (FCC) created new rules that strengthened how broadcasters are expected to comply with the CTA. This 1996 amendment to the CTA included a requirement to label all educational shows as such and designates the days and time period when educational programming has to run (Center for Media Education, 2002).

Self-Regulation of Advertising to Children

Several years ago, the Federal Trade Commission (FTC) was considering a ban on all advertising directed to children. In response, advertisers created the Children's Advertising Review Unit (CARU) of the Better Business Bureau (Dobrow, 2002). The CARU is seen as a very powerful self-regulatory program as advertisers closely adhere to industry guidelines to avoid future government involvement.

CARU evaluates advertising directed to children aged 12 and younger that runs on network and cable television and also in print. There are seven basic principles to the CARU guidelines:

1. Advertisers should always take into account the level of knowledge, sophistication, and maturity of the audience to which their message is primarily directed.

2. Advertising should not exploit the imaginative quality of children by providing unreasonable expectations of product quality or performance. Therefore, a Barbie doll cannot "magically" drive her Barbie Ferrari without the help of a child pushing the car along.

3. Products and content that are inappropriate for use by children should not be advertised or promoted directly to children.

4. Advertisers should communicate information in a truthful and accurate manner and in language understandable to young children.

5. Advertisers should promote positive and beneficial social behavior, such as friendship, kindness, honesty, justice, generosity, and respect for others in their commercials.

6. Positive and prosocial roles and role models should be included wherever possible: Social stereotyping and appeals to prejudice should be avoided.

7. Although many influences affect a child's personal and social development, it remains the prime responsibility of the parents to provide guidance for children. Advertisers should contribute to this parent-child relationship in a constructive manner (Better Business Bureau, 2001).

CARU guidelines suggest that exhortative language (e.g., "Tell your parents to get this today!") be prohibited in messages directed toward children. In addition, the guidelines advise that the use of celebrities and animation in advertisements be minimized. Furthermore, advertising appeals should not suggest that a child could be better than his or her peers by using the advertised product. Finally, the guidelines indicate that advertisements should not frighten children or provoke anxiety, and ads should not promote violent, dangerous, or other antisocial behavior.

There are more specific guidelines for the food and toy categories because they represent the bulk of the products targeted to children. Advertisements for food products, for example, need to provide both audio and video depictions of how advertised foods contribute to a balanced meal (Clark, 1988). Toys that require assembling must make this requirement clear in the commercial; for instance, toys must be shown unassembled as well as assembled, and advertisers must use disclaimers about product assembly (Better Business Bureau, 2001).

CARU functions in a manner similar to the National Advertising Review Board discussed in Chapter 4. CARU can receive or initiate investigations into questionable children's programming, and they are also responsible for receiving, evaluating, investigating, analyzing, and holding negotiations with advertisers who run problematic advertising. They also resolve complaints or questions from any source involving the truth or accuracy of national advertising or an ad's consistency with CARU's Self-Regulatory Guidelines for Children's Advertising. Like the National Advertising Review Board, they refer problems that cannot be resolved to law enforcement organizations such as the Federal Trade Commission.

Criticisms of Advertising Directed to Children _____

There are several problematic areas in the programs and commercials viewed by children.

Advertising Targets Very Young Children

Given the perception that children are becoming older younger, it is not surprising that advertisers and marketers are lowering their target age for many products and services. These marketers are hoping to develop brand loyalty very early, as well as influence children's current purchase decisions. Earlier in this chapter, Ford's *Blue's Clues* promotion was mentioned. This tie-in was a major program related to the Nickelodeon show *Blue's Clues*, which is targeted specifically to young children. As part of the tie-in, the little dog, Blue, has been named the "official spokespup" for Ford's mini-van safety campaign, providing multiple opportunities for little children to develop positive affect toward Ford and the Windstar (Dobrow, 2002). *Blue's Clues* is targeted to preschoolers, and critics have questioned the very young age target of this campaign, as these young children may be especially vulnerable to any problematic aspects of persuasive messages.

Types of Products Advertised

Concerns have been expressed about the types of products that are advertised during children's programming. Specifically problematic for some critics is the high number of food ads in children's programming, given that 9 of every 10 food ads are for sugary cereals, candy, salty snacks, fatty fast foods, and other junk food (Center for Media Education, 2002). These advertised products tend to have low nutritional value and in some cases are unhealthy because they tend to be high in calories and may contribute to a child's energy imbalance. In turn, this may result in obesity (American Academy of Pediatrics, 1995).

There are also issues with toy advertisements. The status of the Chinese Wall in the world of children's television programming is a concern for both parents and legislators, as recently both groups have expressed concerns about toys "starring" in their own television shows (the *Teenage Mutant Ninja Turtles* and *Smurfs* come to mind). Critics argue that these types of programs are merely program-length commercials and question the value of programming developed not by programming professionals but by marketing divisions of toy companies (American Academy of Pediatrics, 1995). The CTA directed the FCC to evaluate whether such programs should indeed be considered commercials and specifically whether the programs should be counted under the total amount of commercial time available to stations. The FCC concluded that only shows that included paid advertising for the toy starring in the program could be classified as a program-length commercial (American Academy of Pediatrics, 1995).

One recent study showed that almost one fifth of all commercials shown during children's television programming was for action figures or weapons (Bradway, 2000). Critics were concerned that these types of toy advertisements could encourage a child to exhibit aggressive behavior. Furthermore, concerns have been expressed about the marketing and advertising of video games, music, and movies in which violent content is a focus. Video games, music, and movies all have their own rating systems to distinguish products appropriate for children from those that are not. A report by the FTC found that these three industries routinely target children under the age of 17 for products that their own rating system deems inappropriate for children or that warrant parental caution due to violent content. The study found that 80% of R-rated movies were targeted to children under 17. Also targeted to these youth were 100% of the music recordings with explicit content labels and 80% of electronic games with mature ratings. In a follow-up report conducted several months after the FTC's first report, the movie and video-game industries were commended for changing their marketing strategies, yet the music industry was further criticized for abandoning promises to enact an industrywide system of ratings and guidelines (Federal Trade Commission, 2000).

Finally, concerns have been raised about collectible products because these types of products and the "collectibility" message can suggest that life is incomplete unless a child owns an array of products. These types of products run the gamut from toy cars like Hot Wheels to Pokemon cards to the extended Barbie line. For example, a child collecting Barbie items is not limited to purchasing dolls, clothes, and the Barbie dream house. It is now possible to purchase a remote controlled Ferrari Spyder for Barbie to drive and sparkle horse dolls for Barbie and her friends to ride. This idea of "one is not enough" is problematic for some critics, as children begin early to view consuming as a never-ending process.

Inappropriate Role Portrayals

As previously mentioned, children learn how to act from observing how others act. Part of this observation process includes learning appropriate gender behaviors—that is, how girls behave and how boys behave. Researchers have noted, however, that some problematic role portrayals are often seen on television commercials. First, there are fewer portrayals of girls than there are of boys (Bradway, 2000). Echoing portrayals of adults in advertisements, girls are generally seen in the home and boys are seen outside the home (Smith, 1994).

More ads are aimed at boys than at girls, and boys and girls are seen in ads for different types of products (Smith, 1994). Boys are seen driving vehicles and using building equipment and are seen building and taking things apart. Boys are also featured in advertisements for science and math toys. When boys play with other boys, they play with male toys such as trucks and computers. Girls are seen playing with dolls, housekeeping equipment, and products relating to vanity. When girls play with other girls, they play with girl toys such as dolls. When boys and girls play together, though, they play with boy toys (Smith, 1994).

Types of behavior seen in ads also differ: Girls tend to be inactive, playing quietly in the house, whereas boys are active and are often seen playing outside. Girls are portrayed as gentle, serene, and passive, while boys are portrayed as aggressive, noisy, and active (Smith, 1994). Deviations from the gendered behaviors can appear, but they are rare. In a recent study, for example, only 13% of commercials showed girls doing stereotypically boy behaviors (e.g., riding a go-cart) and only 3% of commercials showed boys doing girl behaviors.

Commercial production values differ depending on whom the ad is targeted to. Commercials targeted to boys are noisier; there is more talking, sound effects, and music as the focus (e.g., with a jingle) in commercials targeted to boys than in commercials directed to girls. Commercials targeted to girls tend to feature background music with minimal conversation. It has been observed that commercials are even edited differently depending on whether they are targeted to boys or girls. Commercials with boys use frequent cuts, which create a more active and exciting commercial, whereas those with girls use fades and dissolves, which create a more passive and dreamlike commercial.

Corporate-Sponsored Education

A final problem outlined by critics is the commercialization of education. Public schools, in particular, are becoming sponsorship opportunities for companies. The trend toward corporate-sponsored education began in earnest in 1990, when a company called Channel One was created. Channel One provides a daily 12-minute TV news program to 8 million students in 12,000 schools in the United States. Schools participating in the Channel One learning community receive TV sets for each classroom at the school, two VCRs for school use, and a satellite link, all at no cost. During this news program, 2 minutes of commercial time are available for advertisers to purchase. The commercials, and the TV news show, reach 40% of all teenagers in the United States.

In addition to programming on Channel One, corporations can also create a presence in the classroom by providing teaching materials to schools. These materials can include items such as corporate videos, posters, and learning kits with company logos and emblems. Critics are concerned that such sponsored materials may not provide objective information. For example, Procter & Gamble provided environmental curricula to teachers stating that disposable diapers are good for the earth, and McDonald's provided nutritional information promoting the healthy aspects of fast food. The Campbell Soup Company has provided science curricula that included an experiment to show that Prego spaghetti sauce (owned by Campbell's) is thicker than Ragu (Jacobson & Mazur, 1995).

In addition, corporations have started to sponsor aspects of the schools' physical plants', including school buses, bulletin boards, gyms, cheerleading teams, and book covers. Many of these programs provide funding for areas that school budgets may not cover and may also provide additional revenue to schools and school groups. However, critics suggest that any type of corporate participation runs counter to the primary function of schools in our society, which is to cultivate good citizens. To develop an informed citizenry, critics claim, schools need to create a distance from consumerism.

Intended Effects

Obviously, the intended effects of child-targeted advertising recognize that children exert two types of influence over purchases: direct influence, where children control the actual purchase decision (e.g., for candy), and indirect influence, where children are a strong factor in the decisions made by their parents or by other adults. However, other intended effects of advertising directed to children are evident.

Educate Children

Advertisers argue that advertisements are providing consumer education to children; that is, they teach children how to evaluate products, brands, and claims. Many advertisers work under the assumption that children today are much more sophisticated now than when current adults were children. In fact, several studies have shown that about half of all kindergarten students understand that the purpose of commercials is to sell them something (Bandyopadhyay, Kindra, & Sharp, 2002). Most researchers agree that when children reach the age of 8, they are savvy enough to understand and comprehend messages about products directed to them (Bandyopadhyay et al., 2002).

Entertain Children

Like adults, children like some commercials and actively dislike others. Many children see commercials merely as entertainment, and they have no interest in the product being advertised. The entertainment value is important because many critics argue that any advertising is bad for children. Advertisers mention industry reports that show commercials have neither a positive nor negative effect in the mental health development of children. This suggests that the entertainment value of advertising is nondetrimental to children.

Educational Programming Is Supported

Advertising funds the vast majority of the programs on television, including programs directed to children. The FCC stipulates that all networks air 3 hours of educational programming per week to maintain their licenses (Bandyopadhyay et al., 2002). It would be difficult for stations to fulfill this requirement without advertising support.

The quality of children's programming is improving: A recent study by the Annenberg Public Policy Center found that more than three fourths of commercial broadcasters' educational programs met the letter of the FCC guidelines. The ABC network and several companies that provide syndicated programming for children were responsible for the most valuable programming. Additionally, the report found that educational programs contained very little violence, a departure from what is generally available on television (Jordan, 2000). On the whole, it seems that educational programming provides a win-win environment for stations, advertisers, and children.

Unintended Effects

Critics and medical experts warn that excessive exposure to advertisements and other mass media causes psychological and physical problems among children. Some specific unintended effects are described next.

Children Confuse Fact and Fiction

Children become confused as to what is fact and what is fiction, and in particular, many children may be unable to separate advertising information from programming content. For example, after seeing commercials for Flintstones vitamins, one third of children believed that Fred Flintstone and Barney Rubble, characters from *The Flintstones* television show, were experts in nutrition (Figure 10.4). Although many other children can recognize that advertising is different from the programming they are watching, they may not necessarily understand the persuasive nature of advertising (Bandyopadhyay et al., 2002). The idea of puffery is unknown to them. If an advertisement suggests that the advertised product is "the best in the universe," children tend to take that at face value and do not critically analyze the message.

Figure 10.4 Products and messages may confuse children

Stereotyped Gender Attitudes Are Created

Exposure to advertising imagery creates misinformation on gender roles. Children who are heavy TV viewers have a more stereotypical view of sex roles than do children who are light TV viewers. Children who watch a lot of TV, for example, predict that they will hold stereotypical adult jobs when they grow up (Greenfield, 1984).

Development Is Diminished

In a recent report, the American Academy of Pediatrics (AAP) recommended that children under the age of 2 should not watch television at all. Recent research on early brain development shows that babies need human contact to develop socially and emotionally. Children need more than a voice or an image on television to develop. Television provides only two-dimensional interaction with children, but children also need touch and smell to learn about the world fully (American Academy of Pediatrics, 1995).

As children grow, increased levels of television viewing have specific effects on their learning skills. One study showed that children who watch 4 or more hours of TV per day spend less time on schoolwork and have poorer reading skills than children who watch fewer than 4 hours (Center for Media Education, 1997). Television programming and commercials can develop in children something called the "2-minute mind," a short attention span that results in a child's impatience with anything that requires more thinking than what's needed for a commercial break.

Children Are Poorly Socialized

A range of socialization issues has been blamed on television in general and advertising in particular. A recent study showed that children who watch 4 or more hours of TV per day play less well with friends and have fewer hobbies than children who watch fewer than 4 hours (Center for Media Education, 1997). The idea that television is a proxy peer suggests the origins of peer pressure; that is, the media suggest what you need to own to be cool or one of the in-crowd, and children who do not have those things are often ostracized. In addition, with exposure to violent imagery in advertising for video games, films, and music recordings, critics worry that children would exhibit increased levels of violent behavior. Advertising can foster a sense of entitlement among children that can lead to increased conflicts between parent and child. As children keep asking for things and parents keep saying no, conflicts arise and relationships between parents and children may deteriorate.

Children Are Unhealthy

Advertising and other mass media can create unhealthy children. Children who watch a lot of TV have a greater risk of obesity than children who watch less TV (Center for Media Education, 1997). Today, between 16% and 33% of all children in the United States are obese; that is, their body weights are more than 10% higher than the recommended weight (American Academy of Child and Adolescent Psychology, 2001). A number of factors can contribute to obesity, such as biological factors, yet television has been seen as a strong influence, particularly because children watching television are not outside playing or participating in sports.

Television viewing has also been linked to the propensity for children to use alcohol and drugs, as well as be involved earlier in sexual activity (Center for Media Education, 1997). This may be because violence, sexuality, and drug and alcohol abuse are common themes of adult-oriented television programs that children may see (American Academy of Child and Adolescent Psychology, 2001). Young children are impressionable and may assume that what they see on television is typical, safe, and acceptable; thus, television normalizes problematic behaviors.

How to Approach Advertising to Children

Recently, an article in the trade journal *Advertising Age* gave some tips from both industry lawyers and CARU on how advertisers should develop good advertising for children. These tips included:

- Make clear in the commercial what is and what is not included in the product. For example, if batteries are needed but not included, this fact must be specified in simple language. Also be clear about the amount of assembly required for the product.
- Show the product in a way that a young child would use the product.
- Be accurate in how you show the size of the product, the color, how durable it is, and what the nutritional benefits are.
- Do not mislead in terms of the possible benefits of a product's use; for example, do not suggest that a product will make a child happier, more popular, or smarter.
- Avoid using language that exhorts children to pressure their parents to buy them the product.
- Be careful in matching products with programs. Do not advertise products for older children (say, those over the age of 10) in programs watched frequently by children under 5.

The Future

Advertising to children is legal and will continue to be legal into the known future. Advertisers have the right to advertise to children, but they also should be responsible communicators in the messages that they target to children. It is imperative for advertisers promoting products to children to know and follow the CARU guidelines. In addition, parents should be aware of the types of messages their children are exposed to and help children learn about advertising by watching commercials with them and discussing their purposes. Parents must educate children to be responsible and informed (American Academy of Pediatrics, 1995).

As with any mass-mediated content, the importance of parental involvement cannot be underestimated. A study described in *Advertising Age* of children 7 years old and younger found that only 55% of children said that their parents tried to limit the amount of time they watched TV. In the same study, 59% of responding children said that their parents tried to limit the amount of time they were online ("Try to Keep It Simple," 2002). Large numbers of children can apparently watch and surf what they want without any parental involvement.

Although it is unlikely that advertising directed to children will be prohibited, it is possible that we will see further limitations of the number of commercial minutes on children's television programs. The American Academy of Pediatrics, for example, thinks there should be more limitations on the amount of advertising permitted: no more than 5 or 6 commercial minutes per hour (American Academy of Pediatrics, 1995). Even if messages on television are reduced, though, children have a rich source for more commercial messages on the Internet.

The Internet will allow more opportunities for children to be exposed to advertising messages in a context where the Chinese Wall between advertising and content is often intentionally blurred. One of the first concerns raised about marketing online was the collection of personally identifiable information from both adults and children. The concern with the practice of collecting information from children, though, was addressed by government legislation in the 1998 Children's Online Privacy Protection Act (COPPA). COPPA recognizes that children have great difficulty separating marketing from entertainment and information content online, where there are limits to traditional methods (e.g., bumpers) that can help with this distinction. COPPA restricts what kinds of information can be collected from children and requires Web sites to obtain parental consent before collecting information from children. CARU is involved in the monitoring and regulation of COPPA, and indeed, their activities are influencing Web sites to conform to COPPA standards.

Summary

In this chapter, we examined advertising directed to children. Children are considered a vulnerable population, and they are also seen as valuable to marketers for both their current and their future consumer potential. Children's advertising is likely to continue to be scrutinized and criticized by many in society. However, the self-regulatory structure in place for children's advertising is seen as having a strong impact on the advertising that children see.

In Chapters 11 to 16, we will move from looking at people and ads to examining products, messages, and channels. We will look at a number of controversial products and types of messages and also examine how advertising in a new channel, the Internet, is viewed by society.

11

The Vice Squad

Advertising Controversial Products

The physically fit can enjoy their vices.

—Lord Percival

One reason that we, as consumers, purchase products and services is to complement and enhance our lifestyles. As we discussed earlier in this book, many of our purchase decisions are based on a combination of factors, including the images and messages presented in the advertising for the products and services, the price of the products and services, and our past experiences with the products and services or those of competitors. Most of our purchases are fairly uncontroversial using uncontroversial advertising messages: You rarely hear a media outcry regarding advertising messages in peanut butter commercials, for example.

However, for certain products and services, the situation is somewhat more complex. There are several products and services that individuals and groups believe should not be available for purchase. Sometimes these people believe that products should not be available to the public at large (e.g., certain types of weapons). In other situations, people believe the products should not be available to certain segments of the consumer population (e.g., some believe birth control products should not be available to persons younger than age 18).

A number of products tend to be questioned. Concerns with such products represent a range of issues regarding the products themselves, their target audiences, and the companies that produce them. Advertising is often attacked as a surrogate for the product and its producer. Individuals and groups often find that public demand will not permit a direct attack on the objects of their disfavor, and so they attack the ads that sell these products (Nicosia, 1974).

The Nature of Controversial Products

A range of products and services has been considered controversial in the past and may continue to be considered controversial, at least by certain segments of the population, in the future. We can further examine the nature of controversial products and services by grouping them into four broad categories: (a) products and services seen as a "rite of passage"; (b) sexually oriented products; (c) products that make blatantly excessive promises about results; and (d) products produced by companies with questionable production policies.

Rite of Passage Products

Many products are thought of as controversial because using them is akin to an individual's independence; that is, young people use the products so that they can be viewed as more adult. In addition, the products can represent a statement of individuals' striving for self-identity. Behaviors such as smoking cigarettes, drinking beer, and gambling are seen as part of the rite of passage from childhood to adulthood in our culture. Advertising messages tend to present these products as the means of initiation into the adult world, and the images associated with the products include courtship and staying up late. Therefore, individuals and groups that are concerned with children growing up too fast and facing adult problems too early are also likely to be concerned with advertising for these types of products.

Sexually Oriented Products

The category of sexually oriented products is in a way a subsegment of the rites of passage category. Many products associated with a rite of passage have either direct or indirect associations with sexuality. Products including birth control pills and devices and even feminine hygiene products are problematic for individuals who believe that private matters should be kept within families, and a public discussion of sexuality is inappropriate. For some of these individuals, advertising concerns are specifically related to concerns with sexual behavior among youth. Some believe that the act of advertising products that promote sexuality either directly or indirectly tends to mainstream the products and make them and the resultant behaviors socially acceptable. This becomes problematic to persons who believe the resultant behaviors, such as premarital and nonmonogamous sexual relations, are inappropriate and in some cases morally wrong.

Products That Make Blatantly Excessive Promises

A third category of controversial products is those that consistently mislead the public. As you learned in an earlier chapter of this book, the

Federal Trade Commission (FTC) has the power to regulate national advertising that misleads consumers. However, two specific product categories—lotteries and diet pills—have consistently been questioned and criticized for their misleading tactics. You may not think that lotteries and diet pill advertising are similar, but in this case, they are.

Both products use advertising messages that focus directly on the end result of purchasing and using the product: either winning the lottery or losing weight. In such advertising, the messages suggest great results but are misleading because advertising messages rarely explain the poor odds of success. Such advertisements emphasize that purchasing the product is the "easy way out" over hard work and provide instant gratification over prudent investments of time and energy (e.g., saving money for long-term gain or committing to a long-term diet program for good health). Advertising messages suggest that luck is the only thing individuals need to win a lottery (Figure 11.1 a and 11.1 b) or that new scientific breakthroughs mean individuals no longer have to diet to lose weight ("State Governments and Lotteries," 1999) (Figure 11.2). More important, any risks associated with purchasing and using the products (e.g., loss of finances or health) are rarely mentioned (Abelson, 1991).

State lotteries are exempt from the FTC truth-in-advertising standards because the advertisements are purchased by the individual states and do not run on a national basis. Restrictions and constraints on advertising messages for state lotteries vary by state: Some states require that the odds of winning must be displayed in the advertising, and in other states, advertising messages cannot induce people to play by using a message such as "go out and buy a ticket today" ("State Governments and Lotteries," 1999). Several states have few restrictions on the content of lottery advertising.

Diet drugs are regulated by the FTC and also by the FDA (if they are considered over-the-counter drugs and not herbal remedies). Many diet drug advertisements are direct-response advertisements that attempt to generate sales based on a single exposure to the ad. Therefore, many diet drug ads will run in several publications for a brief period of time (e.g., they may run in several magazines with a June cover date). By the time the FTC has investigated the diet drug ads, the campaign would have completed its run and would have generated responses and sales from consumers. Therefore, the goal of the message (to sell products) is completed by the time the FTC can investigate and ask that the ads be stopped (Abelson, 1991).

Company Philosophy

Associations with lifestyle choices are not the only reasons some individuals believe that advertising for certain products should be banned. Other products are controversial because of the overall company philosophy that may or may not be presented in an advertisement. For example, companies that produce products in Third World countries have labor practices that many consider questionable, and advertising and purchasing these companies' products

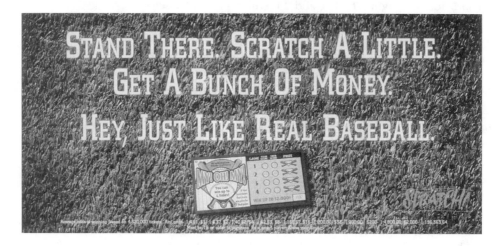

Figure 11.1a and b   Ads promote state lotteries.

appear to support and condone the companies' behaviors. Animal testing is a similar issue: Purchasing products by companies that use animal testing is seen as condoning this practice, which some see as unfair to animals. Another questionable production practice is that of genetically engineered foods: Many are concerned with biotechnology's role in producing the foods we consume and the long-term effects of such practices. Regardless of the practice, opponents and critics believe that banning the advertising of such products can negatively affect their purchase and possibly prohibit the success of the category itself.

To Ban or Not to Ban Controversial Advertising?

Individuals and groups support advertising bans of controversial products for several reasons. As mentioned in the previous section, banning advertising for controversial products may result in a decrease in the use (and possible abuse) of the specific product category. Banning advertising messages for controversial products, especially on television, may protect youth in particular from an onslaught of advertising messages that may be problematic. Finally, banning advertising for controversial products will result in products being stigmatized in society, and some believe that there will be societal pressure to eliminate some controversial products from society as a whole.

However, banning advertising is a complex process, and there are numerous concerns with banning specific types of advertising from a range of groups. These concerns involve issues of freedom of speech, effectiveness of advertising bans, and government power in general.

Figure 11.2 Diet pill ad promises that one can take pills and lose weight.

Freedom of Speech

As we discussed in Chapter 4, the First Amendment provides protection for a wide range of commercial messages for products and services. Any type of ban on advertising that is proposed, then, is likely to come under the scrutiny of the legal system and of various industry groups. The American Advertising Federation (AAF) makes its policy in this matter clear. The AAF states that the "US Supreme Court has affirmed that truthful commercial speech enjoys the free speech protections of the First Amendment. The government's right to ban a product does not give it the right to ban speech about the product" (American Advertising Federation, 1999).

The Supreme Court tends to reject bans on advertising as unconstitutional when complaints are based on concerns with the products themselves and not with the messages. The courts have also recognized the important role consumer information plays in our society today. In 1993, for example, the Supreme Court refused to ban advertising messages about liquor because a consumer's interest in the free flow of information is more important to consumers than their interest in the day's most urgent political debates (Peck, 1993). A complete ban on some types of commercial speech would give the government an opportunity to censor nonmisleading speech about a legal product, leaving no other channels open to the product or service, and consumer choice could be compromised. If free speech is to be meaningful today, exceptions for any speech that some may believe is fraught with problems cannot be made (Peck, 1993).

Effectiveness of Banning Ads

The AAF suggests that assumptions regarding advertising restrictions and product purchases are flawed and states that restricting product advertising will not greatly affect use of the products. This is particularly germane when thinking about products that promote questionable behavior, since advertising bans are not likely to advance any government interests in reducing the abuse or use of products or services. The AAF points to experiences from other countries that illustrate that banning product advertising has not resulted in a decline in the consumption of those products. The U.S. Supreme Court itself stated that keeping users of a product ignorant in order to manipulate their choices does not work (Chafetaz, 2000).

In fact, some suggest that advertising mainstreams products in a positive way and that showing products as mundane consumer products can take away some of their mystique. In this way, advertising can provide images that normalize behaviors and make them less glamorous (Hanson, 2001). Additionally, it has been suggested that banning advertising will force marketers to channel advertising dollars to other areas that may be possibly more influential. The tobacco industry, for example, has cut back on advertising in the United States and now promotes products abroad, as well as invests more funds in in-store point-of-sale advertising.

Fear of Subsequent Bans

Overall, the advertising industry is concerned about any bans on commercial speech. The industry points out that even extreme political parties have the basic liberty of freedom of speech and argues that most consumer products are probably much less dangerous than some extreme political groups. In addition, there are concerns in the industry that bans on advertising for one product or service inevitably will lead to bans on the advertising of other products and services. The AAF warns that censorship is contagious (American Advertising Federation, 1999), and it fears that any potentially dangerous product could have its voice restricted. For example, butter and eggs can be considered unhealthy because they can lead to high cholesterol levels, so banning advertising for butter and eggs, and products made with butter and eggs, could lead to improved public health. This could help lower our nation's health care bill. But would you want to live in a world where you couldn't see an advertisement for butter and eggs or for anything containing butter and eggs? Wouldn't it be possible to find something potentially dangerous about almost every product and service that we consume? Where would the line be drawn?

Approaches to Controversial Advertising

Given advertising's power to influence large groups of people, there are several strategies available to advertisers and to other groups to counteract any potentially problematic messages. Suggestions about banning advertising are often seen as paternalistic because groups advocating bans assume that consumers do not know what is good for them and cannot be trusted to make decisions for themselves when they are exposed to advertising (Peck, 1993). Obviously, groups including women and minorities are as capable of resisting the lure of advertising as any other groups are (Jacobson & Mazur, 1995). However, other approaches that are used in the industry to address controversial messages are provided in this section.

Temperance or Moderation Messages

Right now, some industries that promote controversial products also provide funding for informational advertising that educates and promotes moderation in the use of the controversial product. If bans were placed on controversial advertising, messages promoting moderation would also be cut back. This could work against other efforts (e.g., public service messages) that promote abstinence or moderation. Perhaps a more reasonable alternative would be to require advertisers of certain controversial products and services to match product advertising with moderation messages on a dollar-for-dollar basis.

Warning Labels

Tobacco advertising carries warning labels, and it is possible that other products that result in demonstrable health problems could also be required to include some type of warning messages. Warnings would not necessarily have to feature an abstinence or moderation message but could state the long-term effects of continued use and/or misuse of the controversial product.

However, others suggest that warning labels have an effect opposite of what is intended. Specifically, if warning labels portray products as forbidden fruit, the products are made more attractive to young people (Fox, Krugman, Fletcher, & Fischer, 1998). We will discuss the controversy regarding warning labels in more detail in the next chapter.

Content Restriction

It has been proposed that certain types of images be prohibited in messages for controversial products. For example, some feel that celebrities should not be used in advertising for controversial products that appeal to youth (e.g., rock 'n' roll stars appearing in beer advertisements). Consumers, particularly young consumers, are highly influenced by celebrities in advertising. Athletes in particular add a "healthful" aura to many products or services that are not healthy, such as alcoholic beverages and high-fat snack foods. Positive feelings toward celebrities translate to trust in a product and its benefits, which may be an erroneous association (Dyson & Turco, 2002).

Tax Issues

Currently, most advertising expenses are tax deductible. It has been suggested that tax benefits should be reconsidered, and advertising dollars should not be tax deductible and perhaps even taxed themselves. There are currently "vice taxes" on products like alcohol and tobacco, which help to repay the demonstrable social costs of the products. Some suggest that tax deductions for advertising expenditures other than price advertising should be eliminated; therefore, any ad that features a message that does not include price (a key piece of consumer information) would not be tax-deductible. Others suggest that advertising space costs be taxed for certain questionable products and services. For example, a condom manufacturer running a print campaign would have to pay an additional 10% to the government over the amount spent on the advertising cost for its magazine schedule. Such tax strategies are seen as discouraging advertising without overtly violating freedom of speech (Murray, 1989).

Summary

In this chapter, we provided a brief introduction to some of the general issues and debates regarding controversial products and services. The following chapters are devoted to an examination of several different controversial products. In Chapter 12, we will look at tobacco and alcohol products. In Chapter 13, we will examine direct-to-consumer advertising of prescription drugs, and in Chapter 14, we will examine the only type of advertising messages that have complete protection under the First Amendment: political advertising. We will also discuss advertisers that use a type of strategy called socially responsible marketing in Chapter 15 and then closely evaluate the newest advertising channel—the Internet—in Chapter 16.

12

Two of a Kind?

Tobacco and Alcohol Advertising

If I give up drinking, smoking, and fatty foods, I can add ten years to my life. Trouble is, I'll add it to the wrong end.

—P. J. O'Rourke

Tobacco and alcohol advertising are often lumped together in discussions about controversial products. These two categories comprise a range of individual products (e.g., cigarettes, pipes, and cigars for tobacco and beer, wine, and "spirits," or what we sometimes think of as hard liquor, for alcohol). The two categories have several things in common. First, there are restrictions on who can buy the products. According to state and federal law, consumers must be at least 18 years old to purchase tobacco and at least 21 years old to purchase any type of alcohol products. Both products, then, fall under the rite of passage category of products described in Chapter 11.

Second, there is a risk of abusing both products. Some tobacco products are highly addictive, and addiction to tobacco has been shown to cause a range of health problems. Although alcohol products are less addictive than tobacco, there is still a risk of abuse, and overuse of alcohol can cause physical impairments (which can lead, for example, to drunk driving), addiction, and health problems.

Third, both categories tend to be highly taxed by government. Taxes of cigarettes and alcohol vary by state, and they fund many different projects, including schools and roads. Finally, both categories, along with firearms, have a special government agency devoted solely to monitoring the sales and marketing practices of the products in the category: the Bureau of Alcohol, Tobacco and Firearms (BATF).

In this chapter, we examine the current state of advertising thought regarding tobacco and alcohol products and discuss and evaluate some of the current controversies in both areas. Controversy is nothing new to these two categories: tobacco and alcohol advertising are probably two of the most thoroughly examined and criticized categories of all advertised products. Although there are distinct differences between the two, it is interesting to note that much of the criticism against advertising of both tobacco and alcohol is similar. The industries' responses to these criticisms are varied and broad. In this chapter, we depart from our traditional "intended and unintended effects" framework to focus on the substantial breadth of critical analysis of tobacco and alcohol advertising.

Regulation of Tobacco and Alcohol Advertising

Tobacco and alcohol advertisers have used a range of messages to promote their products. Interestingly, in the not-too-distant past, health-oriented messages were used, particularly for cigarettes. In the first part of the 20th century, for example, several cigarette companies made claims about the health benefits of smoking. Camel cigarettes advertised that more doctors smoked Camels than any other cigarette; another ad for Camels stated that smoking was beneficial because it provided a "a harmless restoration of the flow of natural body energy." Different cigarette brands were positioned as "just what the doctor ordered" and "recognized by eminent medical authorities." An ad for Kent cigarettes suggested that the product's micronite filters offered the greatest health protection in cigarette history. However, subsequent inquiries found that these filters were made the same material used to filter the air in hospital operating rooms, asbestos, which causes lung cancer ("Tobacco Advertising in the United States," 1997).

However, in the past few decades, government and industry have been much more involved in the evaluation and regulation of advertising messages for tobacco and alcohol, as well as in product packaging and labeling for both product categories. This section outlines the applicable regulations for each industry.

Regulation of Tobacco Advertising

Advertising for the tobacco industry is one of the few types of advertising that is regulated by law. Advertising of cigarettes, smokeless tobacco, and little cigars is prohibited on radio, TV, and other forms of electronic media (including the Internet) regulated by the Federal Communications Commission (FCC). The Federal Trade Commission (FTC) is also involved with regulating messages and first became involved with tobacco advertising in the 1930s, when it sought to prevent tobacco companies from claiming the health benefits from smoking discussed earlier ("Tobacco

Advertising in the United States," 1997). Today, the FTC can take action to stop a print advertisement for cigarettes, cigars, or a smokeless tobacco product from running in a print medium if it is deceptive or unfair. The FTC also enforces various federal requirements mandating health warnings on advertising, point-of-purchase displays (i.e., any display of tobacco products at grocery stores, convenience stores, etc.), and on the packaging of tobacco products. The BATF is part of the U.S. Treasury Department and is primarily involved in taxation issues for tobacco products. The only laws the BATF enforces that relate to the advertising of tobacco products are prohibitions against (a) lotteries associated with the products and (b) indecent or immoral images attached to such packages.

Much of this government regulation has recently taken a backseat to states' attorneys general and their actions against the large tobacco companies, including Philip Morris, Brown & Williamson, and R. J. Reynolds, collectively known as "Big Tobacco." Throughout the 1990s, numerous states brought lawsuits against Big Tobacco for a range of issues, including illegally marketing to and targeting minors and violating states' consumer protection and antitrust laws. In 1997, the attorneys general of several states met to negotiate a comprehensive settlement with the tobacco industry, which included public health provisions, full Food and Drug Administration (FDA) regulatory authority over tobacco, and severe restrictions on tobacco advertising and marketing. In November 1998, an agreement was reached with Big Tobacco. The 46 states and five territories that had not yet settled their lawsuits against the industry unanimously approved and joined the settlement agreement. The agreement stands today as the largest financial recovery and most comprehensive settlement in history (Washington State Attorney General's Office, 2002).

The agreement, known as the Master Settlement Agreement (MSA), accomplished the following:

- States received funding for tobacco prevention and control.
- Tobacco companies were required to take down all billboard advertising, including advertising in sports arenas.
- Tobacco advertisers could no longer use cartoon characters to sell cigarettes.
- Tobacco companies could not market or promote their products to people under the age of 18.

Later in this chapter, we examine the implications of this agreement on the tobacco industry and its advertisers.

Regulation of Alcohol Advertising

Both the FTC and the BATF regulate alcohol advertising. The FTC can act if an alcohol advertisement is deceptive or unfair. The BATF also has jurisdiction over deceptive or misleading alcohol labeling and advertising. The BATF is guided by the Federal Alcohol Administration Act (FAAA), which specifically outlines problematic areas with regard to advertising alcoholic beverages. Like advertisements for all other products, advertisements for alcoholic beverages must be truthful, and any claims provided in the advertisements must be substantiated. The FAAA stipulates that advertising must not represent the use of alcoholic beverages as being therapeutic or curative: Language that suggests these benefits, such as the words "bracing," "invigorating," and "pickup" or the phrases "clears your throat" and "relaxes you," cannot be used.

Advertising messages cannot suggest that using alcohol improves an individual's athletic abilities. While athletes and athletic activities can be used in advertising and product labeling, the BATF is vigilant in investigating any messages that mislead consumers based on such imagery. The BATF has historically taken the position that the depiction of athletes on alcoholic beverage labels and advertising is often deceptive and misleading because it implies that consuming alcohol is conducive to athletic skill or physical prowess and does not hinder an athlete's performance. Athletic imagery used in advertising messages tends not to present any negative consequences from consuming an alcoholic beverage, and thus, the messages are likely to be misleading. If athletes are used in advertisements, the BATF requires that they are not to consume or look like they are preparing to consume alcoholic beverages. Such a presentation would be an implied suggestion that the beverage was being used to enhance performance.

In addition, alcohol advertisements, by either their content or their placement, may not be directed to underage consumers (i.e., individuals under the age of 21). Some broadcasters and publishers place additional restrictions on where or when alcohol advertisements can run. Until 1996, a voluntary policy within both the spirits and the television industries banned advertisements for spirits, or hard liquor. Many broadcasters still do not accept ads for products other than beer or wine, although many cable networks air advertisements for spirits.

Whether advertising messages should include price information for alcoholic products has also been highly controversial. Many are concerned that advertising low prices might encourage consumption by individuals who cannot afford the product at full price or might cause overconsumption due to stocking up because of a good price. Price advertising for alcoholic beverages has been analyzed by the Supreme Court, which has said that the government may not ban price advertising in the case of alcoholic beverages to stifle demand.

Criticisms of Tobacco and Alcohol Advertising

Have we come a long way, baby, since those misleading health-related advertisements for cigarettes mentioned earlier? Do the current regulatory efforts by the FDA, the FTC, and the BATF have an impact on who sees the messages and the effects of the messages in society today? Many critics believe that even with the current regulatory climate, tobacco and alcohol advertisers have too much power and influence in today's market. This section examines such criticisms and concerns.

It has been argued that the MSA is not working in terms of minimizing the advertising presence and marketing influence of tobacco manufacturers. The MSA was designed to hit Big Tobacco in their wallets and provide mechanisms to decrease overall category advertising spending. However, the five largest tobacco companies spent a record $8.24 billion on advertising a year after the MSA was signed (Mazzetti, 2001). The MSA's stipulation against targeting children was also apparently ignored by Big Tobacco. Advertising in magazines popular with children, such as *Sports Illustrated* and *Rolling Stone,* increased after the settlement (King & Siegel, 2001). Additionally, the promotion of tobacco products via in-store displays increased after the billboard ban took effect in 1999 (Campaign for Tobacco Free Kids, 2000). Finally, the funds that state governments were awarded have not been applied to tobacco cessation programs in many states, as stipulated in the MSA. Instead, in a period of weak economic growth in many parts of the United States, the funds have gone instead to tax cuts, roads, and other projects.

Industry agreements to refrain from airing hard liquor advertising in broadcast media have generally been altered and weakened. Today, major spirits manufacturers are considering reintroducing their products over network television, and television executives and government agencies are examining whether voluntary policies are effective. As both the spirits and the broadcasting industries continue to pursue the possibility of airing commercials on network television, experts are starting to examine what type of government intervention may be necessary and appropriate in society today.

Concerns with both tobacco and alcohol advertising encompass a range of issues. These include questions and concerns regarding the different groups of consumers that are targeted, the types of imagery used in advertising, and the influence of warning labels on consumer behavior.

Targeting Issues

Targeting Children and Teenagers

Critics suggest, and research supports, that both tobacco and alcohol advertising target children under the age of 18. The imagery seen in advertisements in both product categories is arguably made to be attractive and entertaining to children. Of course, the campaign that most people are aware of is the infamous "Old Joe Camel" campaign for Camel cigarettes (Figure 12.1). Old Joe was a cartoon character, which tobacco giant R. J. Reynolds said

Figure 12.1   Camel cigarettes' spokesanimal, Old Joe

was developed to appeal to adults. During the course of the Old Joe campaign, research found that awareness of Old Joe as a representative of Camel cigarettes was very high among a range of demographic groups, including children. Old Joe was as familiar as Mickey Mouse among 6-year-old children, and Camel's market share among teens increased from 1% to 33% in the few years when Camel ran the Old Joe campaign.

Young people have often been attracted to the idea of smoking and drinking. Young adults and children see these behaviors as a way to develop their own identity, in that smoking and drinking can be seen as a sign of maturity, discernment, and independence (Hastings & MacFadyen, 2000). Tobacco and alcohol advertisers also recognize that certain imagery has cross-appeal to both adults and to children. Anthropomorphic images such as Anheuser-Busch's talking amphibians (Figure 12.2) and frisky Dalmatians are examples of such a cross-appeal. In addition, advertisers place some tobacco and alcohol messages in magazines with high readership among young people, such as *In Style, Spin,* and *Rolling Stone* (Mazzetti, 2001). Beer advertisements also appear frequently in sports-oriented TV programs that generate huge viewership numbers among a range of viewers, including children. Although the percentage of children in the total audience of a program like the Super Bowl may seem low compared with other groups, the percentages must be evaluated in the context of the program's total audience. For a program like the Super Bowl, which features a plethora of beer advertising, the overall large total number of people watching the program means that a lot of children are seeing beer ads.

Earlier in Chapter 5, we discussed concerns with product placement in movies and television. Tobacco and alcohol products have been placed in movies with PG and PG-13 ratings (Sager, 1999). Other product placement with direct influence on children has included placing beer company logos on children's toy cars and tobacco logos on T-shirts (Jacobson & Mazur, 1995).

Figure 12.2 Some of the critters used in Anheuser-Busch advertisements

The abundance of promotional imagery is having an effect on children. A recent study showed that 8- to 12-year-olds know more types of alcoholic beverages than names of U.S. presidents. Research also suggests that awareness of beer commercials on television leads to favorable beliefs about drinking in children 10 to 12 years old and increases their intention to drink as adults (Leiber, 1997). Critics argue that exposure to advertising also can lead to product usage among kids and that product usage may then result in significant health problems among children.

Youth tobacco consumption has been called the single most important public health issue of our era (Peracchio & Luna, 1998, p. 51). Every day, 2000 children and teenagers under the age of 18 begin smoking. One third will eventually die from a tobacco-related disease (Peracchio & Luna, 1998). Studies indicate that a majority of eighth graders and almost all high school seniors have experimented with alcohol, and more than one fourth of high school seniors reported consuming five or more drinks during the 2 weeks prior to the study period (Fox, Krugman, Fletcher, & Fischer, 1998).

Although the evidence supports that both alcohol and tobacco companies target youth, the reasons each industry targets them differ. Cigarette companies lose more of their customers each year than any other product: 434,000 people die from smoking-related diseases each year, and an additional 1.5 million stop smoking every year. Thus, the tobacco industry needs to attract about 2 million new users each year just to break even in terms of product usage. The key demographic for Big Tobacco to reach is teenagers, since between 85% and 90% of smokers start smoking during their teen years (Peracchio & Luna, 1998).

The alcohol industry is not in quite the same hurry as the tobacco industry, but instead, they want children to develop positive attitudes toward alcohol at a young age and want to encourage teens to purchase specific brands of alcohol when they become "legal." The number of beer commercials kids see, for example, is related to their awareness of different brands of beer. The higher children's brand awareness, the more likely they are to have a positive set of beliefs about the social aspects of drinking beer. In addition, brand awareness is related to the likelihood that children will have a higher expectation to drink as an adult.

Since alcohol and tobacco advertising often portray drinking and smoking as glamorous and desirable acts with few or no negative consequences (Figure 12.3), children and youth can be persuaded to form favorable beliefs and attitudes toward smoking and drinking, which may eventually contribute to undesirable behaviors. Studies have shown that among teens and young adults, stronger intentions to drink as well as more frequent drinking were related to higher exposure to TV and print ads for alcohol (Mehta, 2000).

Targeting College Students

In addition to the under-18 crowd, both tobacco and alcohol advertising target college students. At this age, most consumers can legally buy tobacco and many can legally buy alcohol, and both categories prize this group as impressionable young consumers. College students alone drink over $4.2 billion worth of alcohol each year. College campuses are often immersed in a drinking culture to the extent that universities allow school insignia to be used on shot glasses and beer mugs (Jacobson & Mazur, 1995). Although many critics recognize that college students' decisions to smoke and drink often come from peer pressure, the images presented in advertising positively reinforce such decisions.

Targeting Other Vulnerable Populations

Aside from children, youth, and college students, other consumers are seen to be particularly vulnerable to the messages promoted by the tobacco and alcohol industries. Individuals in inner-city neighborhoods, who demographically tend to be black, often have little health education and may not be aware of the hazards of smoking and drinking to the extent that individuals living outside inner-city areas are. In one magazine targeted to blacks, *Essence,* about 12% of revenues generated from advertising are from tobacco companies. Big Tobacco also contributes to the NAACP, National Urban League, and United Negro College Fund, and evidence suggests that tobacco money has bought the support, or at least the silence, of some black leaders regarding health issues and smoking among blacks. Today, about one third of blacks smoke compared with only one fifth of whites (Kiefe & Lewis, 2001).

These health issues are serious and widespread. Black women contract lung cancer 58% more often than white women, and black women have a 50% greater

Figure 12.3 A glamorous night in an ad for Captain Morgan's rum

rate of heart disease compared with white women. Black men have a 20% greater rate of heart disease than white men do. Regardless of gender, blacks disproportionately suffer higher rates of death, disease, and injury from alcohol and tobacco than whites (Indiana State Department of Health, 1992).

Some tobacco products are targeted specifically to women. Messages for brands such as Virginia Slims and More suggest that cigarettes are agents of women's progress and that smoking is the embodiment of liberation for women (Figure 12.4). Today, women comprise the fastest-growing group of smokers, and about one fourth of all women over the age of 18 smokes. Lung cancer has surpassed breast cancer as the leading cause of death from cancer in women (Indiana State Department of Health, 1992). Advertising and other mass media have created a mythic connection between smoking and thinness. Cigarettes targeted to women have names like "slims" and "thins," and nearly 40% of women who smoke say they do so to maintain their weight (Jacobson & Mazur, 1995).

Never come between a woman and her journal. Unless you want to be tomorrow's topic.

VIRGINIA SLIMS
It's a *woman* thing.

© Philip Morris Inc. 1998

8 mg "tar," 0.7 mg nicotine av. per cigarette by FTC method.

SURGEON GENERAL'S WARNING: Quitting Smoking Now Greatly Reduces Serious Risks to Your Health.

Figure 12.4 Virginia Slims suggests smoking is a "woman thing."

Types of Imagery

Both tobacco and alco-
hol advertising associate
with sports and athletic
activities and imagery.
Tobacco companies, for
example, sponsor a range of
sporting events, including
horse racing, auto racing,
golf, motorcycle racing,
sailing, skiing, bowling,
rodeos, ice skating, and ten-
nis. Such sponsorships link
cigarettes with activities
requiring aerobic and respiratory fitness. Beer and
other alcoholic beverages
are also associated with
athletes and athletic events;
for example, Coors beer
recently ran a campaign
that honored athletes such
as former quarterback John
Elway. Messages featuring
athletes perpetuate both the
brands' and the consumer's
denial of the potential consequences of smoking and
drinking (Indiana State Department of Health, 1992).

Figure 12.5 Rush hour after work is time for a Jameson whiskey.

Not only is athletic imagery an issue, but critics view other lifestyle imagery as inappropriate. Both tobacco and alcohol advertising images give an unrealistic view of what the products do, how they make the consumer feel, and how they fit in with an individual's lifestyle. Alcohol, for example, is portrayed as a reward at the end of the workday (Figure 12.5). Many advertisements connect alcohol with magic, and without it, your life is dull, mediocre, and ordinary (Figure 12.6). Images also imply that drinking is risk free: No one in an alcohol advertisement is ever seen as sloppy drunk or pulled over by a police officer for driving under the influence. Tobacco images connect smoking with beautiful, clean tropical locations and healthy outdoor lifestyles (Figure 12.7). Smoking and drinking are often seen as a complement to a celebration of life.

Alcohol is seen as having the ability to make an individual attractive to the opposite sex; it is also pictured as an aphrodisiac or a romance enhancer. Perhaps more than any other product category, alcoholic beverages

Figure 12.6 This Kahlua ad connects the product with magical imagery.

associate sexual imagery with products. Beer drinkers on television are generally portrayed as young, sexy, successful, and active, an image many young adults are eager to achieve (Fox et al., 1998).

Issues With Warning Labels and Moderation Appeals

A final category of concern addresses warning labels and moderation appeals. Cigarette warnings are mandated by a federal policy passed in 1984 and must be included in both product advertising and packaging (Fox et al., 1998). Cautionary statements on alcohol labels are mandatory, but including cautionary statements in advertising messages for alcoholic beverages is voluntary (Fox et al., 1998). Industry guidelines recommend that marketers create moderation appeals that run in tandem with their product advertising; moderation messages for these product categories are not required by law.

Warning labels and moderation messages are designed not only to remind current users of their risky behavior but also to alert nonusers (e.g., adolescents) that behaviors like smoking and drinking are not risk-free. Thus, such warning labels are designed to attempt to counteract advertising messages for the products.

Studies have shown that "warning messages currently mandated by the government are not particularly effective in communicating health risks to the adolescent audience" (Fox et al., 1998, p. 67). Warning labels have been seen as having the ability to increase awareness and knowledge of the attributes of a product (i.e., they have an effect on the user), but they have no impact on perceived risks and behaviors among some or all of drinkers

Figure 12.7 Parliament's ad suggests a beautiful, pristine tropical feel.

(i.e., the effect is not necessarily seen as negative). The messages appear to have more impact on lighter product users than heavy product users.

Adolescents in particular play down the negative consequences of smoking and drinking behaviors because many youth perceive of themselves as invulnerable. Thus, it is difficult for them to relate to any consequences that may occur in what they perceive as the distant future. In fact, warning labels may have an adverse effect on adolescents because they may believe that any product that is "that bad" must have some good things about it (Fox et al., 1998).

Moderation messages for alcoholic beverages, also known as responsible drinking messages, present other problems. First, the content of the messages themselves suggests that responsible drinking always will include a message to drink; that is, the message is not to abstain but only to limit drinking (Leiber, 1997). Moderation messages also tend to leave the definition of what constitutes responsible behavior up to the consumer. This may result in consumers having difficulty determining what moderation is because the message provides minimal direction and instruction.

Industry Responses

Given these concerns, the advertising environment today is becoming even more restrictive for tobacco and alcohol products. There have been discussions in the press and within the industry recently about extending bans on advertising of both products. The NBC television network recently considered accepting liquor advertisements in their prime-time programming but quickly reconsidered, and some have called for a ban on tobacco advertising in magazines. While we will discuss each of these issues in turn, it is important to note that both industries assert that many factors contribute to smoking and drinking, and advertising alone is not the primary factor that determines whether an individual will smoke or drink. Influential factors include whether the individual considers smoking and drinking as positive or negative behaviors, whether the individual has a family member that smokes and/or drinks, and the individual's socio-economic status (Peracchio & Luna, 1998). In a study of American youth aged 12 to 17, for example, 62% of respondents rated their parents as an influence on what affects their decisions about drinking. Only 4% mentioned that advertising is a leading influence on their decisions (Fisher, 1993).

Both industries suggest that they are in mature product categories and that advertising is merely intended to persuade current users to switch brands (Figure 12.8). Thus, instead of increasing the overall consumption by converting nonusers to users, the objective is to encourage users to switch brands and then to create brand loyalty among brand switchers so that one advertiser gains market share while another one loses (Hastings & MacFadyen, 2000; Nelson, 1995). Banning advertising, then, would be prohibiting truthful communication directed to individuals who are legally able to purchase the product or service and already do so.

Obviously, First Amendment issues are at stake. Tobacco and alcohol are legal products for many individuals to purchase. In July 2001, the Supreme Court overturned a set of advertising and point-of-sale restrictions that Massachusetts's attorney general imposed on tobacco products. These regulations banned advertising of tobacco products within 1000 feet of schools or playgrounds viewable from outside a store, and were designed obviously to limit children's exposure to tobacco advertising. Because tobacco manufacturers have taken down most of their outdoor display boards, this type of ban would primarily affect signs posted at stores and would include signs that said cigarettes were for sale (without giving any price or product attribute information). The Supreme Court said that Massachusetts's advertising restrictions on cigars and smokeless tobacco went too far. Justice Sandra Day O'Connor wrote that "these regulations would constitute nearly a complete ban on the communication of truthful information about smokeless tobacco and cigars to adult consumers." The Supreme Court suggested that government cannot reduce the adult population to receiving messages only appropriate for children. This principle was seen as important not only for tobacco but for any company with a product that might be seen as inappropriate for youth.

Should Spirits Advertising on TV Be Banned?

NBC recently considered breaking a more than 60-year-old voluntary industry ban on network broadcast advertising of hard liquor. Since 1936, hard liquor advertising has not appeared on network television, such as ABC, CBS, NBC, and Fox, although networks have always aired commercials for beer and wine. The absence of hard liquor advertising (and the presence of wine and beer advertising) on network TV has caused criticism. Specifically, the absence of hard liquor has created a perception that spirits are somehow more dangerous than beer or wine and thus deserve harsher social, political, and legal treatment (Distilled Spirits Council of the United States, 1996).

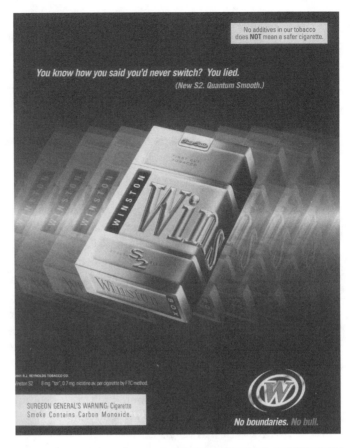

Figure 12.8 This Winston ad suggests that their target audience is potential switchers.

As you might have noticed, though, the television landscape today is much different from 1936. Today, the growth of cable and independent television networks has fragmented television audiences to a great degree. As a result, the distilled spirits industry believes it can direct its messages more precisely to adult audiences than would have been possible when the voluntary ban first went into effect.

NBC decided to accept advertisements for hard liquor in December 2001, citing several reasons for doing so. At the end of 2001, hard liquor ads were already seen on several cable networks, as well as 400 local stations and cable systems (Grossman, 2001). NBC, with a noticeable lack of sports programming compared with the other major networks, cited that they had a lack of beer advertising that resulted in a shortfall of revenue. By accepting hard liquor advertisements, the network hoped to increase its revenue in a broadcasting environment where hard liquor advertising appeared to be generating general acceptance.

With its decision established, NBC set guidelines for the acceptance of hard liquor advertising campaigns. These guidelines included the network's promise to run spots only on programs where 85% of viewers were 21 or older; almost all of NBC's prime-time shows would qualify to receive hard liquor spots given this requirement (Friedman, 2002). Any commercial scheduled before 9 P.M. would be approved on a case-by-case basis, and all spots would be accepted to air after 9 P.M. Most important, though, any spirits advertiser would have to run 4 months of branded social-responsibility messages before brand messages would air. Such commercials could include a message such as, "Drink responsibly this weekend. This message is brought to you by Seagrams." Total spending for these social-responsibility messages had to represent a minimum of 20% of the total advertising budget to be spent on NBC. Other guidelines included implementation recommendations. For example, actors in commercials for spirits had to be at least 30 years old (compared to 25 years old for beer ads), and like beer ads, no one could be shown drinking in a spirits spot (Friedman, 2002).

In light of NBC's decision, some groups called for legislation to ban hard liquor advertising on television. In response, the spirits industry argued that it is difficult to develop any type of persuasive argument for why federal law should allow advertising of beer and wine but not hard liquor (Jahnke, 2001). A comparison of the two industries shows that the beer industry is profitable, whereas the spirits industry is not, and this difference has been attributed to the presence (or absence) of television advertising (Modzelweski, 1996). From 1980 to 2000, beer's share of the total alcohol market rose from 53% to 58%, and wine's share increased from 10.7% to 12.3%. During the same period, hard liquor's market share declined from 36.6% to less than 29% (Grimm, 2002).

In response to comparisons with the tobacco ban, the spirits industry noted that spirits could not be directly compared to tobacco because spirits are not necessarily addictive. In fact, moderate consumption of spirits beverages (one drink per day for women, one or two for men) can provide significant health benefits to some consumers, such as reducing the risk of heart disease in postmenopausal women and in middle-aged men (American Council on Science and Health, 2000).

The industry also referred to the research record on the effects of alcohol advertising, which suggests that there is a limited relationship between advertising and behaviors related to health (Leiber, 1997). An FTC study conducted in the 1980s showed no relationship between alcohol advertising and consumption or alcohol advertising and abuse of alcohol (Crawford & Graham, 1985). A U.S. Senate subcommittee report could not find evidence to conclude that advertising influences nondrinkers to start drinking or that advertising increases consumption. In fact, in what has been termed the "definitive review" of research from around the world (Hanson, 2001), researchers found that advertising has no influence on alcohol consumption and has no impact on experimentation with alcohol or its abuse (Fisher, 1993, p. 150).

A range of groups opposes government regulations banning alcohol advertising. The U.S. Department of Health and Human Services (1990), for example, is against banning or imposing any more restrictions on advertising than currently exist. The group Mothers Against Drunk Driving (MADD) has said it had never been opposed to responsible alcohol advertising in any medium (Grossman, 2001). A recent article in the trade journal *Advertising Age* reported that Congress was currently quiet on whether it would propose regulation of liquor advertising on television. The article suggested that it is unlikely that either Congress or the FCC would oppose liquor advertising on television, since NBC's guidelines were seen to represent a reasonable approach to airing such spots.

However, NBC abandoned plans to accept hard liquor advertising in March 2002, citing concerns from the American Medical Association as well as from legislators (Elliott, 2002b). Although no other networks are indicating accepting spirits advertising, at least one network, CBS, said that it may eventually begin running such advertising (Flint, 2002). The other networks seemed hesitant to alienate beer company sports sponsorships or to deal with a public backlash to spirits advertising on television: About 70% of consumers think it is dangerous to have liquor ads on television (Center for Science in the Public Interest, 2001), and more than 72% support the current voluntary restrictions (Grimm, 2002). Additionally, almost 50% of Americans believe that more restrictions on liquor advertising are needed, but only 14% believe that more restrictions on beer advertising are needed.

Even if a ban on hard liquor advertising continues, we are likely to begin to see more liquor brand names over the airwaves. A wave of new products, known as "malternatives," are sweet, low-alcohol beverages that fall under beer regulations for advertising. These new products contain the names of major alcohol brands: Guinness promotes Smirnoff Ice, Anheuser-Busch advertises Bacardi Silver, and Miller's offering is called Skyy Blue (Figure 12.9). These may serve to enhance awareness of hard liquor brand while keeping to the letter, if not the spirit, of current regulations.

Should Print Advertising for Tobacco Products Be Banned?

In the early 1990s, tobacco companies were among the leading spenders in magazines, but their overall spending in magazines has decreased significantly since that time (Leiber, 1997). Philip Morris said that it was cutting back on print media in the year 2002: Philip Morris represents about 40% of tobacco industry magazine spending, and such a decrease is alarming to the publications that still accept tobacco advertising (DiPasquale & Fine, 2002). Still, several groups suggest that tobacco advertising should be subject to further restrictions, particularly with

YOUR NIGHT JUST GOT MORE INTERESTING.™

NEW BACARDI SILVER PREMIUM MALT BEVERAGE WITH NATURAL CITRUS FLAVORS.

PREMIUM MALT BEVERAGE. 5% ALCOHOL BY VOLUME.

Figure 12.9 Bacardi Silver is one of many "malternatives" or "alchopops" promoted today.

regard to its appearance in magazines.

One reason goes back to a recurring theme in this book: the Chinese Wall. The Society for Women's Health Research conducted research that showed that 73% of women prefer women's magazines to other media sources as a reference for health information. The society also found that magazines that advertise cigarettes are far less likely to run stories about the health effects of smoking (Society for Women's Health Research, 1998). Thus, there is an implicit relationship between tobacco advertising and coverage (or lack of coverage) of health issues due to tobacco use and abuse. Eliminating tobacco advertising might positively affect the coverage of health issues in print today.

The next reason has been touched upon in this chapter, and that is the exposure of cigarette advertising in print to children. Tobacco advertisers continue to run in publications like *Rolling Stone*, where 23% of total readers are under the age of 18, according to both the Simmons Teen Survey and the Simmons National Consumer Survey. *Rolling Stone* still carries ads for R. J. Reynolds brands in practically every issue, and advertising presence by that tobacco company is expected to increase. *Rolling Stone* also carries ads for tobacco products produced by Brown & Williamson. Tobacco advertising in the magazine is frequently positioned near editorial stories featuring performers popular with teens, such as Sarah Michelle Gellar, the star of the TV show *Buffy the Vampire Slayer* (Kuczynski, 2001).

Not surprisingly, most publishers of magazines that still accept tobacco advertising said they were comfortable running the tobacco ads and are against a regulatory ban. The publisher of *People* magazine, Peter Bauer, said in a statement that magazines were not legally restrained from accepting tobacco ads and that the guidelines laid out by the MSA applied only to the tobacco companies, which could choose to follow them or not (Kuczynski, 2001). A majority of individuals surveyed in an AP poll were similarly opposed to advertising restrictions and supported advertising and promotions for tobacco products (Associated Press, 1995).

The publisher of the trade magazine *Advertising Age*, Scott Donaton, argues that publishers should voluntarily ban tobacco advertising from pages. Publishers have the freedom to decide which ads they will and will not accept, and they should take the moral high ground and ban tobacco advertising. However, Donaton believes that it is wrong for government to dictate what a magazine's policy should be, and left to their own devices, magazines would do the right thing (Donaton, 2001). A recent study showed that as of November 2001, half of 190 monitored magazines accepted tobacco ads and half did not. Of the ones that do not accept tobacco ads, only three magazines accept corporate advertisements for tobacco companies such as Philip Morris ("Magazines That Do Not Accept Tobacco Advertising," 2001). This is an important consideration because publishers must face the economic reality that if magazines voluntarily refuse to take tobacco ads, other nontobacco subsidiaries of the tobacco companies may also stop advertising in the magazine.

The other economic reality is that a ban on magazine advertising would not eliminate product messages. The tobacco companies would merely find yet another outlet for their marketing funds. Philip Morris, for example, has reportedly shifted funds from magazine advertising to store displays, direct marketing, and promotions (Bercovici, 2002).

Summary

In this chapter, we examined two of the most controversial products in advertising today: tobacco and alcohol. While tobacco products are strictly regulated, alcohol products are less so. Currently, debates continue as to whether further restrictions on such products are appropriate, although manufacturers, especially spirits manufacturers, have valid reasons for why restrictions on advertising should be relaxed.

In the next chapter, we will examine direct-to-consumer advertising for prescription drugs. Like tobacco and alcohol product advertising, a range of groups is concerned with such messages. However, there are valid reasons why advertising for prescription drugs should be allowed to continue. In all these cases, only time will tell what the actual societal limitations on advertising messages will be.

13

Doctor's Orders

Advertising Prescription Drugs

Words are, of course, the most powerful drug used by mankind.

—Rudyard Kipling

What do the following images have in common? Recently married couples enjoying time together. Grandparents and their grandchildren. A t'ai chi class in the park. Animated stomachs dancing to a rendition of an Elvis Presley song. All these images, and more, have been seen in advertising for prescription pharmaceutical drugs. Today, advertisements promoting prescription drugs are as prevalent on TV and in magazines as are ads for cars, toys, and soda pop. Indeed, 99% of Americans have seen an advertisement for a prescription drug in the past 6 months (Media-DailyNews, 2002).

The United States leads the world in the development of pharmaceutical products and produced about half the drugs introduced around the world between 1975 and 1994 (Tanouye, 2000). The primary target group for prescription drugs is older adults—those individuals aged 65 and older. These older adults make up 12% of the U.S. population but are the purchasers of more than 35% of all prescription drugs. People over the age of 65 fill between nine and twelve prescriptions each year compared with two or three prescriptions per year for people between the ages of 25 and 44 (Tanouye, 2000).

What you may not realize is that prescription drug advertising directed to consumers, as it appears on television today, has only been in its present form since 1997. Prescription drug print advertising directed to consumers has been used since the late 1980s. The relatively late introduction of such advertising is due to the medical community's historical resistance to consumer-oriented prescription drug advertising, also known as *direct-to-consumer* (DTC) advertising.

Traditionally, physicians have considered themselves the "gatekeepers" to health care and have desired (and received) tight control over the information that was conveyed to patients. As far back as 1555, for example, the Royal College of Physicians in London feared that patients would use prescribed medicines improperly, and they decreed that physicians must neither teach people about medicines nor tell them the names of medicines. While the medical community has certainly loosened up a bit in terms of the amount of information they provide to patients, the control over drug choice persisted among the medical professions for more than 400 years (Pharmaceutical Research and Manufacturers of America, 2000). This role of doctors as gatekeepers to deliver information about pharmaceutical products is the primary system used around the world. Today, the United States and New Zealand are the only two countries that allow DTC advertising.

The Food and Drug Administration (FDA) has statutory authority over all aspects of DTC marketing, including the regulation of prescription drug product labeling and both DTC and physician-oriented advertising. This responsibility has grown significantly during the past decade, as increasing numbers of pharmaceutical firms turn to DTC advertising for their products. For example, when DTC drug ads on television were first approved in 1997, advertising spending in the pharmaceutical industry was about $220 million per year. Three years later, DTC advertising spending had increased more than tenfold to $2.5 billion, with the bulk of this money ($1.7 billion) going toward television advertising (Belkin, 2000; Hall, 2001). In the year 2001, total television spending increased to about $2.8 billion (Peterson, 2002). Today, the pharmaceutical industry is one of the leading advertising spenders in the United States. However, this spending increase has raised concerns about rising pharmaceutical costs and about the growing role of DTC advertising within American society.

Many of these concerns stem from the fact that DTC advertising is clearly successful at achieving its goal. Prescriptions for DTC-advertised drugs increased by 34.2% in 1999 compared with 1998, while the number of all other prescriptions written increased by only 5.1% (Charatan, 2000). However, the rise in the number of prescriptions being written has consumers, the government, health care providers, and the pharmaceutical industry concerned with the effects that the increase in sales has with issues such as drug pricing, doctor-patient relationships, and the medicalization of drugs in society.

History of DTC Advertising

The modern pharmaceutical industry has been in existence since the 1940s. Before that time, most drugs were naturally occurring substances such as digitalis and opium (Clark, 1988). Penicillin was one of the first synthetic substances developed by the pharmaceutical industry, which began to grow substantially in the 1950s. Today, a small group of American, German, and

Swiss multinational companies dominate the pharmaceutical industry (Clark, 1988).

The pharmaceutical industry is unique in several ways. First, it is based not only on production but also on creation: A company is successful in part because of the new products it develops. Thus, much of the costs involved in product development occur long before the drug is on the market. Second, it a truly international business, with international sales necessary to recoup the investment costs.

Pharmaceutical companies have always targeted physicians and other health care providers through a number of different channels, including direct mail, personal sales, and advertisements in medical journals. In 1962, the Kefauver-Harris drug amendment set strict guidelines for all pharmaceutical advertising in the United States. There are four basic attributes to the amendment. First, it requires that advertised drugs be proven safe and effective, and the advertisement must not be false or misleading (before the amendment, drugs could be advertised to medical professionals before they received FDA approval). Second, the advertisements must present a fair balance of the risks and benefits of using the drug. Third, they must contain facts that are material to the product's advertised uses. Finally, and probably most important, all promotional material must include a *brief summary* (Henney, 2000). The Code of Federal Regulations describes the brief summary as a statement that provides all the information from the product's approved labeling to facts regarding side effects and contraindications. It includes all information that is found under headings such as cautions, special considerations, important notes, and the like. While the original use of the term *brief summary* included effectiveness information, later references by the pharmaceutical industry and the FDA do not. The FDA's Division of Drug Marketing, Advertising, and Communications (DDMAC) explains that this is because the advertising itself usually provides sufficient information regarding effectiveness in promotional messages about pharmaceutical products.

Until 1981, all prescription drug advertising was directed to physicians and other medical professionals. In 1981, the FDA received a proposal from a pharmaceutical firm that requested the FDA's approval to advertise directly to consumers. This proposal was instigated by the growth of managed care organizations (MCOs), which limited physicians' influence in prescribing medications to what is known as a *formulary*, a list of drugs selected by the MCOs (Peyrot, Alpersetein, Doren, & Poli, 1998). In addition to the growth of formularies, two other practices had the pharmaceutical industry concerned with the future of physician-oriented marketing. First was the increased use of utilization review systems, which are studies that show processes and outcomes of care. Such studies might encourage a range of treatments, including nonpharmaceutical ones, for physicians to consider. Second was the increase in pharmaceutical risk-sharing agreements, when physicians share the risk of financial loss with other participants if the total costs of services provided to patients exceed the anticipated volume of service. All three situations had the ability to limit the effect of physician-oriented advertising on physician prescription writing (Kravitz, 2000).

When the FDA received the request, individuals working at the FDA were concerned whether DTC advertising could serve two masters: the promotional interest of the drug manufacturer and the public's health needs (Henney, 2000). The FDA asked for a voluntary moratorium on DTC advertising in the early 1980s so it could fully examine the issue. Subsequently, the FDA surveyed consumers on their attitudes and opinions toward DTC advertising. The study showed that DTC advertisements could successfully communicate a large amount of pertinent information regarding both the risks and the benefits of prescription medications (Henney, 2000). The majority of consumers responding to the FDA's study thought the DTC advertising would be useful yet also believed that their physicians would be the key decision makers when prescribing drugs.

In 1985, the FDA decided to sanction DTC advertising. The agency announced that such advertisements would be subject to the same criteria as physician-directed advertisements: Most important, any advertisement that included both the product's name and its purpose (i.e., what problem it treated) had to provide the brief summary (Pharmaceutical Research and Manufacturers of America, 2000). DTC advertising began in 1988 with Upjohn's magazine advertisements for the hair-growth product Rogaine. The effect of DTC advertising was seen immediately: When Upjohn started advertising, Rogaine's sales increased from $87 million (preadvertising) in 1988 to $143 million in 1991 (Nayyar, 1992).

At first, most physicians were opposed to DTC advertising. However, as early as 1991, the American Academy of Family Physicians reported that acceptance of DTC advertising was increasing among medical professionals. The academy attributed this change to physicians' observations that DTC advertising encouraged consumers to seek needed medical care. In 1992, the American Medical Association (AMA) reversed its blanket policy against DTC advertising. Recognizing, however, that many physicians were still opposed to DTC advertising, the current AMA policy condones such advertising on a case-by-case basis (Peyrot et al., 1998).

DTC advertisers considering television realized that including the brief summary in a television advertisement would result in a long and incredibly boring execution. In the late 1980s, the FDA would only allow manufacturers to avoid the brief summary requirement by announcing only the drug's name (also known as a *reminder advertisement*) or by announcing only what condition the drug could treat (also known as a *health-seeking advertisement*). Advertisers were quick to try these tactics, primarily because they were hesitant to provide negative information about drug risks in their advertising (Bunis, 2000). DTC advertisers found, however, that reminder advertisements and health-seeking advertisements both confused consumers and were not effective for sales (Pharmaceutical Research and Manufacturers of America, 2000).

To DTC advertisers considering television advertising, the brief summary requirement was a challenge that seemed insurmountable. Advertisers had already discovered that the brief summary for print advertisements could require one to three additional pages to include all the required information (Food and Drug Administration, 1995). In the mid-1990s, the pharmaceutical industry argued that implementing the brief summary requirement on television and radio was extremely expensive since the information could not be included within the constraints of a 60- or 30-second radio or TV spot. The industry also argued that DTC advertising offered immense educational and public health value and that the existing FDA standards were neither practical nor consumer friendly (Food and Drug Administration, 1995). The industry asked for and received a reevaluation of the television guidelines by the FDA.

In 1997, the FDA released a draft set of guidelines for broadcast advertising, and a finalized set of guidelines was released in 1999. This new set of guidelines eliminated the brief summary requirement, replacing it with a requirement called the *major statement*: a reduced brief summary containing the drug's major risks and contraindications (the details of the guidelines and the FDA review process are specified in the next section of this chapter). This change made broadcast advertising a viable option for the pharmaceutical industry.

Once the FDA approved replacing the brief summary with the major statement, DTC advertising became a reality for many pharmaceutical companies. In fact, spending increased in the 60% to 70% range during 1999 and 2000 (Goetzl, Klaassen, Teinowitz, & Sanders, 2001). DTC category spending continued to grow even during the post-September 11 recession that caused most other advertisers to cut back on their budgets.

Recently, however, spending has stalled. There has been a dearth of new drug launches, as well as a number of delays in approvals for new drugs (Goetzl et al., 2001). Additionally, the FDA recently approved changing several allergy drugs' availability from prescription to over-the-counter. These situations would all affect spending in the category (Goetzl et al., 2001).

The Current FDA
_____ Guidelines for DTC Brand Advertising

Today, the FDA sanctions three different categories of DTC advertising:

1. *Health-seeking advertising.* This type of advertising provides information on a specific condition (e.g., diabetes) but does not mention a branded product. Health-seeking advertising can include the name of a

Figure 13.1 This health-seeking ad provides information about the skin disease melasma. It does not provide specific information about a prescription drug.

pharmaceutical manufacturer in the ad (e.g., "This message brought to you by Glaxo-Wellcome") (Figure 13.1).

2. *Reminder advertising.* This type of advertising contains a brand name but does not make any claims about the product or mention what the drug is used for. An example would be a television spot that announced "It's time for Claritin" with no mention that Claritin is an allergy drug. Print ads can also be used for reminder ads (Figure 13.2).

3. *Brand advertising.* This is what comes to mind when we think of DTC advertising: Messages that contain a brand name as well as product-specific information about the drug, including effectiveness (Peyrot et al., 1998) (Figure 13.3).

Any of these three types of advertisements can appear in print and/or broadcast media.

Print Advertisements

The Federal Food, Drug, and Cosmetic Act requires that anyone who advertises prescription human and animal drugs in print media (i.e., in magazines and newspapers) must disclose certain information about the drugs' uses and risks. Such advertisements must contain information relating to the drugs' purpose, side effects, contraindications, and effectiveness in an information disclosure known as the brief summary. Print advertisements must include the brief summary in its entirety: Specifically, the brief summary must contain information regarding each of the risks that are included in the package insert approved by the FDA.

The brief summary typically occupies an entire magazine page of small type (Kaplar, 1998) (Figure 13.4). Obviously, providing such information is much more feasible in print media than in broadcast media such as television and radio (Pharmaceutical Research and Manufacturers of America,

2000). Therefore, DTC print advertisements today currently function largely as repositories of highly technical data that are similar to a Web site or pharmacological reference work (Kaplar, 1998).

Television Advertisements

FDA guidelines are explicit in their requirements for television advertisements. A condensed version of the brief summary, called the *major statement*, is required. The major statement requires a "fair balance" of risk and benefit information. Drug advertisers are required to list the most important risks and side effects in their advertisements. To compensate for the lack of a complete brief summary, the FDA requires that advertisements contain alternative methods of acquiring information, such

Figure 13.2 A reminder ad for the prescription drug Vioxx. The ad does not mention the condition that the drug treats.

as through toll-free telephone numbers, Web site addresses, print advertisements in specified magazines, and health care providers. Providing these information sources is known as *adequate provision*. The information sources selected for inclusion in the advertisements have to account for patient privacy as well as consumers' varying levels of media and technology access. For example, if a television ad used the placement of a print ad in a magazine to fulfill its adequate provision requirement, it must also provide a toll-free telephone number or an address where people can write for further access to package labeling information. Clearly, no-cost or very low-cost methods of receiving the brief summary must be available. If a Web site is featured, the Web page must provide access to package labeling. Television advertisements may also suggest that pharmacists and physicians can provide additional product information. Alternatively, pharmaceuticals can provide

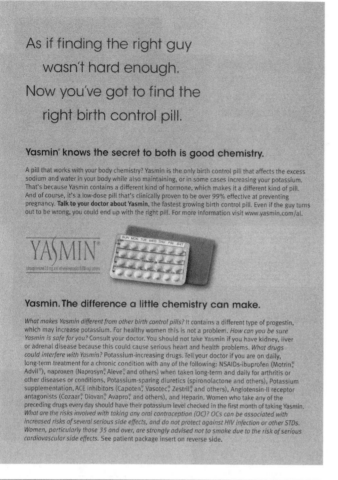

As if finding the right guy

wasn't hard enough.

Now you've got to find the

right birth control pill.

Yasmin‌ knows the secret to both is good chemistry.

A pill that works with your body chemistry? Yasmin is the only birth control pill that affects the excess sodium and water in your body while also maintaining, or in some cases increasing your potassium. That's because Yasmin contains a different kind of hormone, which makes it a different kind of pill. And of course, it's a low-dose pill that's clinically proven to be over 99% effective at preventing pregnancy. **Talk to your doctor about Yasmin**, the fastest growing birth control pill. Even if the guy turns out to be wrong, you could end up with the right pill. For more information visit www.yasmin.com/al.

Yasmin. The difference a little chemistry can make.

What makes Yasmin different from other birth control pills? It contains a different type of progestin, which may increase potassium. For healthy women this is not a problem. *How can you be sure Yasmin is safe for you?* Consult your doctor. You should not take Yasmin if you have kidney, liver or adrenal disease because this could cause serious heart and health problems. *What drugs could interfere with Yasmin?* Potassium-increasing drugs. Tell your doctor if you are on daily, long-term treatment for a chronic condition with any of the following: NSAIDs-ibuprofen (Motrin‌, Advil‌), naproxen (Naprosyn‌, Aleve‌, and others) when taken long-term and daily for arthritis or other diseases or conditions, Potassium-sparing diuretics (spironolactone and others), Potassium supplementation, ACE inhibitors (Capoten‌, Vasotec‌, Zestril‌, and others), Angiotensin-II receptor antagonists (Cozaar‌, Diovan‌, Avapro‌, and others), and Heparin. Women who take any of the preceding drugs every day should have their potassium level checked in the first month of taking Yasmin. *What are the risks involved with taking any oral contraception (OC)? OCs can be associated with increased risks of several serious side effects, and do not protect against HIV infection or other STDs. Women, particularly those 35 and over, are strongly advised not to smoke due to the risk of serious cardiovascular side effects.* See patient package insert on reverse side.

Figure 13.3   A brand advertisement for the prescription
drug Yasmin

brochures with package labels to publicly accessible sites, including pharmacies, doctors' offices, grocery stores, and libraries. The FDA suggests that multiple sources should be used to fulfill the adequate provision requirement.

Advertising Review Process

Currently, all advertising is reviewed and approved by the FDA's DDMAC. DTC advertisers have the option of submitting their advertisements for comments before broadcast or submitting the advertisements (or in most cases, storyboards and scripts) simultaneously to the FDA and the television stations for approval (Food and Drug Administration, 1998c). Commercials do not have to receive FDA approval before airing, although the FDA urges pharmaceutical advertisers to have their messages cleared prior to running (Woods, 2001). The review process takes about 4 weeks (DTC Perspectives, 2002).

Because many advertisements are precleared from either storyboards or scripts (i.e., the finished execution is not evaluated before clearance), the FDA carefully monitors creative executions once they air in any medium. From 1997 to 1999, the FDA sent about 70 notices to advertisers that their promotional messages violated regulations; in most cases, the advertisement overstated the product's effectiveness or the extent of its approved use. Companies have historically complied with any changes requested by the FDA (Henney, 2000).

Intended Effects

Proponents of DTC advertising recognize several beneficial intended effects of such messages. Most of the intended effects have to do with empowering consumers regarding their own health care.

Consumers Learn Information About Health Care Choices

Despite the FDA's original concerns about DTC advertising, research shows that consumers are generally receptive to these advertisements. In a survey of *Wall Street Journal* subscribers, 72% agreed that pharmaceutical companies should play an active role in informing consumers about medical conditions and possible treatments (Pharmaceutical Research and Manufacturers of America, 2000). Consumers take an interest in making their own health care decisions and believe pharmaceutical manufacturers serve as a helpful information source. In fact, 76% of adults think DTC advertising helps them take an active part in their health care, and 72% feel DTC advertisements educate consumers about the benefits and risks of pharmaceuticals (Pharmaceutical Research and Manufacturers of America, 2000). In 11 different public opinion and advertising surveys of consumer perception of DTC advertising (conducted from 1999 to 2001), most consumers indicated that they benefited from what they see, hear, and read about drugs (McInturff, 2001). In these studies, consumers cited benefits including the belief that they were better informed, had more choices, and had become more involved in their health care (McInturff, 2001).

Physicians also see the benefit of DTC advertising. One study showed that 65% of doctors agree that DTC advertising raises awareness of health treatments among consumers, and

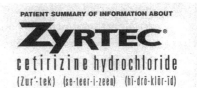

PATIENT SUMMARY OF INFORMATION ABOUT

ZYRTEC®
cetirizine hydrochloride
(Zur'-tek) (se-teer-i-zeen) (hī-drō-klōr-īd)

This summary contains important information about ZYRTEC. It is not meant to take the place of your doctor's instructions. Read this information carefully before you start taking ZYRTEC. Each time you fill your prescription, be sure to read the summary that comes with it. It could contain new information. Ask your doctor or pharmacist if you do not understand any of this information or if you want to know more about ZYRTEC.

► **What Is ZYRTEC?**
ZYRTEC is a prescription medicine for certain types of allergies in adults and children age 2 years and older. It is an antihistamine and is available as a tablet or syrup.
When you have allergies, your body releases a natural chemical called histamine that causes the sneezing, runny nose, hives, and other symptoms of allergies. ZYRTEC helps block histamine from causing these symptoms. ZYRTEC treats:

Seasonal allergies ("outdoor allergies")
During certain times of the year, there may be high levels of pollens in the air from ragweed, grass and trees. A person allergic to any of these may develop sneezing; itchy, runny nose; and red, itchy watery eyes.

Perennial allergies ("indoor allergies")
All year long, things such as dust mites, animal dander, and molds are in the air. A person allergic to any of these may have symptoms every day such as sneezing; itchy, runny nose; postnasal drip (dripping from the nose down the back of the throat); and red, itchy eyes and tearing.

Continuing (chronic) hives
Some people may get red, itchy bumps on their skin called hives. The bumps can be small or large. The cause of this type of hives is not always known. ZYRTEC helps relieve the itching of these hives and shortens the length of time they last.

► **What Should I Tell My Doctor Before Taking ZYRTEC?**
Only your doctor can decide if ZYRTEC is right for you. Before you start ZYRTEC, be sure to tell your doctor if you:
• are taking any prescription medicines
• are taking any over-the-counter medicines you can buy without a prescription, including natural/herbal remedies
• have ever had any kidney problems or are on dialysis
• have ever had any liver problems
• are pregnant, think you might be pregnant, plan to become pregnant, or are breast-feeding
• have ever had an allergic reaction to any medicine

► **Who Should Not Take ZYRTEC?**
People who have ever had an allergic reaction to cetirizine or any of the ingredients in ZYRTEC, or to the medicine hydroxyzine (also called Atarax®*) should not take ZYRTEC. Your doctor or pharmacist can give you a list of these ingredients.

► **ZYRTEC And Other Medicines**
Some medicines can affect how well ZYRTEC works. While on ZYRTEC, check with your doctor or pharmacist before starting any new prescription or any medicines you can buy without a prescription, including natural/herbal remedies.

► **How Do I Take ZYRTEC?**
ZYRTEC comes as tablets (5 mg or 10 mg) as well as a syrup (5 mg/teaspoon). ZYRTEC can be taken with or without food at any time of the day. Your doctor will prescribe the dose that is right for you.

ZYRTEC Tablets
Adults and Children 12 Years and Older: Take ZYRTEC once a day.

ZYRTEC Syrup
Use a medicine spoon to measure the exact dose of ZYRTEC syrup prescribed by your doctor.
Children 6 to 11 Years: Give ZYRTEC syrup once a day.
Children 2 to 5 Years: Depending on your child's condition, the doctor may want you to give the child the full dose once a day or half the dose twice a day. Follow your doctor's instructions.

► **What Are The Possible Side Effects?**
Like all medicines, ZYRTEC may cause some side effects. These effects are usually mild to moderate. The most common side effects in adults and children 12 years and older are:
• feeling tired or sleepy   • dizziness
• dry mouth   • sore throat

Children under the age of 12 years may have side effects such as headache, sleepiness, sore throat or stomachache.
ZYRTEC may cause other less common side effects besides those listed here. If you want more information or develop any side effects or symptoms you are concerned about, call your doctor.

CAUTION: Some people may feel sleepy when taking ZYRTEC. Be careful doing things where you need to be alert (such as driving a car or using dangerous machinery). Do not drink alcohol or use other medicines that make you sleepy while taking ZYRTEC.

► **What To Do For An Overdose?**
In case of accidental overdose, call your doctor or poison control center right away or go to the nearest emergency room.

► **How Should I Store ZYRTEC?**
Store ZYRTEC tablets in a dry place and in the original container. Store at room temperature (59°-86°F or 15°-30°C). ZYRTEC syrup can be kept in the refrigerator or at room temperature (41°-86°F or 5°-30°C). Keep ZYRTEC and all medicines out of the reach of children.

► **For More Information About ZYRTEC**
This sheet is only a summary. If you have any questions or want more information about ZYRTEC, talk with your doctor, healthcare provider or pharmacist. You can also visit the ZYRTEC Internet site at www.zyrtec.com or call 1-888-244-7354.

► **General Advice About Prescription Medicines**
Do not use ZYRTEC for a condition for which it was not prescribed. Only a doctor can prescribe ZYRTEC. Do not share your ZYRTEC with other people.

*Atarax is a registered trademark of Pfizer Inc.

Manufactured/Marketed by   Marketed by
Pfizer U.S. Pharmaceuticals   **ucb** Pharma

001113-115-342A-19   ZY105313   © 2002 Pfizer Inc. February 2002

Figure 13.4 The brief summary from the Zyrtec ad

more than 50% of surveyed physicians believe that DTC advertising leads people to treatment (Woods, 2001). The fact that many DTC ads include 800 numbers and Internet sites adds to the information benefits of the advertising.

DTC Ads Develop Trust in Messages and in Medication

The Television Bureau of Advertising found that consumers ranked DTC broadcast advertisements as "trustworthy" more often than any other product category (Goetzl, 2000b). This is a result of the presence of the major statement: Consumers are more likely to trust advertisements that present both positive and negative product attributes. This idea of trust is important because Americans tend to distrust the current health care system. (Weissman, 1998). Consumers give similar preference ratings to DTC television and print advertisements, although problems with television advertising not allowing consumers to take the time to study the information have been voiced (Sibley, 2000).

Increased Awareness of a Variety of Diseases

DTC advertising helps to increase awareness of diseases that go under-diagnosed and undertreated (McInturff, 2001). The importance of this effect cannot be overlooked because the consequences of not seeking appropriate treatment can be dire for individuals, families, and society. For example, untreated diabetes can lead to blindness or limb amputation. Unchecked high cholesterol levels can lead to heart attack or stroke, and cholesterol-lowering drugs can cut this risk by about 30%. Failure to treat depression can result in suicide, and high blood pressure can lead to stroke, heart attack, and kidney failure (Holmer, 1999).

Increasing awareness of diseases, and their subsequent treatment options, can create a healthier society. DTC advertising has been shown to provide this important information. A recent study by *Prevention* magazine and the FDA showed that advertising messages are seen to instigate conversations between patients and their doctors, allowing doctors to give general health recommendations to patients, not necessarily just a prescription for the drug under discussion (MediaDailyNews, 2002). The same study showed that about one fourth of respondents said their relationship had improved with their doctor after such conversations (MediaDailyNews, 2002). The overwhelming majority of doctors also believe that DTC advertisements have had a beneficial effect on their doctor-patient interactions (MediaDailyNews, 2002).

DTC advertising instigates dialogues between patients and physicians, which allow new information to be diffused quickly and safely into the health care system (Kolassa, 2001). Advertising can also provide "mainstreaming" of disease and treatment by breaking down fears or hesitancy some patients have about taking their medicine. One doctor stated, "If I have to prescribe a medication and they've heard of it because they've seen it associated with pretty pictures on television, it might lower their resistance to taking it" (Bunis, 2000).

Unintended Effects

Many unintended effects generate concern among physicians, policy-makers, and the public. A number of researchers are involved in analyzing the validity of these concerns, as conflicting information regarding these unintended effects exists.

Compliance With Treatment

One surprising unintended effect of DTC advertising was that advertising can facilitate greater compliance with medical recommendation (Roth, 1996). Specifically, advertisements serve as reminders to consumers to refill their prescriptions and to take their already-prescribed medications. Thus, consumers are more mindful of their own health (McInturff, 2001).

Incomplete Information

There is a perception that consumers do not get the full information story in DTC advertising, resulting in skewed perceptions of prescription drugs. The DDMAC, for example, has voiced concerns that marketers overemphasize drug efficacy while downplaying the major statement (Belkin, 2000; Goetzl, 2000a; Newman, 2000).

A study of DTC print advertisements found that 35% did not present a fair balance of information. This lack of balance tended to be errors of omission; that is, several side effects considered important by the pharmacists reviewing the advertising were left out of advertisements (Roth, 1996).

Messages, particularly broadcast messages, can provide distractions from the important risk information, which also may limit the information value of the advertisements. Broadcast advertising introduces more complex forms of communication, with changing scenes, motion, and sound. These features can serve either to reinforce messages or to distract consumers from important information. Comprehension rates of information presented in advertising will vary based on presentation modality (e.g., through audio, visuals, and text). For example, the FDA has cited several DTC advertisements for presenting risk information only in audio form, while the visual content of the commercial presented a background of busy graphics (Food and Drug Administration, 1997).

The FDA has issued warnings to several manufacturers to change the audio portions of the major statement because the statements currently lack fair balance (Food and Drug Administration, 1998c, 1999). For example, a commercial for Claritin was cited for having risk information that was read so quickly that it would be difficult for consumers to understand the risks (Food and Drug Administration, 1997). Similarly, FDA letters have cited advertisements' supers (i.e., text-only information) for lack of prominence, readability, and contrast (Food and Drug Administration, 1998a, 2000).

Misinformation is problematic because the level of information provided in DTC advertising is likely to influence consumer attitudes toward drugs. In a study of DTC print advertising, a correlation was found between consumers' attitudes toward prescription drugs and the depth of the risk-related information within an advertisement. This correlation was, surprisingly, negative. Consumers gave higher safety and appeal ratings to drug advertisements with smaller amounts of risk information (Davis, 2000). Morris, Brinberg, Klimberg, Rivera, and Millstein (1986) also found evidence of consumer misconception about efficacy. After viewing an arthritis drug advertisement designed by the researchers, some respondents believed that the advertised drug was more effective than aspirin for arthritis. The advertisement, however, did not make any such claims. This suggests that there is a preconception that prescription drugs are superior in efficacy to over-the-counter alternatives, and consumers may have a tendency to overestimate a prescription drug's efficacy or benefits (Morris et al., 1986).

Information Overload

Information overload has been defined as an individual's finite capacity to process information. It can result in what the FDA has termed "dysfunctional consequences" when consumers stop trying to make sense of the information (Food and Drug Administration, 1998b).

For DTC advertising, the concept of information overload has been used in the context of examining the complex language in the brief summary, as well as the degree of sensory overload that could be generated from multiple communication methods present in an advertisement (a television advertisement in particular). Competing messages between audio, video, and supers can create a state of information overload among consumers. The FDA has subsequently cited a number of DTC advertisements for providing competing messages or mutually distracting messages in a single execution. For example, one commercial presented the major statement in the video part of the advertisement while a competing message about other risk information was presented in the audio part.

Lack of Retention of Important Information

There is poor retention of information in DTC advertisements, particularly risk information (Sullivan, Schommer, & Birdwell, 1999). This finding, coupled with Davis's (2000) research, suggests that consumers use risk-related information to form an opinion about a drug's safety and appeal, but they do not remember the details of the information used to form that opinion.

In contrast, Schommer, Doucette, and Mehta (1998) found that consumers are noticing those details. Respondents were able to recall more than 60% of the tested information when questioned directly after viewing a DTC television advertisement, even if such information was shown for a brief time. However, they also found over 50% of the respondents did not recall what was seen as the most important promotional claim in the message, suggesting that the communication of both benefit and risk information led to problems in learning and comprehension. They also hypothesized that the small print in print advertising stimulated the same response (Schommer et al., 1998) (Figure 13.5).

Misinformation Regarding Governmental Role

Some consumers may be misled regarding the government's role in DTC advertising. Bell, Kravitz, and Wilkes (1999) suggest that one reason consumers are receptive to DTC advertising is because the government regulates the products. However, many consumers are unaware of the degree to which the advertisements are (or are not) regulated. Nearly 50% of consumers believe that the government approves DTC advertisements before they are broadcast. As mentioned earlier, actual approval may be done while the commercial is airing or may be based only on storyboards (Bell et al., 1999). Additionally, 43% of consumers think the FDA only allows advertising for "completely safe" drugs, and 21% believe that only "extremely effective" drugs are allowed to employ DTC campaigns (Bell et al., 1999). The same study found that consumers with misconceptions about DTC regulation were more likely to have a positive view of DTC advertising. This may lead to a false sense of trust in DTC advertisements and can subsequently result in misconceptions about drug benefits and risks.

Costs of Prescription Drugs Increase

The average price per prescription for new drugs (i.e., those that were introduced in 1992 or later) was $71.49 in 1998. For drugs on the market before 1992, the average price was $30.47. Some see this as support for the claim that advertising has raised the price of drugs to consumers (Kopp & Sheffet, 1997). Prescription drug prices in the United States are the highest in the world, and marketing costs are often higher than research costs (Tanouye, 2000). Consumers are asking their doctors to prescribe name brands when less expensive generic drugs that are just as effective are sometimes available.

Television advertising in particular seems to be blamed for increased prices. One physician suggested,

It took forty years to get it.

And ten minutes to do something about it.

Welcome to the age of Botox® Cosmetic. Finally, a simple, non-surgical procedure that can dramatically reduce even your toughest wrinkle within days. One ten-minute treatment - a few tiny injections - relaxes the muscles between your brows that cause lines to form. And keeps them relaxed up to four months. Botox® Cosmetic has been widely tested. And now it's approved by the FDA. So it's really up to you. You can choose to live with wrinkles. Or you can choose to live without them.

Ask your dermatologist, ophthalmologist, or plastic surgeon about Botox® Cosmetic. Or call toll-free or visit our website for a listing of Botox® Cosmetic Network physicians.

The most common side effects are headache, respiratory infection, flu syndrome, temporary eyelid droop, and nausea. Botox® Cosmetic should not be used if there is an infection at injection site.

Please see additional important information on the following page.

It's not magic, it's

BOTOX
Cosmetic
Botulinum Toxin Type A

1-800-BotoxMD
www.BotoxCosmetic.net

Figure 13.5 Note the small print information in an advertisement for Botox Cosmetic

"The advertising has got to be expensive and you better believe the medicines that are advertised are not available by generic. They are among the most expensive medications on the market and so I have great concerns about forcing my patients to pay for all that direct-to-consumer advertising for these expensive medications." (Bunis, 2000)

Congressional representatives have blamed DTC advertising in part for rising health care costs and are investigating cutbacks in spending (Teinowitz, 2001a).

Unnecessary or Inappropriate Prescriptions

DTC advertising rarely mentions lifestyle changes or other treatments that are less costly for the sick (Kravitz, 2000). For example, the heartburn drug Nexium is sometimes used to treat ulcers (Figure 13.6). However, many patients would be better off taking a single, cheaper treatment of antibiotics for ulcers (Moore, 2001). Alternatively, a patient may respond to an over-the-counter treatment for the same disorder.

Of greater concern, though, is when drugs become the panacea for all types of problems (Roth, 1996). Someone with a case of the sniffles might not need Claritin, yet drug-taking behavior is quickly becoming mainstreamed in our culture (Woods, 2001). Patients may not wish to hear options other than pharmaceutical options. In fact, one study found that if patients were refused an advertised prescription drug, 50% of the patients would register disappointment and 15% would consider switching physicians (Kravitz, 2000).

Additionally, DTC advertising can contribute to the problem of medicalization, which is a process by which nonmedical problems become defined and treated as medical problems (Kawachi & Conrad, 1996). This can divert consumers from other sources of information and create a society whose members consistently feel like they are sick (Mintzes, 2002).

Challenge to Physician's Authority

Although several studies have shown that physicians are increasingly approving of DTC advertising, it is important to note that many physicians have issues with it. Many physicians (and patients) believe it is the doctor's responsibility to serve as advocates for patients and for public health (Hoffman, 1999). Several studies in the 1980s showed that physicians had negative attitudes toward DTC advertising, viewing it as a challenge to their medical authority (Peyrot et al., 1998). More recently, almost half of the respondents to a survey said that DTC advertising causes tension between patients and their doctors (Weissman, 1998). These tensions can be disagreements about inexpensive alternatives, recommendations on other classes of the same medication, or concerns regarding drug interactions (Woods, 2001). Overall, DTC advertising may mean that physicians have to spend time disabusing patients of incorrect information.

Doing DTC Advertising

Given that DTC advertising has only been in existence for a brief period, it is still in the formative stage. The fact that the FDA has guidelines, and not regulations, reinforces this point. With that in mind, several areas for DTC advertisers to consider are provided.

Create a Clear Reason for Someone to Consider Learning More About Drugs

This may seem like a general goal of advertising, but it is one that many DTC advertisers forget about. This could be because advertisers generally have 60 seconds for their messages. However, it is estimated that after the required information is provided, marketers have only about 35 seconds left for the advertising message, which is just about the same as any regular advertiser (Ehrlich, 2002). DTC advertisers often want to include reams of research in their messages, but the real purpose of the advertisement, particularly the broadcast message, should be to get people interested enough in the drug to find out more.

Figure 13.6 The "little purple pill" is only one solution for ulcers.

Test Messages With Both the Client and the FDA in Mind

Since the message will be evaluated for two "masters," it is important that the testing of the advertisements with consumers before airing recognizes both masters and encompasses evaluation of the communication of the major statement as well as the key thought of the advertisement.

Provide Positive Messages

Messages should be positive with the belief that people will choose "hope over fear as a motivator for seeking health care solutions" (Jenkins, 1999, p. 4). Jenkins believes ads can save lives if they provide positive messages. The messages must empathize with the sufferer and amplify the ego of the afflicted, not their anger or their fear. Some people initially approach their diseases in states of denial or dismissal. This is based on fear, and marketers must override fear. Advertisers should not make unrealistic promises in their messages. Finally, the messages themselves should strive to become part of the medicine. People must change their minds before they change their bodies. Advertising should suggest that the medication provides hope because hope is the most powerful dimension of the human imagination (Jenkins, 1999).

Avoid Information Overload

The time constraints of broadcast advertising challenge advertisers to address many topics and provide large amounts of information within a constrained space. Recognizing these limitations, advertisers must strive to provide clear, easily understood information and avoid causing information overload among viewers. Using a video image combined with a complementary audio voice-over is the most effective way to ensure comprehension of information (Murray, Manrai, & Manrai, 1998).

The Future

The future for DTC advertising is currently unclear. Earlier, we explained how some legislators perceive DTC advertising as increasing the costs of drugs. In addition, the brief summary recommendation for broadcast advertising is under review by the FDA (DTC Perspectives, 2002). There are concerns that the brief summary is now required only in print advertisements, and the major statement that is used to replace the brief summary is not utilized effectively by broadcast consumer audiences. The FDA is investigating how to enhance the major statement and provide information similar to the content of the brief statement in a way that is more consumer friendly. Such content guidelines for advertising may require messages to take into account a range of treatment options, as well as voluntary disclaimers that suggest that while the advertised drug is effective, other substitutes may be available (Kennedy, 2002).

Congress is investigating reform of Medicare with four potential measures to curb DTC ads. This would force pharmaceuticals to include the brief summary in their television ads, which would essentially eliminate broadcast advertising for DTC drugs. Congress is also considering requiring consumers to pay more for advertised drugs than unadvertised drugs, as well as offering drug companies lower Medicare reimbursements for advertised drugs than unadvertised drugs and limiting the tax deductibility of drugs ads (Teinowitz, 2001a).

Finally, the Internet causes new issues and controversies for prescription drug advertising. Although some countries ban all consumer promotion of pharmaceuticals and see the Internet as a major threat to such bans, the FDA is more concerned about problematic Web-site claims and the online availability of unapproved products (Wechsler, 1998). Internet pharmacies can and do sell experimental and illegal drugs to consumers (Vogt, 2001). Web advertising and pharmaceutical Web sites should be addressed in the same manner as print advertising in the United States, and the FDA has recently launched a program that alerts Web sites to problematic practices (DTC Perspectives, 2002).

Summary

Direct-to-consumer advertising for prescription drugs has been seen to empower consumers and improve doctor-patient relationships. However, others see DTC advertising as confusing to consumers and raising the prices of drugs and of health care overall. The FDA has guidelines for the information content of such advertisements and is reconsidering the guidelines in light of consumer and governmental concerns.

In the next chapter, we will examine a type of advertising for which the government has no say in the content: political advertising. Political advertising is hotly debated during every election cycle, and Congress recently passed a law limiting campaign spending. While campaign finance reform will likely reduce the number of advertisements we see, the controversial content of the advertisements will not change, as these advertisements have complete First Amendment protection. This results in a number of controversial issues surrounding political advertising.

14

We the People

Political Advertising

Well, I guess we get what we deserve, because if you can affect a presidential campaign on a 30-second commercial, if people will not listen to debates, if they're not interested in hearing what the candidates have to say, yet one negative political ad is able to move people, I guess it's our own fault.

—Helen Spivak

In the U.S. advertising industry, political advertising is indeed a horse of a different color. It is unique in so many ways. First, it only occurs for a few weeks every year or every other year. In addition, by law, media vehicles must sell the airtime and space to political advertisers at their lowest rates during the 4 weeks before an election. This explains the prevalence of political advertising on the air during certain periods of the year. Therefore, when we as consumers do see political advertising, we tend to see a lot of it over a very short period of time before elections. Political advertising is also the only type of advertising that has complete First Amendment protection: Political candidates and issue advertisements can (and do) say anything they want.

Political advertising is the focus of attention and research by many different groups, including academics, the mass media, pollsters, and the parties and issues paying for the advertising itself. In this chapter, we examine political advertising in general, as well as the state of political advertising in the year 2002, an election year strongly influenced by the Campaign Finance Reform Act.

Definitions of Political Advertising

Political advertising is defined by the content of the advertising message and the medium in which the message appears. Political advertising includes messages supporting or opposing a candidate for nomination or election to either a public office or an office of a political party. It also includes messages supporting or opposing an officeholder, a political party, or a measure (also known as a ballot proposition) (State of Texas, 1999).

In terms of where the message appears, political advertising includes traditional media, such as print ads published in newspapers and magazines, as well as commercials broadcast by radio and television stations in return for what is known in the industry as consideration. *Consideration* means that the publisher or the broadcaster receives something of value in exchange for publishing or broadcasting the message. Paying for the space and time to run the message is a common type of consideration. Political advertising also includes messages that appear in pamphlets, circulars, fliers, billboards, and other outdoor signage, including bumper stickers.

In most cases, political advertising must include a disclosure or disclaimer statement indicating the sponsor of the message. The norms for disclosures or disclaimers vary by state and occasionally by election. Most disclosure regulations suggest that the statement must include the name of either the individual who entered into the agreement with the entity that is producing and/or airing the message or the entity that the individual represents (e.g., the name of a candidate or the name of the political committee) (State of Texas, 1999). The Federal Communications Commission (FCC), for example, requires all broadcast advertisements to have disclosures regarding the source of funding for the advertisement.

The Role of Political Advertising

The purpose of political advertising is to persuade voters to vote for a particular candidate (e.g., the president of the United States) or to vote in favor of or against a particular issue (e.g., a new tax levy in your community). There is only one winner in each election. This simple fact distinguishes political advertising from advertising for products and services, which use advertising to compete against other products and services in the same category to receive a share of the market (Berger, 2000).

Political campaigning was done differently before the advent of television. In 1948, the last year of campaigns before the widespread adoption of television among Americans, Harry S. Truman made 356 campaign speeches and shook hands with half a million people in his quest to become president (Clark, 1988). In 1952, Dwight D. Eisenhower hired advertising executive Rosser Reeves to develop campaign messages, and political advertising changed forever (Moyers, 1998).

Today, campaign officials use several different methods to bring information to voters about political candidates and issues. These methods include advertising, political rallies, telephone banks, dissemination of position statements, and news coverage. In recent elections, however, the balance of time and effort has tipped toward mass media and away from personal interactions. Mass media advertising gives candidates control over their image to a wide range of people in a short time period. As consumers, we are accustomed to hearing "packaged" information about a product's or service's attributes and benefits in 30 or 60 seconds. In the 50 years that television advertising has been used for political speech, it has become increasingly natural for consumers to learn about their political choices through the same methods as they learn about other purchase decisions that affect their lives.

First Amendment and Political Advertising

Political advertising enjoys complete First Amendment protection. The Communication Act of 1934 stated that broadcasters could refuse all deceptive advertising except for political campaigns (Chang, Park, & Shim, 1998). The Federal Election Campaign Act's 1976 amendment allowed private individuals at political action committees (PACs) to spend unlimited amounts of money on behalf of candidates (Chang et al., 1998). Campaign finance reform has changed this latter circumstance, as we will see later in this chapter. What is most important, though, is that paid political advertising has a high degree of freedom in terms of what the ads can say.

It is generally assumed that the First Amendment to the Constitution, which prohibits Congress from passing laws abridging free speech, also protects paid political advertising. The assumption behind this argument is that the debate between candidates, or between opposing viewpoints on an issue, is equalized if all parties are allowed to spend money on advertising to get their message across.

Obviously, though, every candidate or group with an opinion on an issue does not have resources equal to other candidates or groups. This may result in a lack of balance in the information that is disseminated to voters. For example, a party representing the aspirations of the poor and underprivileged may be at a disadvantage under our current system. Candidates outside the mainstream, such as those for fringe political parties, may also suffer (Carver, 2001).

Impact on Voters

In 1952, the first year of political advertising, total campaign spending for the presidential race was $140 million. In 1988, more than $2 billion were spent on advertising for presidential candidates. In 1952, less than 5% of total campaign spending was on television and radio advertisements. By 1988, 20% of total campaign spending was on advertising (Ansolabehere & Iyengar, 1995). In 1996, presidential candidate Ross Perot spent 75% of his campaign money on television advertising (Devlin, 1997). In 2000, approx-imately $606 million was spent on local and network television ads, although some estimates put the spending at $850 million or higher (Albiniak, 2002). In the 2002 "off-year" elections, advertisers spent over $1 billion on political campaigns (Taylor, 2002), bringing spending to levels similar to automotive and retail advertisers.

Of course, political advertising is not only for national races such as the presidential election. State, county, and local races all include candidates and issues that have funds available for advertising spending. From the president to the local councilperson, advertising is seen as effective because Americans get the majority of their political information from advertisements. In total, political advertisers spent at least $771 million, and perhaps as much as $1 billion, on more than 1.2 million political ads in the 2000 election year. The lower figure, which comes from the political ad-monitoring firm Campaign Media Analysis Group, only covers the nation's top 75 markets (of 210). The $1 billion figure is an estimate by Wall Street analysts.

This continual increase in advertising spending unfortunately does not positively relate to attitudes among Americans toward our government or to actual voting behaviors. There is low public regard for politicians, and the majority of Americans believe that government institutions inflict more harm than good on our general well-being (Ansolabehere & Iyengar, 1995). Voter turnout has been declining each election cycle since 1960 (Ansolabehere & Iyengar, 1995). Many view these declines as directly related to the amount, and the quality, of political advertising that appears today.

The Process of Political Advertising

Most advertisers come to their agencies with a preestablished marketing budget, generally derived from past history or sales of the product or from other products produced by the same company. Some new businesses begin advertising using venture capital funding. The process of political advertis-ing differs from traditional advertising in that fund-raising is integral both before the ads start to run and during the entire election cycle.

Fund-Raising

Two types of funding are allowed for political candidates. Hard money is raised and spent for use in federal elections according to restrictions and regulations of federal election law. Hard money can fund advertisements of expressed advocacy—that is, those messages that say "vote for Candidate X" and are aimed at the general public. Individuals, PACs, and parties can contribute hard money to campaigns, but unions and corporations cannot.

Hard money contributions from these three groups are subject to contribution limits. Candidates can contribute their own funds for hard money, and such contributions are not subject to limits. All hard money contributions must be disclosed to the Federal Election Commission (FEC) (Cantor, 1997).

Soft money, on the other hand, is raised for use in state and local elections and is regulated only by state and local laws. Soft money may not be used for messages of expressed advocacy; that is, messages cannot say "vote for Candidate X." However, messages can discuss the importance of an issue and say, for example, that Candidate X is in favor of the issue. Common sources of soft money are unions, corporations, and individuals. Political parties can also raise soft money for state parties to use in generic messages, party building, and voter operations (Cantor, 1997).

Message Development

Once the fund-raising machine begins, the next step is the development of the message or messages that will be used during the campaign. Political advertisements must get results in a short period of time. Often, political campaigns use a mix of different types of messages to provide a range of information and address a range of objectives (Chang et al., 1998). Four types of political advertising are name identification ads, argument ads, attack ads, and visionary ads.

Name Identification Ads. Early in a campaign, political candidates will use name identification ads (Figure 14.1). These ads are designed to create awareness of the name of the individual running for the office (Kern, 1989). The ads rarely contain any information beyond the individual's name and the office that he or she seeks, given that many in the electorate may have no awareness of the candidate.

Argument Ads. Once name awareness is established, campaigns begin what are known as argument spots (Figure 14.2). These ads present positions on specific issues (Kern, 1989). In particular, they offer information on actions, policy positions, and ideologies (Smith & Kidder, 1996). The sum of these argument messages serves to either influence public opinion about an issue that is being put to the vote or to aggregately position a political candidate in terms of his or her overall platform or agenda. Argument spots do not mention the opposing positions or candidates.

Attack Spots. Argument spots are often followed by attack spots Attack spots focus on the candidate's opponent and negatively position the opponent and his or her views (Kern, 1989). This type of message strategically puts opponents on the defensive. However, attack ads are often used out of

VOTE AL KING IN HOUSE DISTRICT 11

A BALANCED, COMMON SENSE VOICE IN THE STATE LEGISLATURE

Al King for District 11 Committee

Figure 14.1   A name identification ad creates awareness of a candidate's name.

I'm Bill Dwyer. Fighting and winning for you as your Commissioner makes this job worthwhile!

LANE CO Needs Bill Dwyer

Congressman Peter DeFazio says:
"Bill Dwyer is a proven advocate for the people of our area. Seniors, veterans, mobile home park tenants, youth, sportsmen, working families, and small businesses can count on Bill."
—**Congressman Peter DeFazio**
(Oregon Voters Pamphlet, spring 2002)

Senator Bill Morrisette says:
"Bill Dwyer is one of the most effective County Commissioners in Springfield history. He's a community asset we can't afford to lose!"
—**Senator Bill Morrisette**

**RE-ELECT ☑
DWYER
County Commissioner**

Bill Dwyer
A Neighbor You Can Trust!

Authorized and paid for by Bill Dwyer for Lane County Commissioner
5558 Thurston Rd., Springfield, OR 97478

Figure 14.2   An argument ad presents a candidate's position on an issue, such as this ad advocating neighborhood empowerment.

fear—specifically, fear that the opposition will attack first or that the candidate will appear weak if he or she does not attack or counterattack. Attack ads appear to be used most often in very close races (Ansolabehere & Iyengar, 1995).

For many observers of political advertisements, attack ads are useful tools in political campaigns because a certain amount of conflict and attack is useful to point out the differences between candidates (Kern, 1989). Attack ads also tend to expand the scope of the political discussion because they may force candidates to address issues that they do not wish to address. In addition, attack ads tend to draw attention from voters, and the news media, to the campaign more than any other type of political advertisement (Ansolabehere & Iyengar, 1995).

Visionary Spots. Immediately before the election, candidates revert to positive visionary appeals (Figure 14.3). These optimistic spots give voters a final, positive reason to vote for the candidate (Kern,

1989). Such spots focus on the image and the personal characteristics of the candidate (Smith & Kidder, 1996).

On the Air: Broadcast Consideration

The final step is to place the advertisements in television, radio, and print vehicles. America is one of the few nations to allow political advertising in broadcast media (Clark, 1988). In many other countries, parties and candidates tend to

Figure 14.3 An optimistic image in a Bush ad

be allotted a certain amount of free airtime; in the United Kingdom, for example, the amount of time allotted is based on the size of the political party (Clark, 1988).

As you may already know, the Federal Communications Commission (FCC) regulates political access to the airwaves. The FCC is responsible for monitoring political advertising and for overseeing the equal opportunity or equal-time rights of candidates on broadcast programs. The Communications Act provides that legally qualified candidates for public office are entitled to receive, upon request, equal facilities to those used by their opponents for the same office, under certain defined circumstances. Therefore, one station must ensure that Candidate X and Candidate Y receive equivalent amounts of coverage in its evening news program.

Additionally, the same station must give both Candidate X and Candidate Y the same opportunity to purchase and air commercials. As previously mentioned, stations must also sell the airtime at the lowest cost on the station's rate card for the specific part of the day or at no more than the rate charged to its favorite advertisers for that rate and class. These rate regulations are in effect for the 45 days before the primary and the 60 days before the general election. To get the lowest rate, the ad must contain the candidate's voice or photo likeness in connection with a message that the advertisement is affiliated with the current campaign (Chambers, 2002).

The screen that we discussed in Chapter 4, in terms of a television station's ability to evaluate and refuse television commercials that are not in the public good, is inapplicable for political advertisements. Television stations cannot turn down any political advertisements, regardless of any issues with either the technical quality of the ads or any claims made in the messages. A candidate could conceivably out-and-out lie about an opponent in an advertisement, and the station must accept the spot (Clark, 1988).

Intended Effects

As with all types of commercial messages, political advertising has both intended and unintended effects.

Provide Information to Voters

Political advertising has an important role to inform the public on issues, ideas, and public policy problems. This is a key intended effect because most American voters receive little political information from traditional news sources, and candidates are not able to meet every voter during the course of a campaign (Clark, 1988).

Most critics note that there is a high level of policy content in political advertising, much more than most people tend to recognize. As a result, political advertisements contain more information than most types of advertising, and most of this information has a high utility for voter decision making. This information makes voters aware of basic differences between candidates (Moyers, 1998). Additionally, information provided in commercials that directly contrasts two candidates or two opinions on a measure helps to engage voters actively. Such advertisements clearly take a position and provide evidence to support it, which challenges viewers to assess their own opinions and decisions (Smith & Kidder, 1996).

Help Voters Form Opinions

Like all other advertising, political advertising is designed not only to inform voters about candidates, issues, and positions but also to allow voters to develop differentiated images of candidates or the issues (Ansolabehere & Iyengar, 1995). Thus, political advertising tries to persuade voters to think or feel in a certain way. Political advertising can be highly persuasive; attack messages in particular can be highly influential to voters (Berger, 2000). Attack ads, with their negative messages, derive their impact from a broader range of variables than do positive messages. In an attack ad, voters hear not only what an opposing candidate stands for but also the (usually negative) consequences of that stance. This is important because more people are apt to vote against something they do not like than for something they do like (also known as selecting the lesser of two evils) (Chang et al., 1998). This may be the reason that attack ads are seen as a beneficial tool in campaigning, particularly to provide winning margins in the late stages of an election (Smith & Kidder, 1996).

As a whole, political advertising helps people determine whether candidates feel the same way about certain issues. Kathleen Hall Jamieson, a political researcher at the Annenberg School of Communications at the University of Pennsylvania, finds that the most persuasive messages are the ones that already resonate with large parts of the population. Undecided voters, the ones who truly have not made up their minds, can be highly persuaded about voting one way or another based on issues about which they already feel strongly (Wisconsin Public Television, 1996). Finding that important message is a central goal of most political campaigns.

Reinforce Common Values

Elections serve the function of bringing communities together as a whole, and advertising helps in this process by reinforcing the common values of the community. Jamieson cites images such as parades, flags, and candidates with their spouses, children, and pets as some of the ways that advertising promotes common values of patriotism, community spirit, and family. Such images also suggest the vision of the future held by the candidates. Although some critics may argue that these images are only cheap symbolism, Jamieson disagrees. She believes it is an important part of reconstructing citizenry as a community during election cycles, which are truly one of the few times that individuals come together to make decisions for communities as a whole (Wisconsin Public Television, 1996).

Increase Voter Turnout

Advertising has been shown to affect voter turnout in that the more money spent on advertising during an election, the higher the turnout. Some analysts contend that only positive advertising increases turnout. However, even advertising that is seen as negative, such as attack advertising, can increase voter turnout, particularly among voters who are registered as independents (Freedman & Lawton, 2000). This may be due to variations in what voters consider negative. Some attack ads, particularly ones that criticize an individual's voting record, are seen as "very" or "somewhat" fair in terms of campaign conduct. However, other types of messages, particularly with regard to the activities of family members, are seen as unfair (Freedman & Lawton, 2000). Another study suggested that negative advertising creates a negative public mood, which increases voter turnout because people want to change that mood (Leshner & Thorson, 2000).

Unintended Effects

Government Irrelevance

Some critics suggest that political advertising, particularly messages that use highly emotional appeals, is irrelevant to government situations today. In 1964, for example, one of the most emotional television advertisements, the Daisy ad, used the emotional hot button of nuclear weapons to draw distinctions between the incumbent presidential candidate, Lyndon Johnson, and his challenger, Barry Goldwater. This ad begins with a little girl in a field picking petals off a daisy and counting (similar to Figure 14.4). When the count reaches 10, her image is frozen and a male voice commences a militaristic countdown. When the countdown reaches 0, the commercial shows a nuclear explosion and President Johnson's voice is heard saying, in a voice-over, "These are the stakes: to make a world in which all God's children can live or to go into the darkness. Either we must love each other or we must die." A white super then read: *On November 3rd vote for President Johnson*. This ad ran only once, but the coverage it received in various news media was enough to make voters think that Barry Goldwater was willing to use nuclear warfare in virtually any situation (Schmideg, 1999).

As effective as this ad was, however, it galvanized voters around an issue that really was not very important at that time. The more important concern of government and of the citizenry was what the government was going to do about Vietnam (Moyers, 1998). Therefore, emotional advertising such as the Daisy ad trivialize the political conversation and can be misleading in terms of what the true issues really are (Moyers, 1998). The bottom-line effect may be that citizens feel that our government is irrelevant (Welke, 1999). Citizens may believe that politicians are out of touch with their needs and concerns.

Limited Information Leads to Lack of Debate

When voters rely heavily on advertising, the campaigns have a high level of control over the amount of information that is made available to the public. There is a limited amount of information that can be conveyed in 30 seconds, even if a candidate has a large budget for advertising. Thus, there will always be information that voters do not know. Particularly in situations where few attack ads are provided, the debate will be limited. Even when attack ads are used, there is little or no room for rebuttals from opponents at the same time in front of the same audience (Welke, 1999).

Diminished News Coverage

The increased use of political advertising results in diminished coverage of the campaigns in traditional news media. The trend today is for news organizations to focus not on the activities of the campaigns and the candidates but rather on their advertising, particularly their negative ads. This decreases the overall quality of the election coverage (Ansolabehere & Iyengar, 1995).

The number of political commercials in a typical election far exceeds the number of news stories about the election. The news stories that do exist frequently discuss political strategy and

Figure 14.4 The Daisy ad was highly controversial.

rarely discuss public policy. Furthermore, there is a positive correlation between the amount of advertising, particularly negative advertising, and the public's opinion toward the news coverage of an election. In particular, the more negative the advertising messages are in the campaign, the lower rated is the news coverage of the campaign (Ansolabehere & Iyengar, 1995).

Develops Negative Feelings That May Lead to Decisions Not to Participate

Advertising can be a factor in demobilizing voters. If an advertisement contains information that is untruthful, undocumented, or unjustified, voters develop negative attitudes toward the candidate sponsoring the advertisement (Smith & Kidder, 1996). Campaigns containing high levels of negative advertisements have voter turnouts with 5% fewer voters than elections with lower levels of negative advertising (Ansolabehere & Iyengar, 1995). The types of attacks will also influence the voting level: Turnout will vary with consumers' perceived levels of fairness of advertising messages, as discussed in the previous section.

Many critics suggest that attack advertising in particular can be highly problematic because it has what is known as the boomerang effect: the potential to generate negative feelings toward both the candidate sponsoring the ad and the candidate who is the target of the negative message (Chang et al., 1998; Merrit, 1984). These negative feelings toward all the choices in an election may dissuade people from voting because voters disgusted with their choices stay home on election day (Welke, 1999).

Another study provided the interesting result that even positive messages can hurt voter turnout. Two researchers found that voters who "feel good" about a campaign are more likely to say they voted, when in reality they did not vote. This is called the "over-reporting" problem (Leshner & Thorson, 2000).

Harms the Advertising Industry as a Whole

Political advertising reflects badly on the advertising industry as a whole, and advertising industry leaders have expressed concerns with political advertisers' lack of accountability and their unwillingness to adhere to a code of ethics. The apathy engendered by political advertising may damage the credibility, and perhaps even the persuasiveness, of traditional commercial advertising (Iyengar & Prior, 1999). This is seen as especially germane in the case of attack advertising, where the argument that such messages are effective is seen as ethically beside the point (Smith & Kidder, 1996).

The Future (Is Now)

Many different groups, from public interest groups to the candidates themselves, recognize that political advertising, particularly campaign spending, is out of control. In 2000, more than $500 million in soft money went into the coffers of national parties and was unregulated. After intense deliberation, legislation was passed to better regulate campaign spending.

McCain-Feingold Law

President George W. Bush signed the McCain-Feingold bill into law on March 21, 2002. The law raises hard money contributions from individuals from $1000 to $2000 per candidate per election. There is a cap on any one individual's contributions: Individuals may only contribute $37,500 to candidates and $57,500 to national party committees and political action committees, for a total of $95,000 per individual in any election cycle. If candidates are running against millionaires who fund their own campaigns (e.g., past candidates Steve Forbes and Ross Perot), individual contribution limits can be raised as high as $6000 depending on the wealthy candidate's own donations to his or her own campaign (Associated Press, 2002).

The McCain-Feingold bill has the greatest effect on unregulated soft money contributions. Many traditional sources of soft money are no longer allowed to contribute to campaign coffers. Contributions to candidates and issues from national political parties are now banned. State and local political parties can use up to $10,000 for the promotion of certain political activities such as voter registration and party-building activities. Additionally, private corporations and union organizations can no longer fund broadcast ads that mention a federal candidate within 60 days of a general election or 30 days of a primary. In fact, only advertisements paid for with regulated hard money can run in these periods prior to election days (Associated Press, 2002).

In addition, non-US citizens are prohibited from making contributions to federal, state, and local elections. A final point of the law states that federal property cannot be used to solicit voters or contributions. No longer will candidate staffers be able to make telephone calls for support or donations from their offices (Associated Press, 2002). The law went into effect on November 6, 2002, the day after the off-year elections across the country.

Many regard this legislation as a compromise that is a beginning to genuine campaign reform. The soft money ban helps put a limit on the total amount of fund-raising candidates can do. However, the doubling of hard money limits is predicted to keep overall contributions and spending at a very high level. This spending will be at the state level as opposed to the national level. Some suggest that this may result in increased partisanship in Washington because many state groups are more ideologically extreme than the national party (Woellert & Walczak, 2002).

Numerous legal challenges against the bill have been filed. Under the provisions of the bill, a court challenge would first be heard by a panel of three federal district court judges, and any appeal would go directly to the Supreme Court, bypassing circuit court appeals (CNN, 2002). At this writing, legal challenges have been filed by Senator Mitch McConnell, who argues that the law violates First Amendment protections, and by the National Rifle Association (NRA), which argues that the law infringes upon the rights of individuals to be heard (CNN, 2002).

Free Airtime

Since the dawn of television, scholars, reformers, and "good government" groups have proposed giving free airtime to political candidates, following a model used by many other countries around the world. Free airtime is not a panacea, but it offers a partial remedy to two of the biggest concerns about political advertising today. First, it would eliminate huge amounts of campaign spending. Evidence indicates that the broadcast industry is a primary beneficiary of the campaign finance system. Many reformers support proposals that guarantee political candidates access to the media at little or no cost. In fact, some suggest that broadcast outlets purposefully increase their favorite advertiser rates several months before the election cycle to capitalize on the influx of money spent on political advertising (Taylor, 2002). Furthermore, stations have been charged with cutting back on coverage of campaigns in their news programs, so advertising will become the primary way for candidates to get their messages to the public (Taylor, 2002).

Second, proponents argue that free airtime would improve political dialogue in the country, since consumers would be exposed to more information than the currently available 30-second sound bites of information about candidates and issues. This addresses the obligation of broadcast outlets to operate in the public interest (Taylor, 2002). Additionally, it will open the airwaves to individuals and groups with less money to spend on advertising and put the candidates' energy on communicating important information about the issues, not in raising funds. Veteran broadcaster Walter Cronkite, honorary co-chairman of the Alliance for Better Campaigns, is quoted as saying, "Free air time would help free our democracy from the grip of the special interests" (Taylor, 2002).

Of all groups opposing free airtime, broadcasters are the most vocal. Government regulation of speech, including speech on broadcast stations, must be both the least restrictive means available and must directly advance a compelling governmental interest (National Association of Broadcasters, 2002). The National Association of Broadcasters (NAB) does not believe that a ban on paid advertising addresses either of these regulatory guidelines. In addition, there is still a cost involved in free airtime, as the time would have to come from other types of paid programming at the station level (Gould, 2002).

Public Financing of Campaigns

Reform advocates have long argued that public financing of campaigns is a necessity for achieving true campaign reform. They argue that by removing private money from campaigns, the playing field is leveled and qualified candidates can run for public office without compromising their independence because they will not have to ask for money from those with a personal stake in public policy. Under most public financing proposals, a candidate must qualify by raising signatures or small donations. Those who accept public money must refuse to use private money to finance campaigns.

Public financing does exist for candidates for U.S. elections for the office of president. Funded by the tax "check off" provision, the federal government will match up to $250 in individual contributions for primary contests and will provide full fund matching for the general election. There is no realistic effort to extend such public financing to other federal elections, although recently four states (Vermont, Maine, Arizona, and Massachusetts) have enacted comprehensive public financing of political campaigns.

Longer Spots

Some critics and politicians advocate that all political broadcast advertisements must last 60 seconds or longer. This would ensure a more in-depth debate on the issues as well as allow candidates to provide messages with more detailed information.

Ban "Leadership" PACs

Some members of Congress have formed "leadership" PACs that raise funds distributed to other members of Congress. Many critics believe that these should be outlawed. It is argued that such PACs can be used as a way for a donor to avoid the direct $1000 contribution limit. Also of concern is that they can be used by senior congressional members to "purchase" the support of other members. Moreover, the officers of these PACs are sometimes from industries with which the lawmakers have oversight. Previous efforts to outlaw these PACs have failed (Newsbatch.com, 2002).

Codes of Conduct

Many states and cities are developing voluntary codes of conduct that participants in the political process agree to uphold. These codes suggest principles that candidates should follow when developing advertising messages and then ask the candidates to agree on these principles. Public opinion serves as both a motivator and enforcer.(Smith & Kidder, 1996). Following are some examples of these codes.

Maine. In Maine, the Code of Election Ethics was passed in 1996. Candidates who agree to the code promise to uphold values of compassion, honesty, responsibility, fairness, and respect (Smith & Kidder, 1996).

Pennsylvania. Pennsylvania adopted advertising guidelines in 1995. The guidelines entreat candidates to practice honesty and respect for others and implore them to meet high standards of accuracy and dignity. Candidates who agree to follow the guidelines and then infringe upon them are asked to withdraw ads.

Delaware. The Delaware Code emphasizes decency, honesty, and fair play, and candidates who agree to the code promise to condemn all tactics that corrupt or undermine the system of free elections, including malicious and unfounded attacks against other candidates. This code was adopted in 1995.

Minneapolis. The Minneapolis code, developed by the CEO of Carmichael-Lynch advertising, provides specific guidelines for tactical aspects of political advertising. Candidates agree to be present in either voice or likeness in all television commercials and in return display a logo that indicates they have agreed to run a clean campaign (Smith & Kidder, 1996).

Doing Political Advertising _____

Until any reforms are enacted, it is possible to provide political advertising that is valuable and can contribute to the political dialogue. To that end, we offer the following guidelines.

Be Informative

When creating political advertising, deal with qualifications and topics that are related to the office or the issue. Advertising should present facts, address concerns, and identify problems that the selected candidate or issue (e.g., tax levy) can address. Candidates in particular should offer solutions through well-thought-out platforms, plans, and programs.

Knowing that attack ads are likely to be used, creators of political advertising should recognize that it is important to balance negative advertising with appropriate information. When using attack ads, focus on voters' vital concerns, as well as controversial situations and issues that influence the role of the elected official in society. If a candidate is the focus of the attack ad, do not be evasive about the attacking candidate's true position.

Present Information in Context

Messages that are vague or ambiguous are highly problematic in all advertising and in political advertising in particular. Vague messages provide numerous opportunities for interpretation by the news media and by opponents. These interpretations may be factually wrong, but they may also be highly persuasive and may receive high levels of airtime. In advertising, then, provide reliable sources with information within a true setting along with the necessary supporting facts. This will ensure accurate interpretation.

Be Inspiring

Whatever the message, advertising should show leadership, raise expectations among voters, and encourage optimism in the future and in our country's political system. Advertising has the ability to generate community spirit and recognize community values; thus, it can also inspire voters to work together to improve communities. It can also help to create confidence in our system of government, which will also serve the purpose of encouraging participation in the election process. Positive messages in particular have been shown to instill a sense of confidence in government (Ansolabehere & Iyengar, 1995).

Inspiration can also be generated with production values. There are different feels to spots using film and spots using video: Film gives a richer texture that is better for a positive, bio-oriented spot. If the campaign has the budget for film over video, then film should be used (Geller & Lawrence, 2002).

Provide a Call to Action

Advertising should give voters the opportunity to find out more about the candidates and where they stand on positions. Advertisers should tell voters how to get more information: through Web sites, toll-free numbers, local offices, and the like (League of Women Voters, 2000). This is just one more way that advertising can encourage belief and participation in our system of government.

Summary

In the United States, we are currently in the midst of political advertising reform. New laws have been passed that will limit the amount of money that can be spent on advertising. Although these laws will be challenged in the courts, at a minimum they turn the public's attention to the important matter of the process of electing officials. We are also seeing reform as states and municipalities look for ways to create better and more informative political advertising messages. The political advertising climate is likely to be in flux for the next several years.

In the next chapter, we will examine socially responsible advertising—advertising that not only sells products and services but also presents messages about making the world a better place.

15

Really Good Goods?

Socially Responsible Advertising

The purpose of advertising is not to sell more. It's to do with institutional publicity, whose aim is to communicate the company's values. We need to convey a single strong image, which can be shared anywhere in the world.

—Luciano Benetton

MAC cosmetics' advertisements for their Viva Glam lipsticks have always had an interesting bent (Figure 15.1). Spokespeople for the lipsticks have included transvestites, rap singers, and in its most recent incarnation, pop superstar Elton John. This campaign's use of high-profile and nonmainstream personalities not only creates a unique brand personality for Viva Glam, but it also draws attention to the fact that MAC cosmetics donates a portion of the sales of every tube of Viva Glam to an AIDS foundation.

This campaign is a good representative of a type of advertising known as *socially responsible advertising*. Many advertisers, in all types of product and service categories, are looking for ways to connect their advertising images to their corporate values. This chapter discusses motivations and implementations of socially responsible advertising and explores the intended and unintended effects of such messages.

Corporate Images and Values

The predecessor of socially responsible advertising was known as corporate image advertising, which began in the 1950s and started to take hold in the 1960s in the United States (Brown & Dacin, 1997). Corporate image advertising presented messages and images about a company that tended not to

Figure 15.1 Elton John and other stars promote MAC's charitable connection with an AIDS foundation.

be product specific but instead gave a broader picture of the company and its role in society. Overall, corporate image advertising was designed to build a mental picture or portrait of a firm among consumers (Brown & Dacin, 1997). For example, corporate advertising for a gasoline company would not talk about fast service at their automobile service stations (i.e., a product attribute) but instead would discuss the importance of sustainable energy systems for our society (i.e., a corporate value) (Figure 15.2).

"I figure that the oil companies pay the motor companies not to put out a vehicle that's cleaner, healthier for our environment."

▲ Alfred Espinosa/Heavy Equipment Operator

We're working with leading auto manufacturers to introduce cleaner fuels and vehicles. In 1999 we voluntarily introduced cleaner low-sulfur fuels six years before E.P.A. mandates. These fuels help reduce ozone pollution and are now available in over 40 U.S. cities. It's like taking 100,000 cars off the road on a summer day.

It's a start.

bp

beyond petroleum

bp.com

Figure 15.2 BP promotes their community involvement in this ad.

During this initial wave of corporate image advertising, the messages tended to focus on a company's core values. Most companies kept a low profile about their nonprofit contributions during the 1960s and 1970s (Bloom, Hussein, & Szykman, 1995). In the early 1980s, American Express introduced the first campaign that connected a corporate core value directly to a charity. In their advertising, American Express announced they were donating a portion of their profits to restore the Statue of Liberty (Webb & Mohr, 1998). During this campaign, advertising announced that American Express donated one cent to the Statue of Liberty every time someone used its credit card. The campaign had excellent results: The number of new cardholders soon grew by 45%, card usage increased by 28%, and more than $1.7 million was donated to support the Statue of Liberty's restoration (Steckel, 1999). American Express went on to promote their Charge Against Hunger program, which continues to donate proceeds from using AMEX cards to Share Our Strength, a nonprofit antihunger organization.

Starting in the 1990s, more companies began using socially responsible advertising and marketing messages. Events such as the celebration of Earth Day in 1990 have provided touchstone causes (e.g., the environment) around which advertisers could connect their values and their products to issues that resonate with consumers (Obermiller, 1995). At the same time, consumers began to search out (and pay more for) environmentally friendly products (Jacobson & Mazur, 1995). In fact, the trade magazine *Advertising Age* named green marketing (i.e., advertising that uses environmental claims) as *the* marketing tool of the 1990s (Jacobson & Mazur, 1995). Thus, the win-win situation of using social issues to sell products began to be investigated by all types of companies.

Definitions

First, let us separate socially responsible advertising from social marketing, another concept that has been gaining attention in the industry. *Social marketing* is the process of using marketing techniques to persuade consumers to adopt the behaviors advocated by a social cause. For example, social marketing uses what we might think of as traditional advertising messages to promote behaviors such as using birth control, stopping smoking, or recycling.

Socially responsible advertising is different. Socially responsible advertising is one aspect of cause marketing. Jonathan Polansky, who works at the Public Media Center in San Francisco, describes cause marketing this way:

> Cause marketing requires an agreement between a non-profit and a for-profit. The deal is struck to maximize perceived benefits to each partner. The for-profit partner is looking to (a) associate its product with a perceived social good and thus boost its appeal to a defined market segment which shares that perception, (b) increase a broader market segment's perceptions of the enterprise as socially-engaged or responsible, (c) derive bottom line benefits from increasing market share in the targeted segment. (Goodwill, 1999)

Another example further distinguishes between social marketing and socially responsible advertising. An advertising campaign that uses social marketing would include a television advertisement to encourage people to recycle; a glass institute or a plastic manufacturer might sponsor the ad.

A socially responsible advertising campaign would be a television commercial promoting a product by using a message that the product was built with 100% recycled parts. The latter explicitly associates a company's values ("we care about the environment") with the values of a specific cause or issue (recycling).

Figure 15.3 A Body Shop ad focuses on self-esteem issues.

With socially responsible advertising, then, companies use social issues as part of the persuasive message in promoting products and services. Such messages recognize companies' broad commitments to all of their stakeholders. Stakeholders are all those in the public who have an interest or a stake in the operations of a specific company. Stakeholders include employees, stockholders, communities where the business operates and sells its products or services, and consumers who buy the products or services. Additionally, stakeholders include people involved with the issue or cause that the company supports ("More Than Just Causes," 2000).

For many companies, socially responsible messages are included in everything that the companies do ("More Than Just Causes," 2000). You are probably familiar with the Body Shop chain: Everything this company does is related to improving living conditions around the world for all manner of living things, including indigenous peoples, animals, and plants. Ads also focus on self-esteem issues (Figure 15.3).

Socially Responsible Advertising

Advertisers can demonstrate that they are socially responsible using three different types of advertising messages: social issues linked with products, social issues linked with corporations, and corporate donations to social issues.

Social Issues Linked With Specific Products

This first type of message features specific social issues in conjunction with advertised products. Kenneth Cole's advertising, for example, has featured AIDS awareness messages as well as pro-gun control messages

Folgers® and the GRAMMY® Foundation
have created Wakin' Up the Music.™
A music program to bring out the full
potential in every child. Grants are
given across the country to support
music education for grades K–3.

To join Shawn Colvin in supporting
Wakin' Up the Music and for more
information, log on to Folgers.com.

Figure 15.4 Music education is linked with coffee in this ad for Folgers.

directly alongside a specific shoe style. Folgers promotes music in schools along with their coffee (Johnson, 2001) (Figure 15.4). With these types of messages, the advertiser uses the product or service to draw consumers into the ad, and then the socially responsible message becomes associated with the specific product, creating a valuable link in the consumer's mind.

Several companies promote their no-animal-testing policy to appeal to consumers who are against such practices. Companies like Aveda cosmetics, the Body Shop, and Trader Joe's all promote their "cruelty free" products in various marketing messages.

Social Issues Linked With Corporations

The second type of message features social issues linked to companies but without a link to a specific product or service. Avon's Breast Cancer Crusade promotes awareness of breast cancer and breast health among women and sponsors fund-raising races that raise money for breast cancer organizations. Although such messages are not tied to a specific Avon product, they do position Avon as a company that cares about and is involved with women's issues.

Benetton is famous, if not notorious, for these types of campaigns. Beginning in 1992, for example, Benetton's advertising has featured HIV awareness messages, one of the most memorable showing a photograph of AIDS activist David Kirby on his deathbed. Other advertising in the Benetton portfolio raised awareness of the conflict in Bosnia, as well as child labor practices. Perhaps their most controversial advertising campaign was a freestanding insert entitled "We on Death Row", which purportedly showed what Benetton termed the "reality" of capital punishment, to increase awareness of the death penalty neither as a distant problem nor as news that occasionally appears on TV (Benetton, 1997).

Corporate Donations to Specific Issues

This third category is the most commonly occurring type of socially responsible advertising today. As depicted in the Viva Glam example at the start of this chapter, advertisers donate a percentage of their profits to a specific cause. This contribution may be the focus of the advertising message, or it may be one of several attributes featured in the message.

This is the most prevalent type of socially responsible message that we see, probably because companies already have some type of donation policy in place. The average company in the United States donates between 1% and 2% of pretax profits to philanthropic causes ("More Than Just Causes," 2000). At the high end of the scale, the ice cream company Ben & Jerry's contributes 7.5% of their pretax profits to a number of different charities, including environmental concerns (one such group is Save Our Environment) and groups battling forced child labor (e.g., the Population Media Center). Ben & Jerry's mention their commitments in their advertising and on their Web site (Zinkhan & Carlson, 1995). The retail giant Target donates 1% of purchases to schools, and customers can select the schools that receive their proceeds. This donation is announced in their advertising media as well as through huge banners in their stores. Target gives more than $1 million each week to local communities ("More Than Just Causes," 2000).

After September 11, 2001, numerous advertisers began directing charitable contributions to victims of the terrorist attacks. The marketers of the Discover card began donating a portion of purchases on their special American flag card to families and victims of the tragedy (Johnson, 2001). Revlon cosmetics recently announced a program in which proceeds from the purchase of specific cosmetics would go to women who were affected by the tragedy (Figure 15.5).

Today's Increase in Socially Responsible Messages

Overall, the past several decades have seen an increase in responsible business development. Today, more than 90% of American businesses are involved in some sort of philanthropic program, although the degree to which they focus on such programs in their messages varies by organization (Murphy, 1999). Having some type of socially responsible orientation is being recognized as an additional cost of doing business ("More Than Just Causes," 2000).

Such initiatives are good for both society and for companies' bottom lines. Socially responsible advertising messages are seen as beneficial to society because they raise the public's general awareness of important social issues. Advertisers with large advertising budgets have the means to

COLOR
AMERICA
BEAUTIFUL

FIRECRACKER   BLIZZARD   TYPHOON   REVLON RED

Now when you select patriotic shades* of Super Top Speed™ nail color, Super Lustrous* lipstick or any Charlie* fragrance, you'll be assisting women who have been most affected by the events of September 11th. And, if you enter our Color America Beautiful contest, you could win a trip to New York City. Just visit revlon.com or ivillage.com/revlon for complete contest and contribution details and to post a photo of how you'd best wear your patriotism on your nails.

A portion of the proceeds will benefit the Revlon Cares Fund*

REVLON
BE UNFORGETTABLE.™

Figure 15.5 Revlon donates a percentage of specific product sales to victims of September 11.

communicate to large groups of people. When advertisers undertake socially responsible advertising, they become advocates for voices that cannot easily be heard in the mass media. Additionally, several other specific reasons for the increase in socially responsible advertising have been identified, including an increase in the number of socially responsible consumers, a change in consumer attitudes toward corporate responsibility, increased interest by a range of causes, and a change in stakeholder concerns (Murphy, 1999).

More Socially Responsible Consumers

Many different types of consumers are becoming more socially responsible themselves. In the past several years, for example, consumers have become concerned with not only the purchasing process but also the production and the consumption process. Today, consumers are examining the degree to which scarce resources are used for making products and evaluating how products are developed and tested. They are also involved in learning how products are disposed of and examining how the consumption process affects the environment. As previously mentioned, processes such as animal testing are problematic to some consumers. Other consumers are concerned about where products are manufactured and the types of labor employed to make the products. Others are interested in the amounts of recyclable materials used in the production process or whether product packaging is recyclable and how much of the product itself is recyclable postconsumption. In sum, socially responsible advertising messages are often highly relevant to specific groups of consumers.

Consumer Attitudes Toward Corporate Responsibility

Along with this overall increase in interest in the production and consumption of products, consumers are also interested in how individual companies address such issues. They are aware that many corporations, especially larger multinational ones, have more resources than many small countries do; therefore, some consumers believe that large companies have a similar or greater ability to effect social change than governments or individuals (Mitchell, 1999). Consumers are also becoming more concerned about how the companies they patronize use their profits (Zinkhan & Carlson, 1995). Consequently, we are starting to see a change in the process of branding. Branding is no longer only a relationship between the brand and the consumer; instead, the branding process can involve information related to both the integrity and the ethical behavior of the corporation producing the brand (Lang, 1994).

Socially responsible advertising serves as one way to distinguish brands (and companies) from one another. The past few decades have seen an explosion of new product and service introductions, as well as a decrease in the actual differentiation between the products and services themselves. Providing information about the behaviors and philanthropy of a company and its brands, and connecting the company and brand to a cause, is one way to differentiate a company's products and services from its competitors (Lang, 1994).

Increased Interest by Causes

The groups involved with causes are highly interested in participating in philanthropic programs such as socially responsible advertising campaigns for several reasons. There is a wide range of causes that truly need all kinds of help, including financial assistance and volunteers, and there are clearly limited opportunities for funding from individual foundations and governmental funding sources. When causes join forces with corporations to develop advertising campaigns, the causes benefit not only from direct financial support but also from increased awareness of causes among consumers. This increased awareness may result in additional financial support from consumers. Causes may also gain volunteer workers since corporate employees may be encouraged to donate time to supported causes (Polonsky & Wood, 2001). Partnerships can also validate causes that have not received attention in the past. For example, the Red Cross is familiar to most Americans, but a cause such as Adopt-a-Minefield is not so familiar. By collaborating with the INC brand of clothing and using former model Heather Mills in their advertisements, Adopt-a-Minefield increases its awareness and possibly legitimacy in the mind of consumers (Figure 15.6).

I·N·C
INTERNATIONAL CONCEPTS

HEATHER MILLS
FOR INTERNATIONAL
CONCEPTS OF INSPIRATION.

Heather Mills and I·N·C,
A partnership designed
to make a difference.
Together we're working
to resolve the global
land mine crisis.
To learn more,
www.landmines.org

Worldwide & USA
Only at:

MACY'S
MACYS.COM
BLOOMINGDALE'S
BURDINES
RICH'S
LAZARUS
GOLDSMITH'S
THE BON MARCHÉ
1·800·417·2698
Also available in
petite & plus sizes.

Figure 15.6   Heather Mills and INC raise awareness of Adopt-a-
Minefield.

Stakeholder Concerns

Corporations are highly concerned with consumers' attitudes toward their products and services. In addition to consumers, corporations are responsible to a number of other stakeholders, including owners (often stockholders), suppliers, employees, the government, and more (Zinkhan & Carlson, 1995). As consumers become more socially responsible, these other corporate stakeholder groups are becoming socially responsible. Stockholders in particular are examining issues of corporate responsibility when they make decisions on which stocks to purchase.

Intended Effects

Given this range of benefits of a socially responsible advertising campaign, there are a number of intended effects in such campaigns. These are discussed next.

Consumers Are Educated About a Range of Issues

An increase in the amount of socially responsible advertising messages means that a range of people in society are educated about a number of different issues, opportunities, and injustices that they may not have been aware of before the advertising campaigns began. The images in many socially responsible messages often show an assertion of universal values and experiences to which a wide range of individuals can relate. Additionally, these values are combined with the concept *politics of realism*, which suggests that advertising images and messages can serve as a vehicle for social change by calling attention to the real world. This means that socially responsible messages provide a worldview beyond the traditional consumer culture that many advertisements picture.

In addition, product or service advertising that features socially responsible messages may reach consumers who rarely notice traditional advertising messages. Some individuals strongly relate to or are highly interested in specific causes, and these people may pay more attention to advertisements featuring the cause than advertisements that do not (Polonsky & Wood, 2001).

Message Attention and Comprehension Increase

Not only do these messages reach a large number of consumers— advertisements featuring socially responsible messages have generated increased message attention and comprehension among consumers. Messages that are socially responsible often resonate strongly with consumers who appreciate advertising with messages that feature enduring and traditional values, often embodied by selected causes (Smith, 2001). Since September 11 in particular, Americans strongly identify with the human side of large multinational corporations, and a majority of Americans feel that it is appropriate for companies to raise funds to support victims of the tragedies. In particular, consumers applaud companies that are donating a percentage of the proceeds of sales to helping victims of September 11 ("Point of Purchase," 2001).

Message Credibility Increases

Consumers find advertisements featuring socially responsible messages to be very credible (Smith, 2001). The credibility of the messages has a strong influence on consumer behavior. It has been hypothesized that this credibility is from the obvious motive in the advertisement (i.e., to support the specific cause) behind the request to adopt a certain behavior (e.g., to buy a product) (Bloom et al., 1995). Socially responsible messages are also more credible because many stakeholder groups consider the messages both courageous and profound, which is somewhat different from traditional advertising. In addition, such messages are more credible because they highlight the interdependence of business and society. Advertisers move away from simple product advertising to talk about their corporation's beliefs and value systems, as well as their roles in society today. This is seen as particularly appropriate after the September 11 tragedies (Mason, 2002).

Socially responsible messages provide the "tipping point" for many consumers when making their purchase decisions ("More Than Just Causes," 2000). For example, a study by Roper-Starch and Cone, Inc. found that when price and quality are equal, two thirds of consumers would choose a brand (or retailer) associated with a good cause. This credibility may also translate into diminished price sensitivity among consumers. One study showed that almost 70% of consumers would pay more for a product from a company associated with a good cause than for a product not associated with the cause ("More Than Just Causes," 2000). Another study showed that almost two thirds of consumers would be willing to pay on average 5% more for a product associated with a good cause (Meyer, 1999).

Improved Corporate Image

Socially responsible messages provide benefits beyond the brand to affect the company in general with overall feelings of goodwill by consumers. A majority of Americans report that they have positive images of companies that support causes consumers care about (Till & Nowak, 2000). However, much of this improved corporate image will depend on the current market position of the brand. Companies that have brands with strong market positions along with a wide set of associations in the consumers' minds will gain *less* from links with good causes than will companies that have weaker, smaller brands (Till & Nowak, 2000). This is possibly because smaller brands have weaker positions in the consumers' mind, and socially responsible messages may be distinctive enough to separate smaller brands from larger brands. Well-established brands are likely to have entrenched positions in the consumer's mind; thus, socially responsible messages may conflict with consumer perceptions of the brand.

Not only does corporate image improve among consumers, but socially responsible messages also improve the company's image among its workers. Specifically, employee loyalty to the firm can increase: One study showed that 90% of employees of firms with socially responsible marketing feel loyal to their firms. This loyalty is especially strengthened if employees can help select the cause that the company supports (Polonsky & Wood, 2001).

Consumer Guilt Is Assuaged

Socially responsible messages that are successfully implemented will often suggest actions that consumers can easily take to affect the problem described in the advertising. This can result in easing any guilt associated with consumer consumption of the product (Jacobson & Mazur, 1995).

For some consumers, guilt is often associated with the purchase of certain products, such as luxury items. These feelings of guilt are likely to decrease when the purchased product is related to a good cause, since the positive feeling of donating to a charity, regardless of how the donation occurs, may offset negative feelings associated with a purchase that may be seen as frivolous (Webb & Mohr, 1998).

Unintended Effects

Socially responsible messages are not free from controversy. In fact, several unintended effects of such messages have been identified.

Alienation of Consumers

Not all consumers will be affected by socially responsible messages, and such messages may even alienate consumers who currently consider themselves socially responsible or socially aware. Many socially responsible or socially aware consumers have strong anticorporate biases (Zinkhan & Carlson, 1995). These types of consumers may see a socially responsible advertising campaign purely as a gimmick and not as any real indication of the corporation's values (Jacobson & Mazur, 1995). Other consumers may be skeptical of firms they think take advantage of them when using cause-related marketing, although these consumers are likely to have a distrust of advertising in general (Webb & Mohr, 1998).

Misleading Consumers

Information that is provided in socially responsible messages can be misleading. Specifically, advertising language can indiscriminately use terminology to suggest that companies and products are more involved in social issues than they really are. One such example is green marketing—that is, marketing techniques appealing to environmentally concerned individuals. Some advertisements may use terms like "environmentally friendly" and "ecosafe" to appeal to like-minded consumers. However, such terminology is not legislated by either the Federal Trade Commission (FTC) or the Food and Drug Administration (FDA), so the language can be meaningless and not at all reflective of the companies' practices (Jacobson & Mazur, 1995). For example, recycling experts suggest that products labeled with the term "recycled" should be made of materials that were diverted from the solid waste stream for use as raw materials in the manufacture or assembly of a new product or package. However, some products labeled as recycled are made from reconditioned or reused parts that would normally be reused anyway. Some contain only 10% recycled material. Although the FTC has guidelines about what the terms associated with green practices should mean, compliance by marketers and advertisers is voluntary, and thus, many such messages may be misleading.

Increased Feelings of Futility

Some consumers may believe that some problems are insolvable and that no degree of corporate effort will be enough. These increased feelings of futility may have negative repercussions on the corporation. Much of this is related to whether the socially responsible campaign chooses a "sick baby" or a "well baby" approach to its messages. The most common approach is the sick baby appeal, which focuses on the problem (e.g., the baby is sick or the ocean is polluted) and emphasizes the severity of the problem (Obermiller, 1995). The advertising appeal then presents evidence of what the company plans to do to address the problem. This is a popular appeal because it assumes that people attend to matters that are important and severe and that consumers will allocate their personal effort to problems that they view as important and acute. However, using a sick baby approach can suggest to consumers that problems are insolvable, and thus, it will alienate consumers from companies as consumers feel helpless to do anything about the problem.

The well baby approach, on the other hand, talks about why the problem is improving or perhaps not a problem any longer (e.g., the baby is well or the ocean is cleaner). It then discusses the company's role in achieving the well baby status. The implication is that the company will continue to watch out for the health of the baby and suggests that consumers may wish to be involved in keeping the baby well.

Increased Feelings of Fear

Socially responsible advertising, especially the sick baby approach as just described, may also create feelings of fear that can be damaging to both consumers and to the message. The underlying goal of the sick baby approach is to create an emotional response among consumers, and a fear appeal is often part of such an approach. For a fear appeal to be successful, the message must provide a coping mechanism that is seen by targeted consumers as a realistic way to manage the fear. If a coping mechanism is not provided in the advertising messages, unreasonable levels of fear can be raised in individuals (Obermiller, 1995).

The Italian clothing retailer Benetton is one company that has been accused of providing numerous images in their print advertising that generate a heightened sense of fear and concern in many individuals. Benetton has been criticized for using its socially responsible advertising to attack the sensibilities of unsuspecting magazine readers (Garfield, 1997). Messages that focus on fear may been seen as devoid of context, and fear is created purely from the shock value of the images in the advertisement. The lack of a coping mechanism further causes consumer concern and possible alienation from the message and the corporation.

Issues Are Exploited

Consumers may see socially responsible advertising as exploitive. The centerpiece of Benetton's controversial Death Row campaign was an insert of photographs and interviews with a number of death row inmates across the United States. The goal of the campaign, according to the company, was to put a human face on the individuals who are on death row. The victims or families of victims received no mention in the message. Bob Garfield, in a critique of Benetton's Death Row campaign, said that "No brand has the right to increase its sales on the backs, on the misery of the fates of condemned men and women, much less their slaughtered victims" (Garfield, 2001b, p. 45).

Many consumers feel that companies that use exploitive messages are opportunistic. When messages trade on the tragedies of others, such as the Benetton campaign, the messages become gratuitous and are likely to alienate consumers (Smith, 2001). Throughout this chapter, we have been discussing the increase in patriotic messages that have been aired since the September 11 tragedies. While much of what we have discussed shows such messages in a positive light, the increase in messages with patriotic themes after the tragedies has been questioned by many in society. A study by advertising agency Leo Burnett found that using patriotism in advertising was considered wrong by half of the respondents to the study (Millard, 2001). U.S. automakers in particular were criticized for using the tragedies to suggest that America needed to "keep on rolling" by buying new cars and helping the economy and furthermore suggesting that its givebacks were a "solemn patriotic duty" (Garfield, 2001a, p. 29). Bob Garfield (2001a) called such messages a "self-serving sales promotion" that was "cynical exploitation of the terrorists' victims and an unforgivable insult to those who grieve for them" (p. 29).

Obviously, there are differences between companies that truly care about the issues they support and companies using messages that are blatantly exploitive, and if a message looks exploitive, it rarely has a positive effect on consumers (Millard, 2001). One example is Philip Morris's donation of food to refugees in Kosovo. While this effort was important, there is a perception that the actual donation was overshadowed by the multimillion dollar marketing campaign Philip Morris used to promote the donation.

Sensationalistic and Voyeuristic

The use of certain images, such as those designed to shock, is seen as being sensational and voyeuristic. Some suggest that these types of images are only used to get publicity and do not reflect any corporate concern for the cause. Benetton in particular has been accused of creating what has been termed a "spectacle of fascination, horror and terror" (Giroux, 1994), with their ads featuring the aforementioned death row inmates as well as AIDS victims.

Although the sensationalistic aspect is criticized by some simply as horrific and exploitive, others see sensationalism as clichéd and one-dimensional. For example, Benetton's advertisement featuring AIDS victim David Kirby rankles some individuals because the advertisement presents what Benetton suggests is a universal image of AIDS victims. This image supports conventional representations that people with AIDS are helpless victims and doesn't recognize the range of images that would more accurately reflect the people currently living with AIDS ("More Controversy, Please, We're Italian," 1992).

Greenwashing

Many corporations are genuinely concerned and involved with the causes they support, but other companies are seen as using socially related advertising messages merely to cover up for poor corporate practices overall. This use of socially responsible advertising is known as *greenwashing*. Some corporations use socially responsible marketing to compensate for behavior that some stakeholders may consider questionable, such as selling unhealthful products or wreaking environmental havoc. Otherwise, socially responsible messages may be diverting consumer attention away from bad business practices.

Earlier, we mentioned a campaign by tobacco giant Philip Morris, which spent several million dollars on a socially responsible television campaign that highlighted their involvement in inner-city education, flood relief, and refugee relief in Kosovo. This advertising campaign was problematic to many, given the issues people have with other products made by the company, particularly their tobacco products (Garfield, 2001b). When the positive focus of a company presented in their advertisements clashes with what consumers already know about the company, consumers' negative feelings about the company are likely to worsen (Palmer, 2001).

Unequal Balance Between Company and Cause

In socially responsible message partnerships, the companies sponsoring the messages tend to have more power in the relationship than the causes being featured, and it is possible that companies may make decisions without taking the cause partners into consideration. Overall, many of the benefits of a socially responsible marketing campaign are corporate focused; that is, the messages contribute more to brands and their image than they do to causes (Polonsky & Wood, 2001). Furthermore, although such programs can create awareness of a cause among consumers, the message can have the unintended effect that consumers come to believe that the cause no longer needs support from other sources because the corporate support might be seen as all that the cause needs (Polonsky & Wood, 2001). Other potential relationships may be damaged, since the company may prohibit the partner-cause from seeking relationships with other competing companies.

Selective Causes Are Highlighted

Today, corporations favor collaborating with causes that are demographically compatible with specific target audiences. Thus, there are concerns that all causes do not have an equal opportunity to become involved with socially responsible messages. For example, child care is a top concern for adults aged 30 to 44. Therefore, companies that target products and services to that group would probably look to collaborate with a cause or an issue related to child care. There are also geographic differences to the concerns of Americans: People living in the West are highly concerned about public education, whereas those in the Midwest appear most concerned about the environment. Therefore, companies with a sales focus in those regions may select causes or issues that would best resonate with those consumers. Overall, the top issues that people in the United States are concerned with are public education, crime, and the environment.

Thus, issues and causes that rate highly with specific groups will get the most attention, and important issues and causes related to poverty and drug abuse are less likely to be contacted for partnerships in socially responsible advertising campaigns. It has been argued that many Americans do not believe their lives are immediately touched by the problems associated with poverty and drug abuse, and so they are less attractive for advertisers ("More Than Just Causes," 2000). The advocacy function of socially responsible advertising, then, may be limited to advocacy that is popular with specific publics.

_____ Creating Socially Responsible Advertising

When considering the implementation of a socially responsible advertising campaign, there are several considerations to evaluate.

Relevance

Companies should select a social issue that is relevant to the company and to the product being advertised. Avon's partnership with breast cancer charities was seen as a relevant issue by many consumers (Murphy, 1999).

A different company, such as a power tool company, might not have been an appropriate match for a breast cancer charity. However, companies should consider a range of relevant causes and not limit themselves to the top "hot button" concerns of consumers. The partnership must be genuinely relevant—that is, seen as something that not every other company is undertaking.

Clarity

Your message should be very clear and transparent. Consumers are exposed to many socially responsible messages and will evaluate not only the company's commitment to the cause but also what the company expects to gain from the partnership (Murphy, 1999). The key word is *partnerships*: Consumers are looking for companies that truly care about a cause or an issue. In terms of media, consumers find that clarity is best achieved through television and in-store mentions; only about a third of consumers think print advertisements provide enough clarity about the partnership (Brabbs, 2000). This also suggests that simple, straightforward messages are most effective.

Demonstrate Caring

The lesson with the Philip Morris corporate campaign was that consumers will question whether corporations really care or whether companies are trying to achieve "innocence by association." Innocence by association is another form of greenwash—that is, diverting attention from bad practices by providing evidence of good practices. The sentiments felt by a company and the values they portray should exist at a deep level throughout the company, or the company may be viewed as hypocritical (Murphy, 1999). Not only should the depth of the commitment exist throughout the company, but it should also be directed by and agreed to among all stakeholders. Managers as well as employees must be committed to the partnership (Gray, 2001).

Assess Commitment

Not only will consumers examine whether the company really cares about the cause, but they will also assess whether the company puts its money where its mouth is. The financial commitment that the company makes should be one that consumers see as being able to make a difference. The size of the commitment should be appropriate for the size of the company. A commitment of $1000 from a small retailer may be seen as adequate, whereas the same commitment from a Fortune 500 company would be seen as exploitive according to some consumers (Webb & Mohr, 1998).

Companies should be aware that the commitment goes beyond the financial contribution or donation to the cause. Companies must commit sufficient resources not only for donations but also for advertising budgets, communications, public service announcements (PSAs), and support of volunteers (Meyer, 1999).

Balance of Cause and Company

Many consumers will view the best commitments as those that are long-term (Murphy, 1999). A long-term commitment works over a period of time (perhaps several years) to create an image of a caring company. Particular care must be taken so that the type of message does not suggest that the cause is providing a product endorsement. Many nonprofits are starting to express concerns about perceptions of partnerships that may be perceived as endorsements. Recently, for example, the American Cancer Society (ACS) partnered with Smith-Kline-Beecham and received a reported $3 million to promote the Nico-Derm antismoking patch. The American Cancer Society views such a program as an educational partnership, and while they will promote the patch, according to an ACS vice president, they "are not endorsing the patch specifically; therefore, there is no liability on ACS for the product itself" (Goodwill, 1999). Some suggest that such partnerships may undermine a cause's reputation and affect public confidence in the cause (Goodwill, 1999).

Provide Solutions

Socially responsible messages should provide solutions so consumers understand not only the company's part but also the consumer's role in addressing the problem. The sick baby approach tends to downplay personal action. For example, the severity of a problem could be described by suggesting that there are only enough resources to last for the next 20 years. With the well baby approach, the importance and effectiveness of individual action are highlighted (think of the Smoky the Bear campaign: Only you can prevent forest fires). A strong socially responsible campaign does not just tell people that the company is helping, but it also tells people how they can help (Gray, 2001). This is one way to ensure that the cause does not get lost in the message.

Track Results

Finally, like all advertising campaigns, socially responsible advertising should be tracked. Campaigns should be evaluated to determine if consumers are aware of the partnership, whether they appreciate the message, and how the message relates to the brand. In addition, tracking should involve examining whether the corporate image is affected in a positive way. Socially responsible campaigns are unlikely to be sustained if their effectiveness cannot be proven (Gray, 2001).

The Future

Like all other types of advertising, socially responsible advertising tends to thrive in good economic times and has less support in tough economic times. Socially responsible advertising messages must continue to be evaluated in terms of outcomes—that is, what entities can gain by engaging in such campaigns.

As you may recall from Chapter 10's discussion of advertising and children, there are boundaries to what are acceptable partnerships and what are not. Some states are starting to consider limiting certain types of partnerships. For example, a bill pending in the Oregon legislation would not allow public buildings to be named after corporations. Similarly, the public has denounced plans for corporations to pay fees to add their names to subway stations in Boston. Public sensitivity may increase in the future, and awareness of public sensibilities will continue to be important.

Summary

Socially responsible advertising campaigns present a win-win opportunity for companies and causes. Companies associate with causes that are seen as important to their stakeholders, and causes increase their visibility among consumers by being featured in advertising messages sponsored by companies. Socially responsible advertising works best when companies truly believe in the causes they support and are not using messages to shock audiences or exploit the causes for visibility and attention.

In the next chapter, we will focus on a single medium: the Internet. The advent of a new medium results in a number of new approaches toward advertising, and the Internet is no exception.

16

The Bleeding Edge

Online Advertising

The Internet is so big, so powerful and pointless that for some people it is a complete substitute for life.

—Andrew Brown

Have you recently clicked the "Close" box for a banner ad that popped up on your screen when you were trying to find some information or download some software? Or deleted an e-mail message with a once-in-a-lifetime special offer? Maybe you are the type of person who doesn't even remember seeing any ads online: You have trained yourself to ignore them, much like annoying little bugs that swarm around you on a summer day.

Frankly, many practitioners in the traditional advertising industry still have not figured out what to do about online advertising. The solution for many agencies has been simply to purchase and absorb an "online" agency into their current agency structure. When this happens, other new online agencies are often founded to stay on the "bleeding edge" of new technology, a focus that is sometimes difficult for larger, more traditional agencies to have.

Loyd (2000) has recently described the bleeding edge as the thin line that separates the possible from the available. The bleeding edge is a derivation of the term *cutting-edge,* as in cutting-edge technology. The difference between cutting-edge technology and bleeding-edge technology is that bleeding-edge infers a technology that is the newest of the new, and the impact of the technology on business, consumers, systems, and society is not yet known. It also implies that a failure of this technology will hurt the business or system in a spectacular way (OIT Network Group, 2002). For advertising, this suggests that some online marketers may implement new types of messages without considering their ability to help the brand and/or its impact on the consumer. This chapter explores some of the issues that have recently arisen with various types of electronic advertising as companies and consumers both struggle to keep up with the bleeding edge.

The Growth of the Internet

Today, more than 275 million people around the world have access to the Internet and its associated offerings (Surveys, 2000). As the numbers of people around the world gaining access to the Internet continues to increase throughout the first decade of the new millennium, the impact of the Internet on many different aspects of society is being examined. For example, issues regarding how the Internet and its content should be used, regulated, and taxed are challenging individuals, governments, and businesses around the globe. For advertising in particular, the role, function, and implementation of advertising online have been examined, evaluated, and criticized by content providers, online visitors, Internet service providers (ISPs), and others.

A Brief History of the Internet

You may be hard pressed to recall life without the Internet. Many of us, though, were at the front lines to examine the evolution of the Internet from a scientific and academic tool to the electronic bazaar that it is today. The Internet, a "network of networks," evolved like many other mass media have evolved. Specifically, contributions by a variety of people from different walks of society have influenced its development.

In 1945, Vanneaver Bush, a director of the Federal Office of Scientific Research and Development, had a vision of an appliance that he termed the "information desk." This information desk was akin to what we think of as a desktop computer system, which Bush saw as capable of handling the problem of the information explosion that had been identified in post–World War II America. Bush's vision of an information desk included the ability to link to other information desks to share information (Stefik, 1999). Bush's conception of the desk stayed as a part of his fanciful imagination until numerous institutions around the world began strategically committing funding and human resources to the development of what we now know as the Internet. Among these institutions are the government, research institutions, academic institutions, and telecommunications providers.

Government Institutions

Government institutions such as the Department of Defense (DOD) were directly involved with developing what we currently consider the Internet.

The DOD created a computer network called the Advanced Research Projects Agency Network (ARPANET) in 1969. ARPANET was developed with a dual purpose: to examine whether computer networking had the potential to become reliable and to link together distinct groups doing military-funded research. These groups included the DOD, military research contractors, and universities. One contribution of the DOD was the development of ARPANET so that the physical equipment supporting the network would be physically dispersed throughout the world. This was designed so that it could survive multiple nuclear attacks and no national government can conceivably regulate the Internet alone (Goldring, 1997).

Research Institutions

Research institutions supported researchers examining ways to best use the network as a research tool. One such institute is the European Laboratory for Particle Physics, also known as CERN. CERN facilitated the research efforts of Tim Berners-Lee, who developed Hypertext Markup Language (HTML), the programming language that essentially makes the World Wide Web possible. Research institutions fostered the values of cooperation and sharing of knowledge among the research community, consisting of government researchers, academics, and private enterprise (Rutkowski, 1997). Among other things, these institutions set and monitor the standards for Internet architecture, usability, the World Wide Web, and other functions.

Colleges and Universities

Academic institutions were among the first groups outside government-supported research to identify the value of this new technology beyond the limited usage on DOD projects. Academic researchers valued the expansion of the network to provide access to the Internet to researchers, other faculty, staff, and students. Often, access was provided at no cost, which encouraged the adoption of the Internet among academic groups. These institutions also took the first steps to make the Internet more user-friendly and available to groups outside the research community. For example, the first graphical Web browser (called Mosaic) was developed at the University of Illinois at Urbana-Champaign and distributed free to anyone who wished to download it, and universities hosted the first free community networks (PBS, 2000). Colleges and universities contributed their values of academic freedom to the development of online content: Varied types of content provided by universities helped to build the base of free and open information online.

Telecommunications Providers

Telecommunications providers support the infrastructure of the information flow. These institutions were instrumental in creating the metaphor of an information highway by providing the paths for individuals and companies to access the Internet. This access is accomplished through a range of technology, including telephone lines, cable networks, Digital Subscriber Lines (DSLs), Ethernets, and more (Skelton, 1997). Telecommunications providers contributed the values of speed and quality to the communication experience.

Growth and Other Developments Contributing to the Internet

Several other factors contributed to the penetration of the Internet through society. First, the development and dissemination of the personal computer in the 1980s increased the access that individuals had to networked environments. The introduction of the Apple Macintosh created the term "user-friendly," and many individuals with no previous want or need for computers began to accept them into their homes (PBS, 2000). On a more global level, significant changes were happening in the structure of governments around the world. Specifically, the 1980s saw changes in the world as numerous societies became free of totalitarian or authoritarian regimes. These global changes set the stage for a global economy (Branscomb, 1997).

The National Science Foundation (NSF) administered the Internet in the United States when ARPANET ceased being strictly a tool for the DOD and became more widely available. The NSF relinquished control over a major part of the Internet in 1993; at the same time, they sanctioned use of the Internet for commercial purposes (Shapiro, 1998). This decision fundamentally altered the structure of the burgeoning Internet, as the portal was opened for a range of entities to consider and create an online presence.

Not long after the NSF's decision, the online service provider Prodigy became one of the first companies to advertise online. Many Internet users, accustomed to a commercial-free atmosphere, were not pleased with seeing advertising online. Some online users reacted by placing black tape on their monitors over the place where Prodigy's ads appeared so they would not have to look at them. Today, instead of using black tape, many users purchase blocking software to minimize the online presence of advertising or simply ignore its seemingly constant presence.

The Internet Today

As previously mentioned, the Internet has continued to grow both in terms of its infrastructure and the size of the online population. Today, the bleeding edge is characterized by four trends: networking, bandwidth, processing speed, and wireless technology.

Networking

The Internet is becoming an indispensable tool today, much like the telephone. Indispensability, in terms of the telephone and the Internet, is related to the number of connections you can make with the technology. Today, more than two thirds of all Americans use the Internet on a regular basis. These users are interconnected through millions of network connections in the United States alone. A network connection enables one computer network (e.g., the one at the journalism school at the University of Oregon) to interact with another computer network (e.g., the one at America OnLine). The actual number of networks is uncountable, but consider this statistic: In 1990, the greater Boston area had approximately 10,000 network connections. In 1996, the Massachusetts Institute of Technology (MIT) estimated that there were 10,000 network connections on campus. Compare those figures to connection potentials today, where a single computer lab at MIT can handle 10,000 network connections. The growth in the number of networks correlates with the growth in usage, as increased demand influences increased ability to connect.

Bandwidth

Bandwidth refers to the amount of data that can be transferred between networks in a fixed amount of time. Today, many networks are connected via fiberoptic cables that carry data very rapidly. Today, it is estimated that there are more than 26.7 million miles of fiberoptic cable crisscrossing the United States. Increased bandwidth allows the delivery of Web content with more bells and whistles to each of us individually.

Problems with bandwidth usually relate to the "last mile"— that is, the wires that carry data from the telephone switch office to your home or business. There, data that have been flowing through fiber-optic cables must be compressed through traditional telephone lines. This means that unless your home is equipped with DSL or a cable modem, it takes quite a while to download many new programs.

Processing Power

Today, a child's interactive toy has more processing power than the Apollo spaceships of the 1960s (Loyd, 2000). Computers are evaluated by the power of their central processing unit (CPU), which is the brain of the computer. Even with an accessible network and high bandwidth, your computer's processing power will also influence what you can and cannot quickly and easily do online. Processing power doubles every month while the costs hold constant (Loyd, 2000), thus increasing our abilities for interaction and other tasks.

Mobility

It is no longer necessary to be wired to take part in the wired world. Digital technology has allowed for explosive growth in a range of personal digital devices, such as cell phones, digital cameras, handheld computers, and the like. These small appliances allow for increased communication opportunities in the mobile environment.

Comparing Online and Traditional Advertising

Current anxieties about Internet advertisements involve concerns with frequency, resource use, intrusion, and privacy, issues heretofore not at the forefront for advertisers (Amis, 1998). For many online users, the basic problem with advertising on the Internet is that advertisers show a lack of knowledge and understanding of how the Internet works. Advertisers try to implement traditional methods online without considering the interactive aspects of the medium. For others, advertisers spend too much time trying to be on the bleeding edge—that is, implementing processes simply to have the most and the flashiest (excuse the pun) bells and whistles in their online presence.

Context Issues

One difference between online and traditional media is the context in which advertising messages appear. Many advertisers compare the Internet to a television network, where advertisers pay for the programming support, and viewers generally receive the content for free. However, the online situation is somewhat different. Specifically, the cost of providing content, entertainment, and information on the Internet is distributed between the companies and the people who are connected to it.

Unlike traditional mass media, the Internet is not a public resource. It is a collection of networks, some of which are paid for and owned by companies, some by government, and some by private individuals or entities. Thus, when information flows from one place to another, the price of transferring the information is split across the originator of the information, the information receiver, and other parties who paid for the equipment in between. This information flow results in a different perspective on advertising from both online consumers (receivers) and the entities providing space for online advertising.

Evaluation Issues

Traditional advertising messages are seen as part of a larger marketing effort that involves other types of communication messages: public relations, sales promotion, and the like. Therefore, it is difficult to pinpoint the actual effect that advertising has on consumer behavior, specifically in the short term. Only direct mail, implemented without any other type of communication support, can demonstrate any possible correlation between message and sales. However, online advertising has not been evaluated in the same way. The immediate effect of online messages has been the traditional way to measure the success or failure of an online message.

Types of Online Advertising

Advertisers have been experimenting with many different types of advertisements online. Since the Internet was commercialized, some advertising units have come and gone, whereas others continue to endure and evolve as technology continues to evolve and as we begin to understand more about consumer behavior online. As of this writing, there are several different types of advertisements that are regularly used by online advertisers.

Banner Ads

A banner advertisement is a graphical Web advertising unit, typically measuring 468 pixels wide by 60 pixels tall (in online unit size terms, a 468×60) (Figure 16.1). Traditionally, banner ads appear at the top of a Web page, and they load prior to other Web content. It is also possible to find banner ads at the bottom of a Web page. Banner ads that appear during the transition from one page to another are known as *interstitial advertisements*. Different configurations of banner ads wax and wane in popularity. As of this writing, one popular size is known as a *skyscraper ad*, which is a long, skinny ad aligned on the right side of a page. Often, these unique sizes are popular because of their novelty.

Banner ads have been evaluated primarily based on click-through rates (CTRs): the number of times a banner ad is clicked so that the viewer is transported from the page hosting the banner ad to the page sponsoring it. In the early days of the Web, click-through rates were generally much higher than they are now: Some banner ads reported CTRs of 40% and

Figure 16.1 Banner ads online

higher. Today, banner ads obtain CTRs of less than 1% on average. This is probably due to the decline in the novelty factor of banner ads. Other possible contributions for the decline in CTRs may be due to technical limitations of computers that limit the ability for bleeding-edge technology to be applied on every system; the poor design of banner ads; an excessive percentage of run-of-network buys, which result in high levels of frequency against average online users; and the accumulated bad experiences of Web surfers (Internet Marketing, 2002).

Currently, researchers are examining how banner ads can provide benefits in terms of branding. If banner ads become viewed as a brand-building tool, it is likely that CTRs will be devalued as a good measurement of Web advertising effectiveness.

Pop-Up and Pop-Under Ads

Pop-up ads display in a new browser window. They cover up the site users are visiting and will not move until users interact with them, usually to manually close them down. Pop-up ads come in many different shapes and sizes and appear typically in a scaled-down browser window with only the Close, Minimize, and Maximize commands available to the user (Internet Marketing, 2002). Pop-ups are seen as superior to banner ads because they interrupt users' surfing patterns. In this way, they are similar to a television commercial while banner ads are more like print ads. However, the unpredictability of their appearances and the effort it takes to close them down are problematic for some consumers.

Pop-under ads display in a new browser window behind the current browser window: Basically, they function somewhat like a pop-up except they do not cover your main browser window but rather hide beneath it. Once online users complete their online activities and close their browsers, the pop-under ads become visible.

Pop-up ads are often shown (and closed) instantly, but pop-under ads linger behind the current browser window, appearing only after other windows have been closed (Internet Marketing, 2002). Pop-under ads are becoming more popular because they do not interrupt an individual's session, and they tend to be larger and present better graphics than pop-up and banner ads.

Both pop-ups and pop-unders tend to generate higher CTRs than traditional banner advertisements. This may lead to increased sales results. However, they are not as good at branding as traditional banner ads.

Home Page Takeover Ads

Home page takeover ads employ animation that takes over an entire Web page, using technologies such as Eyeblaster or DHTML (Hespos, 2002). These advertisements feature quite a bit of movement and sound effects. When visiting a Web page featuring a home page takeover ad, several minutes elapse before the entire advertisement appears, and there is quite a bit of sound and motion associated with these types of ads. A company called United Virtualities originated one type of home page takeover ad that they call *shoshkeles* (http://www.unitedvirtualities.com/shoshkeles.htm).

The uniqueness of these types of advertisements and the fact that they freeze the screen so that the viewer is captive are two reasons we may be seeing more home page takeover ads in the future. Advertisers view home page takeover ads as engaging, interactive, and personalized because the ads are created to appear on specific Web sites that attract a specific target audience (Saunders, 2001). These types of ads usually have a frequency cap so that daily visitors to the site are not overexposed to the message.

E-mail Messages

Electronic mail (e-mail) is arguably the most popular online application today. A total of 45% of Americans, or 87% of the online population, use e-mail on a regular basis, an increase from the 35% of all Americans in 2000.

Figure 16.2 Tide detergent sends out e-mail about cleaning.

For advertisers, e-mail is a very versatile medium. E-mail advertising formats range from simple text to HTML and rich media. Content can be one-size-fits-all or highly customized. The delivery of e-mails can vary from fixed, frequent intervals (e.g., the Tide e-mail, Figure 16.2, a monthly offering that highlights clothing care tips and timesavers), to sporadic intervals, with transmissions occurring only when something newsworthy comes along (e.g., the Gap's e-mail messages, which feature new offerings as well as special bargains on an irregular basis). Sophistication (and the resultant cost) of the message can be very low, very high, or anywhere in between.

More advertisers are using targeted e-mail to reach prospective customers, generally by applying tactics that traditional direct marketers use: buying lists and sending out massive amounts of e-mail to targeted consumers. E-mail marketers recognize that not everyone wants to receive unsolicited e-mail, and therefore, two consumer choices for mail receipt—opt in and opt out—have been developed.

Opt-in e-mail consists of names and e-mail addresses of consumers that have given their permission to be part of the e-mail list or any marketing campaigns that involve the collection or usage of personal data (e.g., one's e-mail address). Opt-out e-mail lists consist of names and e-mail addresses of consumers and excludes consumers that specifically requested not to participate in any marketing campaigns that involve personal data (Grebb, 2001a).

Along with the power of e-mail comes the abuse of e-mail, commonly known as spam. Some online users fail to distinguish between permission marketing (i.e., asking people if they would be willing to receive e-mail, generally through a check box at an online Web page) and e-mail spam (i.e., unsolicited e-mail). Concerns with spam present a major threat to legitimate e-mail marketers, as a glut of messages could make the entire e-mail medium less effective (Internet Marketing, 2002).

Keyword Marketing

Keyword marketing is a tactic that specifically involves the appearance of Web sites on search engine results. Keyword marketing involves a variety of techniques for putting a client's message in front of people who are searching on search engine (e.g., the portal yahoo.com and the search engine Iwon.com) using particular keywords and key phrases. The process involves matching paid messages with the information for which an individual is searching at a search engine Web site. If you were looking for information on a vacation in Cancún, for example, good keyword marketing would place numerous paid messages at the search engine you are visiting in addition to providing a list of Web pages with information about Cancún vacations.

One type of keyword marketing is purchased ad units, such as banners or smaller button-type advertisements, on the search results page when a Web surfer searches for particular keywords and key phrases. Additionally, keyword marketing involves achieving top placement in the actual search listings themselves (Internet Marketing, 2002). This is known as *search engine optimization* and can be done with metatags or through search engine sponsorship. Metatags are tags in a Web page's source code that are used by many search engines to index and rank pages. Advertisers' understanding of how consumers use and search for information on the Web can help determine the best words to use in metatags.

Search engine sponsorships tend to be paid placement, when advertisers buy a specific position in search results. Many search engines will refer to paid placements with euphemisms such as "featured links" or "partner sites." Another option is known as a *paid inclusion*, which is a situation when the search engine will review and index a Web page that pays for inclusion on a timelier basis than other Web pages. This allows the most up-to-date information to be available for indexing. In some cases, then, search engine sponsorships will "outrank" any Web sites that have not paid for sponsorship.

Regulation of the Internet

Despite the fact that many users think that WWW stands for Wild, Wild Web, several different groups are involved with regulation of the Internet in general and with its advertising content in particular. Like traditional advertising, regulation of the Internet is overseen by a number of groups, including the Federal Trade Commission (FTC) and various self-regulatory groups.

The FTC

Of any group based in the United States, the FTC is currently the most involved in regulating advertising messages online, specifically on the World Wide Web. Given their mission to protect against false or misleading advertising, the FTC doubled efforts in late 2001 to address online companies that intentionally or negligently mislead the public (Wood, 2002). According to the FTC, all laws and regulations applicable to print, television and radio commercials, and telemarketing apply to the Internet as well.

The FTC requires that all claims made in online commercial messages be supported by evidence, and all information of pertinence must be provided to consumers. All specific product or service claims require disclosure. For example, online computer retailers must list each component of a computer system, the entire cost, shipping and handling, and delivery date whenever a system is advertised (Wood, 2002). Additionally, the placement of such components is important: Disclosures should be close to the body of the advertisement or the commercial message and on the same page if possible. Hyperlinks should point to disclosures that are not on the same page as the advertised message, and they must be easy for online consumers to find. In addition, online marketers must not include graphics or other devices that could visually distract from the disclosure.

The FTC also evaluates unfair messages online. One particular area that they have been involved with evaluates unfair online service promotions—specifically, "free" services that are not really free. Recently, for example, the Internet service providers Juno and Gateway were sanctioned because they ran online ads that featured an offer of 150 free hours of Internet access for users who signed up for their services. However, the messages did not include the stipulation that all 150 hours had to be used during the first month of service. New subscribers had to spend an average of 5 hours a day online to get the full benefit of these offers. Other Internet service providers have advertised offers that were unfair, such as dial-up access via an 800 number that was not free to all customers (e.g., rural customers had to pay $3.95 per hour for 800-line access) (Wood, 2002). The FTC seeks to have ISPs correct such offers with full disclosure of particulars, and it may seek compensation or redress for consumers who were materially harmed by such messages.

Finally, the FTC is involved in online privacy protection initiatives. The collection and dissemination of personal information by online advertisers and marketers have been a great concern among online consumers. The FTC encourages all online entities that collect personally identifiable information to provide notice that the information is being collected, give consumers the choice to not have information collected, explain how the information is used, allow consumers to review the collected information, and provide the opportunity for consumer redress when appropriate. The FTC monitors online advertisers' privacy policies that spell out a company's policy for information collection and usage. In addition, the FTC has recently announced new privacy initiatives, including enhancing enforcement against online chain letters and other spam, and monitoring the development of the Platform for Privacy Preferences, a technology enabling consumers to specify privacy preferences electronically and screen out sites that do not meet them (Federal Trade Commission, 2002).

Current Laws

The Children's Online Privacy Protection Act (COPPA)

The collection and dissemination of information are a great concern to the FTC. There are special concerns with children online, specifically with regard to the collection of information. The Children's Online Privacy Protection Act (COPPA) went into effect in April 2000 and requires Web site operators to obtain parental permission before collecting any type of personal information from children under the age of 13. The law requires that the type of permission obtained depends on the actual use of the information. For example, if a child's information is only going to be used by the entity collecting it, an e-mail from a parent or guardian providing permission is sufficient. If the child's information is going to be shared with third parties, more detailed and verified information, such as a fax with a photo identification, is required from parents and guardians (Children's Online Privacy Protection Act of 1998, 1998).

Antispam Laws

Although no national law regulates unsolicited e-mail, individual states have addressed online users' concerns with spam. In California, for instance, a 1999 law gives Internet service providers the explicit power to pursue spammers in court. This law allows ISPs to sue spammers for $50 per e-mail, up to a total of $250,000 per day (Amis, 1998). There are similar antispam laws in Virginia, Washington, North Carolina, and Connecticut. The Washington law, for example, prohibits unsolicited e-mail that advertises consumer products with a false or misleading subject line or return address. If you have ever tried to respond to a spam to have your name taken off the list and have the message bounce back to you, you may realize how valuable such laws can be.

Self-Regulation

Several industry groups provide guidelines for online advertisers and marketers. The Direct Marketing Association (DMA), for example, maintains mail and telephone preference services that allow consumers to remove their names from lists and is highly involved with legitimizing the use of unsolicited commercial e-mail (Samoriski, 2002). The DMA provides information to advertisers and marketers as to what are appropriate and inappropriate uses of e-mail. The Interactive Advertising Bureau (IAB) is a not-for-profit association dedicated to maximizing the effects of Internet advertising. The IAB established minimum acceptable privacy guidelines for members, which mirror the FTC's core principles.

Intended Effects

Like any other type of advertising, online advertising has intended effects that can lead to possible unintended effects. Here are some intended effects of online advertising.

Support of Free Content

Although some people advocate that the Internet should be free, most realize that to support the infrastructure and the amount of information content available to those with Internet access, it is necessary to have a commercial Internet. Advertisements help many Web sites finance themselves, ensuring that much of the information available on the Internet remains free (Amis, 1998). Given this ability to provide financial support for the Web, a recent study showed that 72% of online users were not opposed to certain types of advertisements, as long as they were not overexposed to them (Hallerman, 2002).

Efficient Targeting

The Web offers a wide range of content and activity choices. Advertisers have the ability to collect a level of aggregate data on Web site visitors. These two aspects suggest that it is quite possible to reach numbers of consumers who are likely to be interested in a specific product or service and not to reach other consumers who may not be interested. Visitors to a travel Web site, like expedia.com, will be greeted by advertisements for small companies like Palace Hotels, which they will rarely see at other places. Such an ad would cost about what a small local newspaper ad would cost. This makes advertising online efficient for many companies that may not be able to afford a national presence otherwise.

Ads Break Through Clutter

With so much content available to online visitors, online users sometimes suffer from information overload. To break through the huge amounts of information, advertising and otherwise, new advertising units are constantly being developed, tested, and utilized. Many people were surprised at the success of pop-unders (Neuborne, 2001a): X10, a company that promoted the use of pop-unders, was recently the fourth most visited site on the Web, with more visitors than Amazon or eBay. When Web site mypoints.com put a pop-under at the *New York Times* Web site, traffic increased by 66% (Neuborne, 2001a). Even though people complain about online advertising, advertisers recognize that people notice the ads (Hallerman, 2002).

Branding Power

Branding works by creating awareness and a shared emotional commitment to a product or service (Crowell, 2001). Banner advertisements, specifically those using so-called rich media, including audio, video, and Flash, conclusively increase branding effectiveness according to a recent study by the Internet Advertising Bureau. Although 99% of banner ads are never clicked, brand awareness increases for brands advertising with banner ads. Indeed, it has been suggested that traditional banner ads boost brand awareness by 56%, and larger ads boost awareness by 86%.

Unintended Effects

Banner Blindness

Online advertisements are intrusive and annoying to many people. Some advertisers are desperate to find something that works, and they use too many bells and whistles that interrupt consumers' reading, affect consumers' information comprehension, and may ultimately crash users' computers. Additionally, some online users receive constant exposure to the same ads. All these situations lead to the phenomenon of banner blindness, which is the tendency of Web visitors to ignore banner ads, even when banners contain information visitors are actively seeking (Internet Marketing, 2002).

Banner blindness may transfer other online messages. For example, a recent study by Forrester Research saw that consumer interest in e-mail had declined greatly over a 1-year period. Although more than half of respondents thought e-mail was a great way to find out about products and services in 2000, by 2001 almost 40% of respondents said they delete them without reading them (Neuborne, 2001b). The increasing frequency of pop-ups and pop-unders is also irritating consumers, some of whom automatically delete them (Hespos, 2001b).

This may ultimately damage any branding that banner advertisements or other messages might be able to accomplish. Any type of irritation that leads to banner blindness may have the effect of providing negative branding (Grebb, 2001b).

Consumers Feel Misled by Trick Ads

Remember the Chinese Wall from Chapter 3? Well, online, the Chinese Wall is made of Jell-O. Online, it is very difficult for consumers to determine what information is meant to be objective and what information is meant to be persuasive because both types of messages can often be mixed on a single Web page. One particular category of banner ads is highly misleading. These are known as "trick banners" since they try to overcome banner blindness by disguising the fact that they are advertising devices.

Typically, the trick banner makes no mention of the advertiser but can look like an operating system, a game, a dialogue box, or a popular application. While it is common for trick banners to attract a higher-than-average CTR, the quality of the clicks may be somewhat suspect, as visitors are likely to hit the Back button once they realize what is happening. Aside from CTR, there is the issue of visitor satisfaction—or lack thereof. Visitors may feel ill will toward a site that tricked them and may decide not to return. Examples of trick banners can be found at http://www.apromotionguide.com/banexamp11.html.

Credibility of Search Engines Is Compromised

Consumers also feel misled by sponsorship on Web search engines, which damages the credibility of this important Internet application. Recently, Ralph Nader's group Consumer Alert filed a complaint with the FTC against Web search engines that accept paid placements (Sherman, 2001). Sponsorship issues have also been problematic at retailers like amazon.com, where it recently became evident that publishers paid for placement within Amazon's own search engine (The Search Engine Report, 1999). In Amazon.com's case, publishers were paying up to $10,000 for featured treatment on the site. Content partnerships are at many different sites but are especially problematic at retailers who have developed a reputation for independence from larger offline presence (Reuters, 1999).

Advertisements Slow Down the Process

The presence of online advertising slows the computing process because it pinches bandwidth by clogging a computer's Web pipeline (Hallerman, 2002). However, using software to filter out messages may not be the best solution to this specific problem because filtering out advertising messages also consumes bandwidth (Raz, 2002).

Invasion of Privacy

As discussed earlier, the interactive nature of the Internet allows for the collection of information on an individual level that is used by many advertisers and content providers to develop aggregate information for target audience visitor profiles. Some content providers collect and sell an individual's information without the consent of the Web site visitor. These data are collected via registration, online surveys, purchases, and guest books. Information may be collected by a technique called *cookies*, which are information files placed by a Web site on a visitor's computer.

Online users are concerned about the secretive nature of information collection, the type of information collected, and how the information is used beyond the purpose for which it is originally collected. Such practices are not limited only to Web sites. Many Web sites belong to the Double Click network, a giant advertising network where participating Web sites receive banner ads from Double Click, which in turn sells the space on the network to advertisers. This makes it easier for advertisers to place banners ads since they do not have to contract with Web sites individually. A policy called *cookie synchronization* allows Web sites to share information associated with them across all of the sites that are part of the Double Click network. Therefore, if you give your name to one Web site associated with the Double Click network, you are virtually giving it to all the Web sites.

If consumers do not know that information is being collected, they also do not know how to opt out and keep information from being collected. We choose to give information at certain Web sites because of what we get in return. If consumers do not believe that they are getting anything in return from companies like Double Click, it is unlikely that consumers believe information is being treated fairly.

Cost Issues

The business model of the Internet suggests that receivers have to pay for the reception of content, be it Web pages, e-mail, or the like. Obviously, if you are paying your ISP for every minute you spend online, you are paying for the time it takes to receive advertising. It takes time and money to write and maintain filters or to buy filtering software (Raz, 2002). Internet service providers must purchase the equipment to create the space used to handle online traffic and they pass these costs on to us. Very few ISPs are truly free: Even if you receive access through your school, you may be charged a technology fee for the privilege, or the costs are reflected in other areas.

Doing Online Advertising

Anyone thinking about doing an online advertising campaign should not proceed with the idea that anything goes. Anything most definitely does not go, and ignoring legal and professional guidelines about appropriate advertising could generate ill will among many different groups.

First, keep in mind that unauthorized use of private property is trespass. The use of the Internet's resources is a privilege given to people who pay for it and respect the ownership and rights of the people, companies, and governments that built the Internet. To address issues of privacy online, all companies having a presence on the Web should develop an information privacy policy that addresses the five core principles of the FTC.

This policy should be posted on the Web site, with a clear navigation bar for visitors to find it. As part of the policy, you should ask permission to use the information that is collected about individuals, regardless of where you collect that information. Additionally, take the opportunity to educate your customers about their privacy rights. An informed consumer base will help maintain self-regulation. You should also investigate the range of "seal" programs that provide consumer recourse and assurance that your Web site has good information protection practices. The three major seal programs, all with easy-to-find Web sites, are BBB Online, TrustE, and VeriSign (Figure 16.3).

In terms of creating advertising messages that are effective, remember to be interactive and use high-quality images, but do not provide so many bells and whistles that you overload consumers' computers, many of which (at this writing) cannot handle music and full-motion video. Consider how frequently you expose consumers to messages that direct people to your Web site as well as the type of content that you provide at your site. Opt in generates more goodwill than opt out (Grebb, 2001b).

The Future

The Internet is still a very new medium, and so it is anticipated that it will experience tremendous change in the next few years. Currently at the top of the list of questions to address include First Amendment issues with regard to unsolicited e-mail, the legality of ad-blocking software, and the government's role in privacy regulation.

First Amendment Interpretations

Yes, unsolicited e-mail is annoying, and you may strongly dislike it. However, unsolicited commercial e-mail, or spam, may be a form of commercial speech that is protected by the First Amendment. Thus, any restrictions legislated by individual states, as discussed earlier, may be in violation of the First Amendment. Samoriski (2002) suggests that "any legislative restriction or content-based restrictions on unsolicited commercial e-mail must meet the test for commercial speech to be constitutional" (p. 125). The American Civil Liberties Union has recently indicated that advertisers should have the right to send any type of unsolicited commercial e-mail until recipients request that it stop.

The argument against First Amendment protection suggests that advertisers do not have protection because they are passing the cost of advertising from the advertiser to the recipient of the e-mail. Additionally, Internet and network service providers view the overwhelming number of e-mails as causing harm to their own businesses and think the spam should be fined so that the practice becomes unprofitable. Several lower courts have ruled that the First Amendment

Figure 16.3 Seal programs ensure consumer privacy rights are protected online.

Figure 16.3 Continued

does not provide a sender with the right to inundate unwilling recipients with his or her message (Sorkin, 2001). They have also written that advertisers have no right to force speech into the home of an unwilling listener (Sorkin, 2001). In the future, then, we may see more formalized processes for creating a national opt-out list of individuals who do not wish to receive spam, similar to lists of people who do not want to receive phone calls from telemarketers.

Ad-Blocking Software

Ad-blocking software is just what it says: software that keeps advertisements (specifically banner advertisements) from being displayed during the download of an advertising-supported site. Even though many online users experience banner blindness, there is still a demand to physically keep advertisements off sites. Supporters of ad-blocking software say that banner advertisements, particularly large banner ads such as skyscrapers, slow download times significantly (Hespos, 2001a).

Opponents view ad-blocking software as tantamount to stealing. Blocking software is a threat to the ad-supported model for publishing Web content (Hespos, 2001a). Thus, owners of ad-blocking software who view content without ads are enjoying the benefit of the content that is funded with advertiser dollars. Moreover, since online users have to buy the software, they are paying money to third-party software developers who have no real claim to any revenue that stems from publisher-consumer relationships (Hespos, 2001a). Such software can threaten the livelihood of a wide range of content sites. In response, some content providers are denying Web-site access to individuals running blocking software. If this trend continues, we may see a shift from an advertising-supported model to a subscription model.

Some see this issue as boiling down to a question of clutter. When excessive amounts of a Web page are taken up with advertising, slow downloads may force away as many viewers as the number of viewers who are blocking ads. Publishers should consider limiting the number of ads on any given page.

Government's Role in Privacy Protection

Of all areas, the government is most likely to become involved in privacy protection online and enact legislation to limit data collection practices by online advertisers. Numerous groups, including representatives from the Electronic Privacy Information Center, have testified before Congress that federal law, not self-regulation, must govern online profiling by Web advertisers.

In response, online advertisers promise to develop stronger self-regulatory practices. The Internet Advertising Bureau's privacy guidelines require full disclosure to online users; that is, member companies must disclose what information is being collected, how information is used, and the choices online users have about the data collection process. Companies are also required to report third-party distribution of personal information. However, such guidelines are voluntary and not enforceable.

The Internet is a work in progress and as such is volatile not only to changes in technology but also to changes in the world at large. We have seen that world events, such as the September 11 terrorist attacks, reorganize industry priorities in terms of privacy.

Summary

This chapter examined the current state of the art of Internet advertising. Many online users complain about the frequency, intrusiveness, and clutter of online advertising, but research has shown that online advertising in all its many forms can help build brand image among selected consumers. The ever-changing nature of technology and the new applications continually being devised make it difficult for both advertisers and policymakers to keep up with the best way to advertise online.

17

Advertising

Agencies, Values, and the Commons' Dilemma

The morality of an act is a function of the state of the system at the time it is performed.

—J. Fletcher

At the start of the new millennium, the advertising industry is facing a range of challenges. At a recent meeting of the American Association of Advertising Agency's 2002 management conference, organization chairman Brendan Ryan told colleagues that he was worried that respect for and in the advertising industry is not high (Elliott, 2002a). Clients respect work less and less, and consumers rated advertising professionals well below lawyers, auto mechanics, and members of Congress. Ryan blamed this lack of respect on pressures for short-term earnings, pressures from being companies that were publicly traded, and clients' pressures in both these areas. Additionally, he found an industrywide shift from friendly competition and mutual respect to disregard for rivals as highly damaging. Specifically, pressures to get and keep new business cause agencies to treat other agencies with a lack of respect (Elliott, 2002a). Advertising with a short-term focus may also use questionable messages and imagery to break through the clutter, and to register with consumers, occasionally with detrimental effects.

These pressures all can lead to any, if not all, of the issues that we have discussed throughout this book. A short-term focus can lead to the use of stereotyped images to find ways to "move the needle" quickly. Agencies may try to produce eccentric and bizarre commercials to attract attention and win awards, which could lead to new business wins. In tough financial times, agencies may take on projects for clients that in other situations may be ill advised. As we have mentioned throughout the book, advertising is about choices: choices made by an individual in the development of an advertising campaign, choices made by agencies regarding their corporate philosophies and their client lists, and choices made by consumers when focusing on different types of messages. The choices made by agencies and their employees are the focus of this chapter.

Agency reactions to today's pressures can be characterized as a "commons' dilemma": a phenomenon in which members of a specific group (e.g., advertisers) face choices in which selfish, individualistic, or uncooperative decisions seem rational by virtue of short-term benefits, yet produce undesirable long-term consequences for the group as a whole. The idea of the commons' dilemma was outlined in an article "The Tragedy of the Commons" (Hardin, 1968), and the title is an expression you might have heard before. In the article, Hardin looked at the role technology plays in our lives. He suggested that many groups rely on technical solutions to various problems, and if we only look to science and technology to solve problems, the result will be to worsen the situations.

Hardin's ideas about the commons' dilemma can be interpreted in simpler terms in that the choices made by individuals working in advertising can have repercussions that go beyond a single ad campaign. Specifically, an individual's choices will affect advertising's interactions with society as a whole. Each individual is responsible for making the best choices possible so that we as a society do not suffer the tragedy of the commons. Stated differently, the advertising industry should be responsible for avoiding long-term negative consequences for society as a whole

Putting Into Practice

Throughout this book, we have tried to provide workable solutions and techniques to address the issues discussed in each of the chapters. As a way of providing some more "global" ideas to put into practice, we turn to Scott Bedbury and his wonderful book *A New Brand World*. In this book, Bedbury provided seven core values that all brands should pay attention to in the years ahead (Bedbury, 2002). The seven core values are

1. Simplicity

2. Patience

3. Relevance

4. Accessibility

5. Humanity

6. Omnipresence

7. Innovation

The values on this list just as easily apply to how advertisers and advertising agencies should approach the creation and dissemination of advertising messages, and we discuss each of these in turn.

Simplicity

Simplicity involves having a single focus that is not cluttered by extraneous words, images, symbols, and the like. According to Bedbury, simplicity is important because too many brands strive to be everything to everyone, and it is virtually impossible for many brands to meet that goal. This is seen most frequently when brands seek to compete in every available market segment and provide distinctive messages to each target segment. This results in confused messages about the brand among consumers, which can damage the brand in the long term because consumers will have no idea what the brand stands for.

For advertising, simplicity means focusing on the attributes of a brand that will appeal to a single target market. It also means developing a clear and concise message that will communicate the attributes in a meaningful way to the members of the target. It suggests that advertisers realize that they face time and space constraints in their advertising executions and thus must find ways to register ideas quickly with the target.

Simplicity leads advertisers to use recognizable symbols to tell stories. Arguably, the use of stereotypical imagery is one attempt to simplify the communication process.

Simplicity is not taking the easy way out and using the same symbols that you have always used or that others have used before you. It does not require a 180-degree change but rather a subtle change that adds depth and complexity to the symbols you use. It can be as simple as taking the homemaker out of the kitchen and putting her or him at a volunteer stream cleanup. The secret to simplicity is in understanding your specific target audience and in identifying the essential symbols and language that will resonate most closely with them.

The Master Card ad (Figure 17.1) is an excellent example to illustrate the concept of simplicity. It quickly illustrates the results of the adoption of a desired behavior: what will happen if consumers use their Master Card. It also connects a simple image with a simple headline. The intriguing feature of this ad is that the headline attracts attention quickly, yet the payoff is a surprise.

Patience

Patience involves respecting the amount of time it takes for a brand to develop. Bedbury suggests that every brand develops at its own unique pace, and the actual amount of time depends on the overall goals of the

Figure 17.1 This Master Card ad presents a simple message in a concise yet surprising way.

brand. Great brands take a long time to develop, and as Bedbury (2002) warns, "speed is not as important as arriving safely" (p. 58).

Many brands are trying to aggressively increase sales in a short period of time: 3 months, 6 months, or 1 year. Such brands that are trying to move the needle quickly may use advertising techniques that shock or in some other way quickly draw attention to the brand. Yet, although such messages may meet short-term goals, long-term goals with regard to branding become compromised. Specifically, controversial aspects of the advertising message may pass on to the brand itself. Think about brands that use shocking images like Benetton or FCUK: Do we think of them as fashionable brands, or do we think of them as brands with fashionable advertising?

For advertisers, it is important to think about both short- and long-term goals of the brand. It is also important to look at what consumers want, both in the short term and in the long term (Schudson, 1984). Yes, a consumer needs a shampoo to wash his hair tomorrow. However, he is also perhaps looking for a long-term relationship with a brand he can continually trust throughout his life.

The Bombay Sapphire ads (Figure 17.2a and 17.2b) illustrate the idea of patience in several ways. The ads are beautifully designed and very subtle, connecting the idea of sophistication with the product. The more print ads that an individual sees, the stronger the association between the product and sophistication.

Relevance

Relevance is the match of the brand's values to those of consumers. Bedbury (2002) uses the example of one-to-one marketing to describe the increased importance of relevance of the brand to consumers. He points to the increase in the number of customizable products that are available today, which he attributes in part to the growth of the Internet and its ability to collect individual-level information about consumers.

Obviously, one-to-one customizable advertising would be labor intensive and difficult to achieve outside the Internet. Relevance in advertising terms,

Figure 17.2 These ads for Bombay Sapphire feature glassware created by artists and architects.

though, means again going back to consumers and looking at what is important to them. Schudson acknowledges that all advertising serves an information function that helps consumers make rational consumer judgments. Schudson (1984) states that "Even when advertising is not very informative, it provides a modest form of consumer protection, providing consumers some knowledge of the availability of products and so making them less dependent on the local retailer" (p. 239). Therefore, understanding what consumers consider relevant will help advertising be more meaningful for consumers. Even if a minimal amount of information is provided, a relevant image that is unique from other images in advertising can do much to register the brand in the consumer's mind.

The advertisement for Havana Joe shoes (Figure 17.3) can be considered relevant in that it taps into individuals' reactions to the stresses of daily life. Ten people (including an elderly couple and a Hispanic family) are waiting for a bus at the side of a country road. The headline reads "resting never hurt anybody." The tag line, "Go for it," is a twist on other tag lines exhorting athletes to "just do it."

Accessibility

Bedbury (2002) suggests that consumers want to directly connect with brands and with people who are familiar with the brands. Consumers want to know that there are individuals who can help them make purchase

Figure 17.3 Havana Joe shoes encourages consumers to slow down.

decisions. The personal aspect of such communication is becoming increasingly important today, when many individuals feel disconnected due to distance from family and friends and the increased use of technology in our lives.

Again, accessibility as defined by Bedbury (2002) seems separate from the mass-mediated aspect of advertising communication. However, the accessibility of advertising to a large number of diverse consumers has specific benefits. Schudson suggests that advertising has a socially democratizing influence: Let people who are not in-the-know be in-the-know. Distribution of consumer goods is much more egalitarian than the distribution of wealth, and it is the accessibility of advertising messages that does this (Schudson, 1984).

This suggests that advertising messages should serve as a base for all other types of communication associated with the brand. Marketers should look to their advertising agencies for help in developing consistency in the tone of brand messages. The best way to develop this consistency is through advertising that is focused and that understands not only the consumer but also the basic values of the company and the brand. These important core values should be communicated across every aspect of the company. Accessibility will then work hand in hand with relevance, as messages seek to match what the brand has with what consumers can relate to.

Chevy Malibu makes the connection between the company's values and the values of consumers with the simple statement "just like you, we'll be there." In one ad, copy talks about how dads depend on cars with all the "right stuff" to take care of their obligations. A strong visual of a man and his child that underscores the importance of this value to the company and to the consumers.

Humanity

Bedbury (2002) suggests that brands should convey human values whenever they can. This seems a natural outgrowth of the discussion thus far, but it deserves special repeating in the context of humanity. Bedbury suggests that companies must not only stand for specific values but must also show compassion. Companies are increasingly being judged on widely accepted moral obligations. It is important that companies and their brands should not have intent to harm any consumers and citizens of the world.

In Chapter 15, we discussed socially responsible advertising and the importance of connecting the values of the company to the values of the cause that the company planned to collaborate with. The idea of humanity suggests that all brands and companies should think about the values for which they stand and find ways to connect these values with product information to create messages that relate to the target audience. This connection is important because, according to Schudson (1984), the most offensive advertising tends to have the least information content.

The values that the advertising promotes should be values that you can personally affirm. In effect, they are not the values that the company wants to have, but the values that the company truly has. An excellent example that transcends its advertising is S.C. Johnson, which uses the tag line "A Family Company" in all its advertising (Figure 17.4). This tag line suggests the humanity of this very large company because the words *a family company* can be interpreted in a number of ways. It not only suggests that the company's products are good for families, but it also suggests that people who work for S.C. Johnson are treated like family.

Omnipresence

Today, advertising is not only in the traditional mass media vehicles such as television, radio, magazines, and newspapers but also, as we have discussed, in media such as feature films and the Internet. The past decade has seen the rise (and occasional fall) of advertising messages on the back of bathroom doors, on parking meters, and inside the holes on golf courses.

While advertising will continue to support traditional mass media, advertisers and marketers continue to look for ways to get their persuasive messages to break through the clutter. Critics have suggested that many consumers feel assaulted by the vast number of advertising messages that they are exposed to in a single day. Bedbury (2002) states that marketing détente might be achieved if advertisers can select venues or programs that are genuinely relevant to the brand, its values, and the message that it is trying to communicate to consumers. At its simplest, it suggests that messages for

Figure 17.4 S.C. Johnson uses the tag line "A Family Company" on all their advertising and promotional materials.

sports drinks like Gatorade are appropriate and messages for cigarettes are inappropriate at sports venues. At its most complex, it is evaluating the range of meanings that can be derived from a single advertisement and assessing target audience reactions to each of those meanings.

Innovation

Bedbury (2002) writes that advertisers and marketers place a lot of value on the ability to continually innovate and develop new products, services, and revenue streams. Recently, it seems that business transforms itself rather than moves ahead in increments. Fast-food retailers, for example, have moved beyond traditional offerings like hamburgers and now sell salads, wraps, and pita bread sandwiches.

For advertisers, innovation means not settling for the old ways of doing things. This does not mean that the lessons we have learned from a century or more of advertising practice should be thrown away. Instead, we should respect the old ways of doing things yet transform them for specific products and targets and for the current situation in society. The Milk Board's "Got Milk?" campaign is a great example of a campaign that has been around for a long time yet continues to reinvent itself with whimsy and humor. One of the most recent ads features Aerosmith band founder, Steven Tyler, promoting the benefits of milk to people over the age of 35 who are concerned about bone loss (Figure 17.5).

How do we avoid the tragedy of the commons? As we have discussed throughout this book, much of advertising innovation is in making traditional symbols and stereotypes fresh and new by finding ways to portray people and situations in a new light that resonates with the target audiences. We have warned you that this won't be easy, but it is one of the best ways to present advertising that is interesting and relevant and to create persuasive messages that sell your product.

Agencies and Advertising

As you begin your career in this business, you will probably be eager to find work at an agency, and you may not spend time thinking about the type of agency you are going to work for. All agencies are different, and it is important to work for an agency with a value system that matches yours and that is committed to doing good work. One way to find out about an agency is by learning about the individuals who are in charge of agency and by reading the agency's mission statement.

In terms of leadership, look for agencies and organizations with leaders who believe in good advertising. Read interviews with the individuals and try to see what their approaches are to advertising and advertising's role in society. Try to learn what types of value systems they hold and how these values are connected with the agency's work. Most advertising agencies have mission statements, and you should read these statements for clues as to the agency's orientation to its work and to the people who produce the work. Does the agency put the client, and the client's and brand's success, foremost? If so, that is one sign that the agency believes in work that can be good for society. If agencies value more intrinsic goals, such as winning awards, they may be less client oriented and more focused on doing advertising that will get them noticed and publicized. This work may be good and win awards, but it may not be as good for the client if winning awards is not one of the client's goals.

You should look for agencies that are committed to the process and the value of advertising in general, noting that advertising and agencies will always have some degree of conflict with society. Nicosia (1974) wrote,

Figure 17.5 Steven Tyler, in this milk ad, suggests that milk can "make your bones rock hard."

> There will always be differences between the points of view of an individual or an organization and the points of view of society. The history of Western civilizations is essentially a search for a balance between the individual's and the group's interests. This search resembles a pendulum continuously swinging from one extreme to the other, but never coming to a point of rest. (p. 355)

Look for agencies that will recognize and participate in the debate, not merely ignore it or downplay it. Some of this will go back to the agency's view of consumers, as we discussed in the first part of this book. Does the agency approach consumers as active and involved participants in the advertising process or as passive vessels to be filled with a message? Does the agency approach consumers in a way that you, yourself, would like to be treated? Look at the agency's orientation toward research because agencies that approach consumers in an empathic and positive way will likely value and respect the role of research.

Finally, you should recognize that the pendulum's swing, as described by Nicosia, is one that you will occasionally experience in your advertising life. During these times, it is good to remember Schudson's words:

> Advertising is but one factor among many in shaping consumer choice and human values. The question, ultimately, is not one of how people independently arrive at a set of desires. Desires are never independently arrived at, but are socially constructed. The important question is what social conditions will be most conducive to autonomous, rational choice. What is the sum of the influence of advertising, family, school, government policy, and the promotional efforts of private industries on personal values?(1984, p. 241)

As an advertiser, you are responsible, to the best of your ability, for trying to understand how all these social conditions are influencing consumers and their choices.

Conclusion

Advertising can have an influence on individuals in our society and works alongside other types of marketing communications to persuade consumers to adopt certain behaviors. Sometimes it works, and advertised products and services are successes, which helps the economic wheels of our country to turn. Sometimes the advertising does not work, and products fail. Other symptoms of advertising not working have been discussed throughout this book: an overreliance on a consumer culture, a feeling of disenfranchisement among groups that are seen as unimportant to advertisers, clutter in our environment, and the promotion of products and services that may be unhealthy or dangerous to certain groups.

What we hope to achieve with this book is to alert current and future advertisers of the range of choices available and to encourage you to consider the ramifications of each and every choice that you make. Choice is one of advertising's strongest tools; choice gives us the ability to create advertising that is not only effective but that we can be proud of. In our society today, we are overwhelmed with choices and sometimes make expedient decisions to save time as well as to simplify our lives. In advertising, though, we should make choices that help simplify the messages and make them clearer for consumers, even if this process of assessing the impacts of our choices is a complex and time-consuming one. It can only serve to improve individual advertising and the advertising industry in America today.

Bibliography

AARP. (2000). *Are consumers well informed about prescription drugs? The impact of printed direct-to-consumer advertising.* Retrieved February 13, 2003, fromhttp://research.aarp.org/health/2000%5f04%5fadvertising.html

Abelson, R. (1991). Product bans and controversies. *FDA Consumer, 25*(8), 10.

Adams, G. R., & Crossman, S. M. (1978). *Physical attractiveness: A cultural perspective.* New York: Libra.

Adler, R. (1996). Stereotypes won't work with seniors anymore. *Advertising Age, 67*(46), 32.

Adler, R., Lesser, G. S., Meringoff, L. K, Robertson, T. S., Rossiter, J. R., & Ward, S. (1980). *The effects of television advertising on children.* Lexington, MA: Lexington Books.

Ahrens, F. (2002, March 13). *In TV's numbers game, youth trumps ratings.* Retrieved May 10, 2002, from http://www.washingtonpost.com/ac2/wp-dyn? pagename=article&node=&contentId=A16935-2002Mar12&notFound=true

Aiken, K. J. (2002, October). *Direct to consumer advertising of prescription drugs: Current issues.* Paper presented at the Advertising Club of New York.

Albiniak, P. (2002, February 11). For 2002, the buck starts here. *Broadcasting and Cable,* p. 6.

Alexander, D., & Dichter, A. (2002). *Ads and kids: How young is too young?* Retrieved April 13, 2002, from http://www.mediachannel.org/atissue/ consumingkids/

American Academy of Child and Adolescent Psychology. (2001). *Obesity in children and teens.* Retrieved May 2, 2002, from http://www.aacap.org/publi-cations/factsfam/79.htm

American Academy of Pediatrics. (1995). Children, adolescents and advertising (RE9504). *Pediatrics, 95*(2), 295–297.

American Advertising Federation. (1999). *Position statements.* Retrieved April 10, 2003, from http://www.aaf.org/government/position_bans.html

American Advertising Foundation and American Advertising Federation. (2003). *Principles and recommended practices for effective advertising in the American multicultural marketplace.* Retrieved March 10, 2002, from http://www.aaf. org/multi/principles.pdf

American Council on Science and Health. (2000). *Physicians and scientists agree that moderate alcohol use, unlike tobacco use, can benefit health.* Retrieved April 14, 2003, from http://www.acsh.org/press/releases/comparison061600. html

Amis, D. (1998, November 24). *Freedom of speech, advertising, and the Internet.* Retrieved February 19, 2002, from http://www.netfreedom.org/news.asp? item=19

Andersen, A. E., & DiDomenico, L. (1992). Diet vs. shape content of popular male and female magazines: A close response relationship to the incidence of eating disorders? *International Journal of Eating Disorders, 11*, 283–287.

Ansolabehere, S., & Iyengar, S. (1995). *Going negative: How political advertisements shrink and polarize the electorate.* New York: Free Press.

Armstrong, K. L. (1999). Nike's communication with black audiences. *Journal of Sport & Social Issues, 23*(3), 266–286.

Armstrong, L., & Mallory, M. (1992, June 23). The diet business starts sweating. *BusinessWeek*, pp. 22–23.

Arthur, I. (1995). *Make love not war.* Bombay, India: Hindustan Thompson.

Artze, I. (2000, March). Targeting Hispanic consumers. *Hispanic, 13*, 30–31.

Ashmore, R. D., & Soloman, M. R. (1996). Thinking about fashion models' looks: A multidimensional approach to the structure of perceived physical attractiveness. *Personality & Social Psychology Bulletin, 22*(11), 1083–1105.

Associated Press. (1995, August 22). *AP poll: Most would not snuff out tobacco advertising and promotion.* Retrieved April 10, 2003, from http://www.kickbutt.org/learn/ads2.html

Associated Press. (2001, March 10). FCC drops inquiry into "RATS." Ad. Retrieved April 14, 2003, from http://www.newstribune.com/stories/031001/wor_0310010018.asp

Associated Press. (2002). Limits for campaign finances. Retrieved April 5, 2002, from http://www.CNN.com/

Avery, R. J., & Ferraro, R. (2000). Verisimilitude or advertising? Brand appearances on prime-time television. *Journal of Consumer Affairs, 34*(2), 217–244.

Bagdikian, B. (1983). *The media monopoly.* Boston: Beacon.

Bailey, W. T., Harrell, D. R., & Anderson, L. E. (1993). The image of middle-aged and older women in magazine advertisements. *Educational Gerontology, 19*, 97–103.

Baker, C. E. (1976). Commercial speech: A problem in the theory of freedom. *Iowa Law Review, 62*, 1–56.

Baker, M. J., & Churchill, G. A. (1977, November). The impact of physically attractive models on advertising evaluations. *Journal of Marketing Research, 14*, 538–555.

Baker, W. F., & Dessart, G. (1998). *Down the tube.* New York: Basic Books.

Balasubramanian, S. K. (1994). Beyond advertising and publicity: Hybrid messages and public policy issues. *Journal of Advertising, 23*(4), 29–46.

Bamberger, M., Kim, A., & Mravic, M. (2000, October 9). Nothing subliminal about it. *Sports Illustrated, 93*, 28.

Bandyopadhyay, S., Kindra, G., & Sharp, L. (2002). *Is television advertising good for children?* Retrieved January 25, 2002, from the University of Ottawa Web site: http://www.governance.uottawa.ca/english/Publications/Downloads/ Subir/ Tvad2-edit.pdf

Bannan, K. J. (2002, March 5). Companies try a new approach and a smaller screen for product placements: Video games. *New York Times*, p. 6.

Banner, L. W. (1983). *American beauty.* Chicago: University of Chicago Press.

Bass, A. (1994, April 25). Anorexic marketing faces boycott. *Boston Globe*, p. 1.

Bean, L. (2001). Toyota pulls gold-tooth ad, opens dialogue with Jesse Jackson. Retrieved April 14, 2003, from http://www.diversityonline.com/divarch/2001/ aug/0815-1.htm.

Bedbury, S. (2002). *A new brand world.* New York: Viking.

Begeley, S. (2000, November 6). The stereotype trap. *Newsweek, 136,* 66–68.

Belkaoui, A., & Belkaoui, J. (1976). A comparative analysis of roles portrayed by women in print advertisements: 1958, 1970 and 1972. *Journal of Marketing Research, 13,* 168–172.

Belkin, L. (2000, March/April). Primetime pushers. *Mother Jones,* pp. 31–37.

Bell, R. A., Kravitz, R., & Wilkes, M. S. (1999). Direct-to-consumer prescription drug advertising and the public. *Journal of General Internal Medicine, 14*(11), 651–657.

Benetton. (1998). *What we say.* Retrieved January 9, 2002, from http://www.benetton. com/wws/aboutyou/ucdo/index.html

Bercovici, J. (2002). Philip Morris yanks $$ from 80 titles, in big retreat. *Media Life.* Retrieved April 14, 2003, from http://209.61.190.23/news2002/feb02/ feb04/4_thurs/news1thursday.html

Berger, A. A. (2000). *Ads, fads and consumer culture.* Lanham, MD: Rowman and Littlefield.

Better Business Bureau. (2001). *Self-regulatory guidelines for children's advertising.* Retrieved June 10, 2001, from http://www.bbb.org/advertising/caruguid.html

Black Broadcasters' Association. (2002). *Minority ownership report.* Retrieved July 8, 2002, from http://www.thebba.org/NTIA.html

Bloom, P. N., Hussein, P. Y., & Szykman, L. R. (1995). Social marketing. *Marketing Management, 4*(3), 8–12.

Bordo, S. (1993). *Unbearable weight: Feminism, Western culture and the body.* Berkeley: University of California Press.

Bowers, M. (2001, May 18). *Country's founders realized political debate must be free and unfettered.* Retrieved April 5, 2003, from http://atlanta.bizjournals. com/atlanta/stories/2001/05/21/editorial3.html

Brabbs, C. (2000, June 29). Analysis. *Marketing,* p. 27.

Bradley, D. E., & Longino, C. F. (2001). How older people think about images of aging in advertising and media. *Generations, 25,* 17.

Bradway, J. S. (2000, April). *Gender stereotypes and children's television.* Paper presented at the Butte College Mass Media and Society Program, Butte, MT.

Brady, D. (2001, November 8). *Patriotic ads—and minuses.* Retrieved June 4, 2002, from http://www.businessweek.com/bwdaily/dnflash/nov2001/nf2001118_ 7193.htm

Brand, P. Z. (1999, Winter). Beauty matters. *Journal of Aesthetics and Art Criticism, 57*(1), 1–10.

Branscomb, L. (1997). The place of the Internet in national and global information infrastructure. In O'Reilly and Associates (Eds.), *The Harvard Conference on the Internet and society* (pp. 338–352). Cambridge, MA: Harvard University Press.

Brown, H. W., & Barnes, B. E. (2001). Perceptions of advertising influence on broadcast news. *Journalism and Mass Communication Educator, 55*(4), 18–29.

Brown, T. J., & Dacin, P. A. (1997). The company and the product: Corporate associations and consumer product responses. *Journal of Marketing, 61*(1), 68–80.

Brown, W. (2001, October/November). *A deal full of dollars but short on sense.* Retrieved April 4, 2003, from http://www.automag.com/AAOWMagazine/ 2001_octnov/pg42.asp

Bruno, D. (2001, September 6). The Bulgari disconnection. *Christian Science Monitor,* p. 9.

Bunis, D. (2000, February 23). *Direct to you.* Retrieved April 4, 2003, from http://www.salon.com/health/feature/2000/02/23/drug_ads

Burton, S., & Netemeyer, R. G. (1995). Gender differences for appearance-related attitudes and behaviors: Implications for consumer welfare. *Journal of Public Policy and Marketing, 14*(1), 60–75.

Bush, A. J., Smith, R., & Martin, C. (1999). The influence of consumer socialization variables on attitude toward advertising: A comparison of African-Americans and Caucasians. *Journal of Advertising, 28*(3), 13–24.

Butler, R., Lewis, M., & Sunderland, T. (1991). *Aging and mental health: Positive psycho-social and biomedical approaches.* New York: Macmillan.

Cable Advertising Bureau. (2000). *Multicultural marketing resource center.* Retrieved April 6, 2002, from http://www.cab.com

Calfee, J. (1997). *Fear of persuasion: A new perspective on advertising and regulation.* London: Agora.

Calfee, J. (2002). Public policy issues in direct-to-consumer advertising of prescription drugs. *Journal of Public Policy and Marketing, 21*(2), 174–192.

Cameron, G., & Ju-Pak, K.-H. (2000). Information pollution? Labeling and format of advertorials. *Newspaper Research Journal, 21*(1), 12–23.

Cameron, L. (2002). *Evaluating sources of information.* Retrieved November 13, 2001, from the James Madison University Web site: http://www.lib.jmu. edu/library/gold/mod6eval.htm

Campaign for Tobacco Free Kids. (2000). *Big Tobacco shifts ads from billboards to stores.* Retrieved February 11, 2002, from http://www.tobaccofreekids.org

Campbell, K. (2001, September 20). Death of literature? Not just yet. *Christian Science Monitor,* p. 15.

Cantor, J. E. (1997). *Soft and hard money in contemporary elections: What federal law does and does not regulate.* Washington, DC: Center for Responsive Politics.

Carrigan, M., & Szmigin, I. (2000). Advertising in an ageing society. *Ageing and Society, 20*(20), 217–233.

Carver, R. (2001, January 31). *Paid political advertising.* Retrieved January 31, 2001, from http://www.aceproject.org/main/english/me/mec04b.htm

Cebrzynski, G. (2002, February 11). Panda Express lands roles in movies, hit TV show. *Nation's Restaurant News,* p. 6.

Center for Media Education. (1997). *Children and television.* Retrieved January 23, 2002, from http://www.cme.org/children/kids_tv/c_and_t.html

Center for Media Education. (2002). *A field guide to the Children's Television Act.* Retrieved January 25, 2002, from http://www.cme.org/fieldguide.html

Center for Science in the Public Interest. (2001). *National poll shows strong opposition to liquor ads on network television.* Retrieved January 11, 2002, from http://www. cspinet.org/new/oppose_liquorads.html

Chabria, A. (2002, March 25). Revlon will be incorporated into soap opera storyline. *PR Week,* p. 2.

Chafetaz, M. E. (2000, May 20). *Critics who say advertising contributes to alcohol-related problems are way off base.* Retrieved December 10, 2001, from http://www.drkoop.com

Chambers, B. (2002, January 30). *Political advertising.* Retrieved May 14, 2002, from http://216.239.35.100/search?q=cache:q9gGBKmIG4cC:webpages.acs. ttu.edu/barbradl/politicaladvpp.ppt+disclosure+statement+political+advertising& hl=en

Chang, W. H., Park, J.-J., & Shim, S. W. (1998). Effectiveness of negative political advertising. Retrieved April 14, 2003, from http://www.scripps.ohiou.edu/wjmcr/vol02/2-1a.htm

Chaplin, H. (1999). Centrum's self-inflicted silver bullet. *American Demographics, 21*(3), 68–69.

Charatan, F. (2000). US prescription drug sales boosted by advertising. *BMJ: British Medical Journal, 321*(7264), 783.

Chestnut, R. W., LaChance, C. C., & Lubitz, A. (1977). The "decorative" female model: Sexual stimuli and the recognition of advertisements. *Journal of Advertising, 6*(4), 11–14.

Children's Online Privacy Protection Act of 1998, 6501. (1998).

Chocano, C. (2001, May 17). *They give good head.* Retrieved December 3, 2002, from http://archive.salon.com/people/feature/2001/05/17/b_in10nse/

Chura, H. (2000). Coors hikes spending on gay ads. *Advertising Age, 71,* 16.

Chura, H. (2001, November 12). Sweet spot. *Advertising Age, 72,* 1–2.

Clark, E. (1988). *The want makers.* New York: Viking Penguin.

Clark, K. (1953). *The nude: A study in ideal form.* Princeton, NJ: Princeton University Press.

CNN. (1999, February 5). *Study shows black and white viewing habits coming together.* Retrieved January 22, 2002, from the CNN Web site: http://www.cnn.com

CNN. (2002). *Senate approves campaign finance bill.* Retrieved May 6, 2002, from the CNN Web site: http://www.cnn.com/2002/LAW/03/27/campaign.finance.lawsuit/index.html

Coen. (2001, June 11). *Coen's spending totals.* Retrieved March 15, 2002, from http://www.adage.com/page.cms?pageId=454

Courtney, A., & Whipple, T. (1983). *Sex stereotyping in advertising.* Lexington, MA: Lexington Books.

Craig, R. S. (1992). The effect of television day part on gender portrayals in television commercials: A content analysis. *Sex Roles, 26*(5/6), 197–211.

Crain, R. (2001, March 26). Husbands are boys and wives their mothers in the land of ads. *Advertising Age, 72,* 22.

Crawford, C. T., & Graham, W. L. K. (1985). *Cover memo to Omnibus Petition for Regulation of Unfair and Deceptive Alcoholic Beverage Advertising and Marketing Practices* (Vol. Docket No. 209-46, p. 2). Washington, DC: Federal Trade Commission.

Cross, G. (2000). *The all-consuming century: Why commercialism won in modern America.* New York: Columbia University Press.

Crouch, A., & Degelman, D. (1998). Influence of female body images in printed advertising on self-ratings of physical attractiveness by adolescent girls. *Perceptual and Motor Skills, 87*(2), 585–586.

Crowell, G. (2001, May 10). *Banner ads: Defusing the dot-bomb.* Retrieved February 20, 2002, from http://www.workz.com/content/2303.asp

Cuneo, A. (2000). Of contracts and claims: Agencies face liability issues. *Advertising Age, 71,* 25.

Cuneo, A. Z. (2000). Can an agency be guilty of malpractice? *Advertising Age, 71,* 24–25.

Dali, P. W. (1988). Prime-time television portrayals of older adults in the context of family life. *The Gerontologist, 28,* 700–706.

D'Amico, M. F., & Hummel, J. W. (1980, July). *Sex role portrayals in television commercials: 1971, 1976, 1980.* Paper presented at the meeting of the Southern Marketing Association, Urbana-Champaign, IL.

Davis, J. (2000). Riskier than we think? The relationship between risk statement completeness and perceptions of direct-to-consumer advertised prescription drugs. *Journal of Health Communications, 5*(4), 349–370.

Della Femina, J. (1997, March 9). The age boom: A market ignored. *New York Times,* p. 74.

Department of Commerce. (2002). *54% of US now online.* Retrieved April 24, 2002, from the MSNBC Web site: http://www.nua.com/surveys/index.cgi?f=VS&art_id=905357626&rel=true

Dessart, G. (2001). *Standards and practices.* Retrieved January 7, 2002, from http://www.museum.tv/archives/etv/S/htmlS/standardsand/standardsand.htm

Devlin, L. P. (1997). Contrast in presidential campaign commercials of 1996. *American Behavioral Scientist, 40,* 1058–1084.

DiPasquale, C., & Fine, J. (2002). PM: Last call for magazines. *Advertising Age, 73*(5), 1, 31.

Distilled Spirits Council of the United States (1996). *Distillers change advertising code to advance equal treatment.* Available: www.discus.org/mediaroom/1996/prad.htm. Accessed August 5, 2003.

Division of Drug Marketing. (1999, August). *Consumer-directed broadcast advertisements guidance: Questions and answers.* Retrieved July 15, 2002, from the Food and Drug Administration Web site: http://www.fda.gov/cder/guidance/1804q&a.htm

Dobrow, L. (2002). How old is old enough? *Advertising Age, 73*(5), s2.

Dobzynski, J. (2000). *Stereotypes are not evil.* Retrieved April 1, 2002, from http://students.uww.edu/stdorgs/philosophy/mfmoct/page4html

Donaton, S. (2001). Magazines should consider kicking the tobacco habit. *Advertising Age, 72,* 15.

Downs, A. C., & Harrison, S. K. (1985). Embarrassing age spots or just plain ugly? Physical attractiveness stereotyping as an instrument of sexism on American television commercials. *Sex Roles, 13,* 9–19.

DTC Perspectives. (2002). *Interview with Dr. Nancy M. Ostrove.* Retrieved April 17, 2002, from http://www.dtcperspectives.com

Dunn, S. W., & Barban, A. (1986). *Advertising, Its role in modern marketing.* Chicago: Dryden.

Duvert, P., & Foster, R. (1999). *Decoding minority targeted advertisements: A perspective of the representation of blacks in print advertising.* Paper presented at the University of Rochester McNair Program, Rochester, NY.

Dychtwald, K. (1988). *The challenges and opportunities of an aging America.* Los Angeles: Tarcher.

Dyson, A., & Turco, D. (2002). *The state of celebrity endorsement in sport.* Retrieved April 3, 2003, from http://www.ausport.gov.au/fulltext/1998/cjsm/v2n1/dyson.htm

Eagly, A. H., Ashmore, R. D., Makhijani, M. G., & Longo, L. C. (1991). What is beautiful is good, but . . . A meta-analytic review of research on the physical attractiveness stereotype. *Psychological Bulletin, 110*(1), 109–128.

Edenfield v. Fane (123 L. Ed. 2d 543, 113 S. Ct. 1792, 1798 1993).

Ehrlich, B. (2002). *35 seconds to DTC success.* Retrieved April 17, 2002, from http://www.dtcperspectives.com

Eighmey, J. (1999, February 15). Accident prevention in advertising. *Ad Age*, p. 24.

Elliott, R., Jones, A., Benfield, A., & Barlow, M. (1995, June). Overt sexuality: A discourse analysis of gender responses. *Journal of Consumer Policy, 18*, 187–217.

Elliott, S. (2001). *Advertising: Four A's discuss creativity with a purpose*. Retrieved May 2, 2002, from http://www.veridiem.com

Elliott, S. (2002a, April 19). An ad executive tells his colleagues to mend their ways. *New York Times*, p. 2.

Elliott, S. (2002b, March 21). Facing outcry, NBC ends plan to run liquor ads. *New York Times*, p. 1.

England, P., Kuhn, A., & Gardner, T. (1981). The ages of men and women in magazine advertisements. *Journalism Quarterly, 58*, 468–471.

Englis, B., Soloman, M. R., & Ashmore, R. D. (1994). Beauty before the eyes of beholders: The cultural encoding of beauty types in magazine advertising and music television. *Journal of Advertising, 23*(2), 49–64.

Entman, R. M., & Rojecki, A. (2000). *The black image in the white mind: Media and race in America*. Chicago: University of Chicago Press.

Etcoff, N. (1999). *Survival of the prettiest*. New York: Doubleday.

Face reality of new demo. (2001, November 19). *Advertising Age, 72*, s2–s6.

Fazari, L. (1997, July 22). New mag looks at big picture. *Toronto Sun*, p. 47.

Federal Trade Commission. (1999). *FTC reports on industry efforts to avoid promoting alcohol to underage consumers*. Washington, DC: Author.

Federal Trade Commission. (2000). *Marketing violent entertainment to children: A review of self-regulation and industry practices in the motion picture, music recording & electronic game industries*. Washington, DC: Author.

Federal Trade Commission. (2002). *Privacy agenda*. Retrieved April 24, 2002, from the Federal Trade Commission Web site: http://www.ftc.gov

Feingold, A. (1992, March). Good-looking people are not what we think. *Psychological Bulletin, 111*, 304–341.

Ferguson, J. H., Kreshel, P., & Tinkham, S. (1990). In the pages of *Ms.*, Sex roles portrayals of women in advertising. *Journal of Advertising, 19*(1), 40–51.

Ferrante, C. L., Haynes, A. M., & Kingsley, S. (1988). Images of women in television advertising. *Journal of Broadcasting and Electronic Media, 32*(2), 231–237.

Festervand, T. A., & Lumpkin, J. R. (1985). Responses of elderly consumers to their portrayals by advertisers. *Current Issues and Research in Advertising, 8*(1), 203–226.

Fisher, H. E. (1999). *The first sex: The natural talents of women and how they are changing the world*. New York: Random House.

Fisher, J. C. (1993). *Advertising, alcohol consumption, and abuse: A worldwide survey*. Westport, CT: Greenwood.

Fiske, J. (1986). *Understanding popular culture*. Boston: Unwin Hyman.

Fletcher, W. (1992). *A glittering haze: Strategic advertising in the 1990s*. Henley-on-Thames, England: NTC Publications.

Fletcher, W. (2001, November 22). Rub egg off, Fcuk: Your ads are bollocks that just peddle smut. *Marketing*, p. 20.

Flint, J. (2002, January 11). CBS won't take commercials for hard liquor. *Wall Street Journal*, p. 8.

Food and Drug Administration (1995). *Direct to consumer promotion*. Silver Springs, MD: Author.

Food and Drug Administration. (1997). *Warning letter to Merck.* Retrieved September 11, 2000, from the Food and Drug Administration Web site: http://www.fda.gov/cder/warn/jan97/zocor.pdf

Food and Drug Administration. (1998a). *Warning letter to Merck.* Retrieved September 11, 2000, from the Food and Drug Administration Web site: http://www.fda.gov/cder/warn/apr98/6494.pdf

Food and Drug Administration. (1998b). *Warning letter to Pharmacia and Upjohn.* Retrieved September 11, 2000, from the Food and Drug Administration Web site: http://www.fda.gov/cder/warn/mar98/6421.pdf

Food and Drug Administration. (1998c). *Warning letter to Rhode-Puolene Rore.* Retrieved September 11, 2000, from the Food and Drug Administration Web site: http://www.fda.gov/cder/warn/may98/6610.pdf

Food and Drug Administration. (1999). *Warning letter to Hoffman-LaRoche.* Retrieved September 12, 2000, from the Food and Drug Administration Web site: http://www.fda.gov/cder/warn/july99/8089.pdf

Food and Drug Administration. (2000). *Warning Letter to Eli Lilly and Company.* Retrieved September 12, 2000, from the Food and Drug Administration Web site: http://www.fda.gov/cder/warn/july99/8089.pdf

Fox, R. J., Krugman, D. M., Fletcher, J. E., & Fischer, P. M. (1998). Adolescents' attention to beer and cigarette print ads and associated product warnings. *Journal of Advertising, 27*(3), 57–68.

Francher, J. (1973). It's the Pepsi generation . . . Accelerated aging and the television commercial. *International Journal of Aging and Human Development, 4,* 245–255.

Franklin, C. (2000, February 28). The need to look beyond Black History Month. *Advertising Age, 71,* 62.

Freedman, P., & Lawton, L. D. (2000, May). Does campaign advertising depress voter turnout? *The Virginia News Letter, 76,* 1–4.

Friedman, W. (2001, November 19). "Squeeze" play stokes concerns. *Advertising Age, 72,* 41.

Friedman, W. (2002). *Nearly all NBC prime time shows qualify for liquor ads.* Retrieved January 11, 2002, from http://www.adage.com/news.cms?newsId-33734

Galbraith, J. K. (1957). *The affluent society.* Boston: Houghton Mifflin.

Gantz, W., Gartenberg, H., & Rainbow, C. (1980). Approaching invisibility: The portrayal of the elderly in magazine advertisements. *Journal of Communications, 30,* 56–60.

Gardner, M. (2000, November 22). Stereotypes tarnish golden years. *Christian Science Monitor, 92*(253), p. 15.

Gardyn, R. (2000). REtirement REdefined. *American Demographics, 22*(11), 52–57.

Garfield, B. (1997). Benetton's hype: Free publicity for pricey clothes. *Advertising Age, 62*(31), 38.

Garfield, B. (2001a, September 17). Ads must be sensitive, but don't try to profit from grief. *Advertising Age, 72,* 29.

Garfield, B. (2001b). *Mass murder is no occasion for marketing.* Retrieved January 29, 2002, from http://www.adreview.com/article.cms?articleId=861

Garner, D. (2001, December 9). Content. *New York Times,* p. 63.

Garner, D. M. (1997). 1997 body image survey results. *Psychology Today, 30*(1), 30–47.

Garner, D. M., Garfinkel, P. E., Schwartz, D., & Thompson, M. (1980, October). Cultural expectations of thinness in women. *Psychological Reports, 47*, 483–491.

Geller, A., & Lawrence, B. (2002, February). TV production: Trends, tone and technology. *Campaigns and Elections*, p. 63.

Gerbner, G. (1993a). Learning productive aging as a social role: The lessons of television. In S. A. Bass, F. G. Caro, & Y. P. Chen (Eds.), *Achieving a productive aging society* (pp. 350–365). Westport, CT: Auburn House.

Gerbner, G. (1993b). *Women and minorities on television, a study in casting and fate.* Philadelphia: University of Pennsylvania, Annenberg School of Communications.

Gerbner, G., Gross, L., Morgan, M., & Signorelli, N. (1981). *Aging with television commercials: Images on television commercials and dramatic programming, 1977–1979.* Philadelphia: University of Pennsylvania, Annenberg School of Communications.

Gerbner, G., Gross, L., Morgan, M., & Signorelli, N. (1986). Living with television: The dynamics of the cultivation process. In J. Bryant & D. Zillman (Eds.), *Perspectives on media effects* (pp. 17–40). Hillsdale, NJ: Lawrence Erlbaum.

Gibbs, N., August, M., Cole, W., Lofaro, L., Padgett, T., Ressner, J., & Winters, R. (2001). Who's in charge here? *Time, 158*, 40–48.

Giroux, H. (1994). Benetton's world without borders: Buying social change. In C. Becker (Ed.), *The subversive imagination: Artists, society and social responsibility* (p. 198). London: Routledge.

Gobé, M. (2001). *Emotional branding: The new paradigm for connecting brands to people.* New York: Allworth.

Goetzl, D. (2000a). New venture aims to measure effectiveness of DTC drug work. *Advertising Age, 71*(23), 16–18.

Goetzl, D. (2000b). TVB study: DTC disclosures lend credibility to drug ads. *Advertising Age, 71*(24), 6.

Goetzl, D., Klaassen, A., Teinowitz, I., & Sanders, L. (2001, July 23). Dose of reality. *Advertising Age, 72*, 1–2.

Goffman, E. (1979). *Gender advertisements.* Cambridge, MA: Harvard University Press.

Goldman, D. (2002, January 7). Bumping and grinding with Britney rage. *AdWeek*, p. 11.

Goldring, J. (1997). Netting the cybershark: Consumer protection, cyberspace, the nation-state, and democracy. In B. Kahin & C. Nesson (Eds.), *Borders in cyberspace: Information policy and the global information infrastructure* (pp. 322–354). Cambridge, MA: MIT Press.

Goodwill, B. (1999, October). Cause marketing pros and cons. *Broadcast Cafe Newsletter.* Retrieved December 28, 2000, from http://www.psaresearch.com/CRMFEATURE.html

Gordon, J., & Pappas, B. (1998, October 19). A larger dose of reality. *Forbes, 162*, 47.

Gould, J. (2002). *Political television advertisements: Pro.* Retrieved May 14, 2002, from http://www.etext.org/Zines/Intl_Teletimes/Teletimes_HTML/debate_room_9402.html

Gould, S. J., Gupta, P. B., & Graner-Krauter, S. (2000). Product placements in movies: A cross cultural analysis of Austrian, French and American consumers' attitudes toward this emerging international promotional medium. *Journal of Advertising, 29*(4), 41–58.

Gray, R. (2001, May 3). Cause related marketing. *Marketing*, p. 35.

Grebb, M. (2001a, April 3). *Don't forget about email*. Retrieved February 15, 2002, from http://www.bizreport.com

Grebb, M. (2001b, May 11). *Let's talk about privacy—again*. Retrieved February 15, 2002, from http://www.bisreport.com

Green, C. L. (1999). Ethnic evaluations of advertising: Interaction effects of strength of ethnic identification, media placement, and degree of racial composition. *Journal of Advertising, 28*(1), 49–64.

Greenfield, P. M. (1984). *Mind and media: The effects of television, video games and computers*. Cambridge, MA: Harvard University Press.

Grimm, M. (2002). A spirited debate. *American Demographics, 24*(4), 48–50.

Grossman, A. (2001). *NBC drinking in revenue from hard-liquor ads*. Retrieved January 11, 2002, from Yahoo News Web site: http://dailynews.yahoo.com/NBC_drinking_in_revenue_from_hard-liquor_ads_1.html

Grown up women (2000, March 9). *Marketing Week*, p. 57.

Guillen, E., & Barr, S. I. (1994, September). Nutrition, dieting and fitness messages in a magazine for adolescent women, 1970–1990. *Journal of Adolescent Health, 15*, 464–472.

Gulas, C., & McKeage, K. (2000). Extending social comparison: An examination of the unintended consequences of idealized advertising imagery. *Journal of Advertising, 29*(2), 17–28.

Gwinner, K., & Eaton, J. (1999). Building brand image through event sponsorship: The role of image transfer. *Journal of Advertising, 28*(4), 47–57.

Hacker, G. A. (2002, January 10). *Alcohol advertising: Are our kids collateral or intended targets?* Paper presented at the meeting of Leadership to Keep Children Alcohol Free, Washington, DC.

Hahn, H. (1987). Advertising the acceptably employable image: Disability and capitalism. *Policy Studies Journal, 15*, 551–570.

Hall, C., Ijima, C., & Crum, M. J. (1994). Women and body-isms in television beer commercials. *Sex Roles, 31*(5–6), 329–337.

Hall, S. (2001, March 12). *Claritin and Schering-Plough: A prescription for profit*. Retrieved April 17, 2002, from the *New York Times* Online Web site: http://www.nytimes.com/2001/03/11/magazine/11CLARITIN.html

Hallerman, D. (2002, February 20). *Mindshare over matter: Interstitials, pop-ups and pop-unders*. Retrieved March 11, 2002, from http://www.emarketers.com/analysis/marketings/20020220_mark.html

Halprin, S. (1995). *Look at my ugly face*. New York: Penguin.

Hamilton, A. (2001). Stopping those pop-up ads. *Time, 158*(10), 87.

Hanson, D. J. (2001). *Alcohol advertising*. Retrieved February 11, 2002, from http://www2.potsdam.edu/alcohol-info/Advertising/Advertising.html

Hardin, G. (1968). The tragedy of the commons. *Science, 162*, 1243–1248.

Hastings, G., & MacFadyen, L. (2000). A day in the life of an advertising man: Review of internal documents from the UK tobacco industry's principal advertising agencies. *BMJ: British Medical Journal, 321*(7257), 366–371.

Hatfield, E., & Sprecher, S. (1986). *Mirror mirror . . . The importance of looks in everyday life*. Albany: State University of New York Press.

Hays, R. G., & Reisner, A. E. (1990). Feeling the heat from advertisers: Farm magazine writers and ethical pressures. *Journalism Quarterly, 40*, 936–942.

Henderson, S. (1997, February 23). A magazine looks at the plus-side of the fashion world. *New York Times*, p. 41.

Henney, J. E. (2000). Challenges in regulating direct-to-consumer advertising. *MS JAMA, 284,* 2242.

Herrmann, D. (1997). *Query: Origins of the term melting pot.* Retrieved April 14, 2003, from http://www.h-net.msu.edu/gateways/migration/threads/terminology/disc-meltingpot1E97.html

Hespos, T. (2001a, April 19). *The dilemma of ad-blocking software.* Retrieved May 21, 2002, from http://www.clickz.com/media/media_buy/article.php/840581

Hespos, T. (2001b, August 2). *How to make users hate online advertising.* Retrieved February 15, 2002, from http://www.clickz.com/media/media_buy/article.php.844432

Hespos, T. (2002, February 19). *Signs of recovery* [E-mail newsletter]. Media Post Communications.

Hirschman, E., & Thompson, C. J. (1997). Why media matter: Toward a richer understanding of consumers' relationship with advertising and mass media. *Journal of Advertising, 26*(1), 43–60.

Hite, M. (1988). *Adman: Morris Hite's methods for winning the ad game.* Dallas, TX: E-Heart Press.

Hoffman, J. R. (1999). Direct to consumer advertising of prescription drugs. *BMJ: British Medical Journal, 318*(7194), 1301–1303.

Holmer, A. F. (1999). Direct-to-consumer prescription drug advertising builds bridges between patients and physicians. *Journal of the American Medical Association, 281*(4), 380–382.

Homer did it first. (2001, September 8). *Economist, 360,* 92.

Howard, T. (2001, December 31). *Wacky 7up ads agree with men, women of all ages.* Retrieved April 10, 2003, from http://www.usatoday.com/money/index/2001-12-31-main.htm

Howland, J. (1989, December). Ad vs. edit: The pressure mounts. *Folio,* pp. 92–100.

Hranchak, W. (1999, August 5). *Bad addytude.* Retrieved January 15, 2002, from http://www.commando.com/ARCHIVE/post13.html

Hu, J. (2000). *AOL's Schuler defends Time Warner merger as consumer friendly.* Retrieved January 11, 2002, from http://news.cnet.com/news/0-1014-201-2402089-0.html

Humphrey, R., & Schuman, H. (1984). The portrayal of blacks in magazine advertisements: 1950–1982. *Public Opinion Quarterly, 48*(3), 551–563.

Humphreys, J. (2000). *Buying power at the beginning of the new century: Projections for 2000 and 2001.* Unpublished manuscript, University of Georgia at Athens.

Indiana State Department of Health. (1992). *Prevention newsline.* Retrieved November 14, 2001, from the Indiana Prevention Resource Center Web site: http://www.drugs.indiana.edu/publications/iprc/newsline/spring92.html

Internet Marketing. (2002). *Internet marketing dictionary.* Retrieved February 19, 2002, from http://www.marketingterms.com/dictionary/

Irving, H. (1991). Little elves and mind control: Advertising and its critics. Retrieved April 14, 2003, from http://wwwmcc.murdoch.edu.au/ReadingRoom/4.2/Irving.html

Iyengar, S., & Prior, M. (1999, June). *Political advertising: What effect on commercial advertisers?* Retrieved April 10, 2003, from http://www.stanford.edu/~siyengar/research/papers/advertising.html

Jacobson, M. F., & Mazur, L. A. (1995). *Marketing madness: A survival guide for a consumer society.* Boulder, CO: Westview.

Jahnke, A. (2001). *Hard liquor, soft resolve.* Retrieved January 11, 2002, from http://www.darwinmag.com/connect/opinoin/column.html?ArticleID=217

Jenkins, K. E. (1999). Health care communications: Creating messages that help heal. *Business and Management Practices, 2*(8), 4–6.

Johnson, C., & Petrie, T. (1995). The relationship of gender: Discrepancy of eating attitudes and behaviors. *Sex Roles, 33,* 405–416.

Johnson, S. (2001, October 18). *Patriotism for sale.* Retrieved April 14, 2003, from the *Chicago Tribune* Web site: chicagotribune.com/features/columnists/chi-0110180015oct18,0,7073275.column

Johnston-Jones, N. (2001, August 1). Geri-ad-tricks don't go down well. *Brand Strategy,* p. 30.

Jones, M. Y., Stanaland, A. J. S., & Gelb, B. D. (1998). Beefcake and cheesecake: Insights for advertisers. *Journal of Advertising, 27*(2), 33–51.

Jordan, A. B. (2000). *Is the three hour rule living up to its potential?* Philadelphia: Annenberg Public Policy Center.

Joseph, W. B. (1982). The credibility of physically attractive communicators: A review. *Journal of Advertising, 11*(3), 15–24.

Kahle, L., & Homer, P. M. (1985). Physical attractiveness of the celebrity endorser: A social adaptation perspective. *Journal of Consumer Research, 11*(4), 954–961.

Kang, M. (1997). The portrayal of women's images in magazine advertisements: Goffman's gender analysis revisited. *Sex Roles, 37*(11/12), 979–997.

Kantrowitz, B., King, P., Downey, S., & Scott, H. W. (2000). The road ahead: A boomer's guide to happiness. *Newsweek, 135*(14), 56–59.

Kanungo, R., & Pang, S. (1993). Effects of human models on perceived product quality. *Journal of Applied Psychology, 57*(2), 172–178.

Kaplar, R. T. (1998, May). *It's time to remove the brief summary from DTC print ads.* Retrieved November 5, 2002, from http://www.cpsnet.com/reprints/1998/05/dtcprint.pdf

Kawachi, I., & Conrad, P. (1996). Medicalization and the pharmacological treatment of blood pressure. In P. Davis (Ed.), *Contested ground: Public purpose and private interests in the regulation of prescription drugs* (pp. 26–41). New York: Oxford University Press.

Kelly, K. J. (1997, October 15). Chrysler folds. *New York Daily News,* p. 42.

Kennedy, J. P. (2002). *DTC marketing of prescription drugs: Citizen's health.* Retrieved April 17, 2002, from http://www.dtcperspectives.com

Kern, M. (1989). *30-second politics: Political advertising in the eighties.* New York: Praeger.

Kiefe, O. D. W., & Lewis, C. E. (2001). Ten-year changes in smoking among young adults: Are racial differences explained by socioeconomic factors in the CARDIA study? *American Journal of Public Health, 91*(2), 213–218.

Kilbourne, J. (1999). *Deadly persuasion: Why women and girls must fight the addictive power of advertising.* New York: Free Press.

King, C., & Siegel, M. (2001). The master settlement agreement with the tobacco industry and cigarette advertising in magazines. *The New England Journal of Medicine, 345*(7), 504–511.

Kirby, K. (1999, November, 1999). *Rules of the race.* Retrieved February 22, 2002, from http://www.rtnda.org/foi/ror.shtml

Kirk, E. E. (1996, July 16). *Evaluating information found on the Internet.* Retrieved November 13, 2001, from http://www.library.jhu.edu/elp/useit/evaluate/

Klein, N. (1999). *No logo-taking aim at the brand bullies*. New York: St. Martin's.

Koezler, B. (2000). *What's all this talk about branding?* Retrieved March 15, 2002, from http://realtytimes.com/rtnews/rtapages/20000405_branding.htm

Kolassa, E. M. (2001). Maximizing patient choice. Retrieved April 14, 2003, from http://www.pfizerforum.com/english/kolassa.shtml

Kopp, S. W., & Sheffet, M. J. (1997). The effect of direct-to-consumer advertising of prescription drugs on retail gross margins: Empirical evidence and public policy implications. *Journal of Public Policy and Marketing, 16*(2), 270.

Kravitz, R. L. (2000). Direct-to-consumer advertising of prescription drugs: Implications for the patient-physician relationship. *MS JAMA, 284,* 2244.

Krol, C. (1998, February 23). Full figured women a great fit for model. *Advertising Age, 69,* s16.

Kuczynski, A. (1998a, March 29). The incredible shrinking plus-size model. *New York Times,* p. 4.

Kuczynski, A. (1998b, November 9). Some consumer magazines are getting real. *New York Times,* p. 1.

Kuczynski, A. (2001, August 11). *Tobacco industry still advertises in magazines read by youth.* Retrieved February 11, 2002, from the *New York Times* Website: http://www.nytimes.com/learning/teachers/featured_articles/ 20010816 thursday.html

Kvasnicka, B., Beymer, B., & Perloff, R. (1982). Portrayals of the elderly in magazine advertisements. *Journalism Quarterly, 59,* 656–658.

Lagnado, L. (2000, January 20). *Choosing between drugs, necessities.* Retrieved January 19, 2001, from the *Wall Street Journal* Interactive Edition Web site: http://www.msnbc.com/news/215703.asp

Lang, M. (1994, November 19). Building your social marketing skills. *Strategy,* p. 9.

League of Women Voters. (2000). *Tired of negative political campaigns?* Retrieved May 17, 2002, from http://www.cboss.com/lwv/politicalcampaigns.htm

Lee, R. A. (1997). The youth bias in advertising. *American Demographics, 19*(1), 47–50.

Leiber, L. (1997). *Should the government restrict advertising of alcoholic beverages?—Yes.* Retrieved December 11, 2001, from http://www.acsh.org/ publications/priorities/0903/govadyes.html

Leigh, T. W., Rethans, A. J., & Whitney, T. R. (1987). Role portrayals of women in advertising: Cognitive responses and advertising effectiveness. *Journal of Advertising Research, 27,* 54–63.

Leinweber, F. (2001). The older adult market: New research highlights key values. *Generations, 25*(3), 22–23.

Lerner, N. (2001, June 4). Ad World "dumbs down" American males. *Christian Science Monitor, 93,* p. 16.

Leshner, G., & Thorson, E. (2000). Over reporting voting: Campaign media, public mood and the vote. *Political Communication, 17*(3), 263–278.

Liebeskind, K. (2002, February 15). *Affiliate teetotalers.* Retrieved February 15, 2002, from http://www.mediapost.com

Lies about Toyota. (2001, August 10). Retrieved June 10, 2002, from http://www. smartertimes.com/archive/2001/08/010810.html

Limberg, V. E. (2002). *Ethics and television.* Retrieved January 14, 2002, from http://www.museum.tv/archives/etv/E/htmlE/ethicsandte/ethicsandte.htm

Lin, C. A. (1995, March). *Manipulating sex appeals in television advertising*. Paper presented at the conference of the American Academy of Advertising, Waco, TX.

Linder, D. (2002). *Exploring constitutional conflicts: 44 Liquormart, Inc. v. Rhode Island*. Retrieved March 19, 2002, from http://www.law.umkc.edu/faculty/projects/ftrials/conlaw/liquormart.html

Lipke, D. J. (2000a, November). Databasics. *American Demographics, 22*, 40.

Lipke, D. J. (2000b, September). Fountain of youth. *American Demographics, 22, 37*.

Loyd, T. (2000). Postcards from the bleeding edge. Retrieved April 14, 2003, from http://www.linezine.com/2.1/features/tlpbe.htm

Lysonski, S. (1983). Female and male role portrayals in magazine advertisements: A re-examination. *Akron Business and Economic Review, 14*(3), 45–50.

Magazine Publishers of America. (2001). *Marketing to the emerging majorities*. Retrieved April 14, 2003, from http://www.magazine.org/Diversity/articles/ad_pages.html

Magazines that do not accept tobacco advertising. (2001, May 10). Retrieved February 11, 2002, from http://www.tobacco.org/Misc/tob_ad_mags.html

Mand, A. (2001). Site for gay ads debuts. *Advertising Age, 72*(19), 50.

Mandese, J. (1994). Stymied TV nets take promotion to new level. *Advertising Age, 65*(12), s6–s9.

Martin, M. C. (1995). *The influence of the beauty of advertising models on female pre-adolescent and adolescent self-perceptions, self-esteem and brand intentions: A longitudinal study*. Lincoln: University of Nebraska Press.

Martin, M. C., & Gentry, J. (1994, August). *Assessing the internalization of physical attractiveness norms*. Paper presented at the 1994 AMA Educators' Proceedings, Chicago.

Martin, M. C., & Gentry, J. W. (1997). Stuck in the model trap: The effects of beautiful models in ads on female pre-adolescents and adolescents. *Journal of Advertising, 26*(2), 19–33.

Mason, T. (2002, June 6). Analysis. *Marketing*, p. 11.

Masterson, P. (1993, January 11). Many editors report advertising pressure. *Advertising Age*, p. 22.

Mays, A. E., & Brady, D. L. (1990). Women's changing role portrayals in magazine advertisements: 1955–1985 (Working paper: Millersville State University Series). Millersville, PA: Millersville State University.

Mazzetti, M. (2001, April 2). Tobacco is still smokin'. *U.S. News and World Report, 130*, 25.

McCracken, G. (1988). *Culture and consumption*. Bloomington: Indiana University Press.

McDonald, C. (1992). *How advertising works: A review of current thinking*. Detroit, MI: NTC Publications.

McDonald, M., & Lavelle, M. (2001, July 30). Call it kid-fluence. *U.S. News and World Report, 131*, 32–34.

McInturff, B. (2001, March 26). While critics may fret, public likes DTC ads. *Advertising Age, 72*, 24.

McLaughlin, P. (1993, August 29). Madison Avenue discriminates against disabled—just like it does the rest of us. *Southern Illinoisan Plus*, p. 1.

McLuhan, R. (2000, May 11). Internet: Silver surfers join the Internet party. *Marketing*, p. 37.

Media Action Network for Asian Americans. (2001). *Asian stereotypes: Restrictive portrayals of Asians in the media and how to balance them.* Retrieved March 10, 2002, from http://www.manaa.org/

Media audiences. (2000, January 12). Retrieved January 21, 2002, from http://www.asne.org/kiosk/reports/98reports/media_audiences.html

MediaDailyNews. (2002, February 15). *Benefit to public health lost in debate over DTC advertising.* Retrieved March 11, 2002, from www.mediapost.com

Mehta, A. (2000). Advertising attitudes and advertising effectiveness. *Journal of Advertising Research, 40*(3), 67–72.

Melton, G. W., & Fowler, G. L. (1987). Females roles in radio advertising. *Journalism Quarterly, 64*(1), 145–149.

Merrit, S. (1984). Negative political advertising: Some empirical findings. *Journal of Advertising, 13*(3), 27–38.

Meyer, H. (1999, November/December). When the cause is just. *Journal of Business Strategy, 20*, 27–29.

Millard, P. (2001). *Patriotism becomes trendy advertising theme.* Retrieved June 29, 2002, from http://www.bizjournals.com/milwaukee/stories/2001/12/03/

Miller, B., & Sweeney, H. (1999). *Are current DTC ads ineffective?* Retrieved April 9, 2003, from http://www.cpsnet.com/reprints/1999/05/face2face.pdf

Miller, C. (1994, June 6). Give them a cheeseburger. *Marketing News*, p. 6.

Miller, C. L. (1987). Qualitative differences among gender-stereotyped toys: Implications for cognitive and social development in girls and boys. *Sex Roles: A Journal of Research, 16*, 473–488.

Mintzes, B. (2002). Direct to consumer advertising is medicalising normal human experience. *BJM: British Medical Journal, 324*(7342), 908–909.

Mishra, R. (2000, September 13). TV spot gaffe revives decade old suspicion. *Boston Globe*, p. A26.

Mitchell, A. (1999). Marketing. *Marketing Week, 21*, 40.

Mitchell, A. A. (1986, June). The effect of verbal and visual components of advertisements on brand attitudes and attitude toward the advertisement. *Journal of Consumer Research, 13*, 12–24.

Mitchell, A. A., & Olson, J. C. (1981, August). Are product attribute beliefs the only mediator of advertising effects on brand attitude? *Journal of Marketing Research, 18*, 318–332.

Modzelweski, J. (1996). *Liquor deserves equal ad time on TV.* Retrieved January, 11, 2002, from the MIT Web site: http://the-tech.mit.edu/V116/N61/liquor. 61c.html

Mogelonsky, M. (1998, April). Watching in tongues. *American Demographics*, p. 48.

Monteath, S. A., & McCabe, M. P. (1997). The influence of societal factors on female body image. *Journal of Social Psychology, 37*(6), 708–727.

Moore, C. (2001, November). How old are you? *Communication Arts Design Annual*, pp. 10–11.

Moore, P. L. (2000). An overdose of drug advertising? *BusinessWeek, 3682*, 52.

Morant, H. (2000, June 3). BMA demands more responsible media attitude on body image. *BMJ: British Medical Journal*, p. 1495.

More controversy, please, we're Italian. (1992). *Economist, 332*(7744), 70.

More than just causes. (2000, August). *Chain Store Age Executive, 76*, 37.

Morris, L., Brinberg, D., Klimberg, R., Rivera, C., & Millstein, L. (1986). Miscomprehension rates for prescription drug advertisements. *Current Issues and Research in Advertising, 9*(1&2), 93–117.

Morton, J. (1995). Farewell to more family dynasties. *American Journalism Review,* *17*(8), 68.

Morton, L. P. (2001). Segmenting baby boomers. *Public Relations Quarterly, 46*(3), 46–48.

Moyers, B. (1998). *The :30 second candidate.* Retrieved April 10, 2003, from http://www.pbs.org/30secondcandidate/

Murphy, C. (1999). Cause related marketing. *Marketing, 10,* 31.

Murray, N. M., Manrai, L., & Manrai, A. (1998). How super are video supers? A test of communication efficiency. *Journal of Public Policy and Marketing, 17*(10), 24–34.

Murray, W. (1989, March). Taxation of advertising: A violation of free speech? *USA Today Magazine, 117,* 23–24.

Myers, P. N., & Biocca, F. A. (1992, Summer). The elastic body image: The effect of television advertising and programming on body image distortions among young women. *Journal of Communications, 42,* 108–133.

National Association of Broadcasters. (2002). *Campaign finance reform.* Retrieved June 25, 2002, from http://www.nab.org/Newsroom/Issues/issuepapers/issuecfr.asp

National Institute for Healthcare Management Foundation. (2001). *Prescription drugs and mass media advertising.* Washington, DC: Author.

National Telecommunications and Information Administration. (2002). *A nation online: How Americans are expanding their use of the Internet.* Retrieved April 13, 2002, from http://cyberatlas.internet.com/big_picture/geographics/article/0,,5911_969541,00.html

Nayyar, S. (1992, June 29). Green light for drug ads. *Adweek,* p. 9.

Nelson, J. P. (1995). Advertising and U.S. alcoholic beverage demand: A growth-accounting analysis. *Empirical Economics, 22,* 1–20.

Neuborne, E. (2001a, August 13). For kids on the Web, it's an ad, ad, ad, ad world. *BusinessWeek,* pp. 108–109.

Neuborne, E. (2001b, September 3). Irksome and effective. *BusinessWeek,* p. EB6.

Neuborne, E. (2001c, October 1). Stop the zzz-mails. *BusinessWeek,* p. EB6.

New York Times. (2000, September 17). Agency investigates rats ad. *New York Times,* p. 16.

Newman, L. (2000). Avalanche of direct-to-consumer drug marketing brings new questions. *Journal of the National Cancer Institute, 92*(12), 964–967.

NewsBatch.com. (2002). *Background on campaign financing from NewsBatch.com.* Retrieved February 22, 2002, from http://www.newsbatch.com/news-campaignfin.htm

Nicosia, F. M. (1974). *Advertising, management and society.* New York: McGraw-Hill.

Nielsen Media Research. (2000). *Minority television usage.* Retrieved April 10, 2002, from http://www.nielsenmedia.com/ethnicmeasure

Noonan, D. (2000, October 16). A new way to sell smokes. *Newsweek, 136,* 54.

Nordenberg, T. (1998). *Direct to you: TV drug ads that make sense.* Retrieved February 20, 2003, from the Food and Drug Administration Web site: http://www.fda.gov/fdac/features/1998/198_ads.html

Noriega, C. A. (1997, May). *There may be a Frito bandito in your house.* Presented at Chicago/Latino and Native American Student Film and Video Festival Program, Chicago.

Nuiry, O. (1996, July). Ban the bandito: Madison Avenue takes a more sophisticated approach to Latino stereotypes. *Hispanic, 9,* 5–11.

Obermiller, C. (1995). The baby is sick/the baby is well: A test of environmental communication appeals. *Journal of Advertising, 24*(2), 55–70.

Ogletree, S., Williams, S., Raffeld, P., Mason, B., & Fricke, K. (1990). Female attractiveness and eating disorders: Do children's television commercials play a role? *Sex Roles, 22,* 791–797.

Ohanian, R. (1990). Construction and validation of a scale to measure celebrity endorser's perceived expertise, trustworthiness and attractiveness. *Journal of Advertising, 19*(3), 39–52.

OIT Network Group. (2002). *Reference definition of terms.* Retrieved April 25, 2002, from The University of Wisconsin-Platteville Web site: http://www.uwplatt.edu/network/reference/terms/b.html

Ormondroyd, J. (2001, September 18). *Critically analyzing information sources.* Retrieved November 14, 2001, from the Cornell University Library Web site: http://www.library.cornell.edu/okuref/research/skilll26.htm

Owens, M. (2001, April 25). *Four letters too far.* Retrieved July 10, 2002, from http://abcnews.go.com/sections/business/DailyNews/Frenchconnection010425.html

Paff, J. L., & Lakner, H. B. (1997). Dress and the female gender role in magazine advertisements of 1950–1994: A content analysis. *Family and Consumer Sciences Research Journal, 26*(1), 29–58.

Palmer, C. (2001, September 21). Does advertising have a conscience? *Campaign,* p. 22.

Parnes, F. (1997, November 1). Magazine puts a plus on big sizes. *Denver Post,* p. E-01.

Pastore, M. (2002). *Internet key to communication among teens.* Retrieved April 13, 2003, from http://cyberatlas.internet.com/big_picture/demographics/article/0,,5901_961881,00.html

PBS. (2000). *Life on the Internet timeline.* Retrieved June 11, 2001, from http://www.pbs.org/internet/timeline/timeline-txt.html

Peck, R. (1993). Is cigarette advertising protected by the First Amendment? Yes. *American Council on Science and Health Priorities, 5*(3), 1–2.

Peracchio, L. A., & Luna, D. (1998). The development of an advertising campaign to discourage smoking initiation among children and youth. *Journal of Advertising, 27*(3), 49–60.

Perlman, E. (1996, December). Lotto's little luxuries. *Governing,* p. 18.

Perry, N. J., & Rogers, A. (1992, August 10). Why it's so tough to be a girl. *Fortune, 126,* 82–84.

Perse, E. M., & Ferguson, D. A. (1994). Cultivation in the newer media environment. *Communication Research, 21*(1), 70–104.

Peterson, M. (2002, March 8). TV ads spur a rise in prescription drug sales. *New York Times,* p. 13.

Petroshius, S. M., & Crocker, K. E. (1989). An empirical analysis of spokesperson characteristics on advertisement and product evaluations. *Journal of the Academy of Marketing Science, 17*(3), 217–225.

Peyrot, M., Alpersetein, N. M., Doren, D. V., & Poli, L. G. (1998). Direct-to-consumer ads can influence behavior. *Marketing Health Services, 18*(2), 26–32.

Pharmaceutical Research and Manufacturers of America. (2000, February 1). *Quick facts: Direct to consumer advertising.* Retrieved February 11, 2002, from http://www.phrma.org/publications/quickfacts/05.11.2000.189.cfml

Phillips, M. J. (1997). *Ethics and manipulation in advertising: Answering a flawed indictment.* Westport, CT: Quorum.

Pinhas, L., Toner, B. B., Ali, A., Garfinkel, P. E., & Stuckless, N. (1999). The effects of the ideal of female beauty of mood and body satisfaction. *International Journal of Eating Disorders, 25*(2), 223–226.

Pivato, M. (1999, October 10). *Tax advertising.* Retrieved May 10, 2002, from http://xaravve.trentu.ca/vato/Policy/adtax.html

Plous, S., & Neptune, D. (1997). Racial and gender biases in magazine advertising: A content-analytic study. *Psychology of Women Quarterly, 21,* 627–644.

Pogrebin, R. (1997, September 29). Magazine publishers circling wagons against advertisers. *New York Times,* p. 1.

Point of purchase. (2001, November). *Business and Management Practices, 7,* 12.

Pollay, R. W., & Gallagher, K. (1990). Advertising and cultural values: Reflections in the distorted mirror. *International Journal of Advertising, 9*(4), 359–372.

Polonsky, M., & Wood, G. (2001). Can the over-commercialization of cause-related marketing harm society? *Journal of Macromarketing, 21*(1), 8–22.

Polyak, I. (2000). The center of attention. *American Demographics, 22*(11), 30–32.

Popcorn, F., & Marigold, L. (2000). *EVEolution: The eight truths of marketing to women.* New York: Hyperion.

Postman, N. (1985). *Amusing ourselves to death.* New York: Viking.

Powell, J. (2001, August 28). The pulse—Television advertising. *Manchester Guardian,* p. 4C.

The price of DTC success. (1999). *Advertising Age, 70*(30), 14.

Raz, U. (2002). *Advertising on the Internet, or why is spam bad?* Retrieved March 4, 2002, from www.private.org.il/anti-spam.html

Rebek-Wegener, J., Eickhoff-Schemek, J., & Kelly-Vance, L. (1998). The effect of media analysis on attitudes and behaviors regarding body image among college students. *Journal of American College Health, 47*(1), 29–35.

Regan, K. (2001, July 19). *Studies say banner ads work, but.* Retrieved July 8, 2002, from http://www.ecommercetimes.com/perl/story/12127.html

Reinhard, K. (2000, June 15). *The ethics of advertising.* Speech presented at the Umber Center, Goshen, IN.

Reinhard, K. (2001). *De gustibus non est disputandum.* Retrieved October 30, 2001, from http://www.aaaa.org/transcripts/transcripts_main.asp?format= detail&sitew.../transcript8.htm

Reuters. (1999, February 9). *Selling books or screen space?* Retrieved August 15, 2002, from http://www.wired.com/news/news/businesss/story/17810.html

Richards, J. I., & Zakia, R. (1981). Pictures: An advertiser's expressway through FTC regulation. *Georgia Law Review,* (16), 77–134.

Richins, M. (1991, June). Social comparison and the idealized images of advertising. *Journal of Consumer Research, 18,* 71–83.

Riffe, D., Lacy, S., & Fico, F. G. (1998). *Analyzing media messages: Using quantitative content analysis in research.* Mahwah, NJ: Lawrence Erlbaum.

Rodin, J., Silberstein, L. R., & Striegel-Moore, R. H. (1985). Women and weight: A normative discontent. In T. B. Sondregger (Ed.), *Nebraska Symposium on Motivation: Vol. 32. Psychology and gender* (pp. 267–307). Lincoln: University of Nebraska Press.

Rogers, M., & Seiler, C. A. (1994). The answer is no: A national survey of advertising industry practitioners and their clients. *Journal of Advertising Research, 34*(2), 36–45.

Roth, M. S. (1996). Patterns in direct-to-consumer prescription drug print advertising and their public policy implications. *Journal of Public Policy and Marketing, 15*(1), 63–76.

Rothenberg, R. (2001, September 10). Marketing's borders blurred by product placement revival. *Advertising Age, 72,* 24.

Rotzoll, K., & Haefner, J. E. (1996). *Advertising in contemporary society* (3rd ed.). Urbana: University of Illinois Press.

Roussos, D. (1998, October 14). *Top ten reasons to give up dieting.* Retrieved April 30, 2001, from the University of Wisconsin Medical Foundation Web site: www.udoctors.org

Ruggiero, J. A., & Weston, L. (1985). Work options for women in women's magazines: The medium and the message. *Sex Roles, 12*(5/6), 535–547.

"Runner" test. (2001, May 7). *Advertising Age, 72,* 20.

Rushkoff, D. (2000). *Merchants of cool: Interview with Malcolm Gladwell.* Retrieved January 22, 2002, from http://www.pbs.org

Russell, J. T., & Lane, R. (2002). *Kleppner's advertising procedure.* Upper Saddle River, NJ: Prentice Hall.

Rutkowski, T. (1997). Institutional structure for the Internet: Who will control it? In O'Reilly and Associates (Eds.), *The Harvard Conference on the Internet and society* (pp. 325–336). Cambridge, MA: Harvard University Press.

Sager, R. (1999, December). Public drinking. *Reason, 31,* 10–11.

Samoriski, J. (2002). *Issues in cyberspace: Communication, technology, law and society on the Internet frontier.* Boston: Allyn & Bacon.

Saunders, C. (2001). *Fox launches "take over" ads on portals.* Retrieved April 24, 2002, from http://www.internetnews.com/IAR/article/0,,12_783351,00.html

Scanlon, J. (2000). Advertising women: The J. Walter Thompson Company women's editorial department. In J. Scanlon (Ed.), *The gender and consumer culture reader* (pp. 201–225). New York: New York University Press.

Schmideg, P. (1999). *Brother low-rez on Daisy ad.* Retrieved May 10, 2002, from http://members.aol.com/schmideg/daisy.html

Schommer, J., Doucette, W., & Mehta, B. (1998). Rote learning after exposure to a direct-to-consumer television advertisement for a prescription drug. *Clinical Therapeutics, 20*(3), 617–631.

Schudson, M. (1984). *Advertising, the uneasy persuasion.* New York: Basic Books.

Scott, L. M. (1994, December). The bridge from text to mind: Adapting reader-response theory to consumer research. *Journal of Consumer Research, 21,* 252–273.

Shallitt, R. (1999). *The ad from hell.* Retrieved March 20, 2002, from http://www.salon.com/media/col/shal/1999/05/28/kenya/

Shanahan, L. (1999, September 27). Multicultural? Get into the mix! *Brandweek, 40,* 29.

Shannon, A. (1998). *Advocating for adolescent reproductive health in sub-Saharan Africa.* Washington, DC: Advocates for Youth.

Shapiro, A. L. (1998). New voices in cyberspace: The Net could become a vibrant alternative to the media oligopoly. *The Nation, 266*(21), 36–38.

Shavitt, S., & Lowrey, P. (1998). Public attitudes toward advertising: More favorable than you might think. *Journal of Advertising Research, 38*(4), 7–22.

Shaw, D. (1987, February 16). Credibility vs. sensitivity: High, thick wall divides editors and advertisers. *Los Angeles Times,* p. 1.

Shaw, M. (2001, May). *The DTC dilemma.* Retrieved February 20, 2003, from http://www.HealthcareMedia.com

Sheehan, K. (2000). Is thin still in? In Charles R. Taylor (Ed.), *Proceedings of the 2000 Conference of the American Academy of Advertising* (p. 1). Villanova, PA: Villanova University Press.

Sherman, C. (2001). Consumer watchdog files complaint against eight search engines for "crass commercialism." *Information Today, 18*(8), 28.

Shultz, C. J., & Holbook, M. B. (1999). Marketing and the tragedy of the commons: A synthesis, commentary and analysis for action. *Journal of Public Policy and Marketing, 18*(2), 218–229.

Sibley, C. (2000). *Research report: DTC advertising studies.* Greenwich, CT: Coalition for Healthcare Communication.

Siebert, F. S., Peterson, T., & Schramm, W. (1956). *Four theories of the press.* Urbana: University of Illinois Press.

Silent dishwasher ad too quiet. (2000). *Broadcaster, 59*(2), 6.

Silverstein, B., Perdue, L., Peterson, B., & Kelly, E. (1986). The role of the mass media in promoting a thin standard of bodily attractiveness for women. *Sex Roles, 14*(9/10), 519–532.

Simmons, J. M. (1986). Gender differences of nonverbal power cues in television commercials. In E. F. Larkin (Ed.), *Proceedings of the 1986 Convention of the American Academy of Advertising* (pp. R72–R76). Norman: University of Oklahoma Press.

Singer, S. (1991, September). Auto dealers muscle: The newsroom. *Washington Journalism Review,* pp. 25–28.

Singh, S. (2000, July). Modern strategies needed for grey area. *Marketing Week,* p. 20.

Skelton, R. (1997). The next generation Internet. In O'Reilly and Associates (Eds.), *The Harvard Conference on the Internet and society* (pp. 77–91). Cambridge, MA: Harvard University Press.

Smith, A., & Kidder, R. M. (1996). *Political attack advertising.* Camden, ME: Institute for Global Ethics.

Smith, F. (1997). Advertising: Boon or bane? *Consumers Research Magazine, 80*(4), 315.

Smith, L. J. (1994). A content analysis of gender differences in children's advertising. *Journal of Broadcasting and Electronic Media, 38*(3), 323–337.

Smith, T. (2001). *Marketing mood.* Retrieved April 15, 2003, from www.pbs.org/newshour/bb/media/july-dec01/advert_12_27.html

Society for Women's Health Research. (1998, March). *Society calls on women's magazines to "stop pushing cancer!"* Retrieved February 11, 2002, from http://www.womens-health.org/news_article11.html

Soley, L., & Kurzbad, G. (1986). Sex in advertising: A comparison of 1964 and 1968 magazine advertisements. *Journal of Advertising, 15*(3), 46–54.

Soley, L., & Reid, L. (1988). Taking it off: Are models in magazine ads wearing less? *Journalism Quarterly, 65,* 960–966.

Soley, L. C., & Craig, R. L. (1992). Advertising pressures on newspapers: A survey. *Journal of Advertising, 21*(4), 1–10.

Solomon, M. R., & Ashmore, R. D. (1992). The beauty match-up hypothesis: Congruence between types of beauty and product images in advertising. *Journal of Advertising, 21*(4), 23–34.

Sorkin. (2001, February 4). *Technical approaches to unsolicited electronic email.* Retrieved May 22, 2002, from www.sorkin.org/articlers/usf.html

Stafford, M. R. (1998). Advertising sex-types services: The effects of sex, service type, and employee type on consumer attitudes. *Journal of Advertising, 27*(2), 65–82.

Staples, R., & Jones, T. (1985). Culture, ideology and black television images. *Black Scholar, 16*, 10–20.

State governments and lotteries. (1999). *Consumers Research Magazine, 82*(8), 12–13.

State of Texas. (1999, April 26, 2000). *Political advertising: What you need to know.* Retrieved March 13, 2002, from www.ethics.state.tx.us/pamphlet/ polad.htm

Steckel, R. (1999). *Making money while making a difference.* Homewood, IL: High Tide Press.

Steel, K. (1998, March 9). The waif and the babe. *Alberta Report, 25*, 34–35.

Stefik, M. (1999). *The Internet edge: Social, legal, and technological challenges for a networked world.* Cambridge, MA: MIT Press.

Stein, J. (1997, March 6). A new mode of women's magazines. *Los Angeles Times,* p. 2.

Steinhauer, J. (1997, September 27). Strutting their own stuff: Department stores pushing in-house clothing labels. *New York Times,* p. 1.

Stephens, D., Hill, R. P., & Hanson, C. (1994, Summer). The beauty myth and female consumers: The controversial role of advertising. *Journal of Consumer Affairs, 28*, 137–153.

Sullivan, D. (2002). *Lawsuit over paid placements to define search engines.* Retrieved February 4, 2002, from www.searchenginewatch.com

Sullivan, D., Schommer, J., & Birdwell, S. (1999). Consumer retention of risk information from direct-to-consumer advertising. *Drug Information Journal, 22*, 281–289.

Surowiecki, J. (2002, April 1). Ageism in advertising. *The New Yorker,* p. 40.

Surveys, N. I. (2000). *How many online.* Retrieved October 12, 2001, from http://www.nua.ie/surveys/how_many_online/index.html.

Sutherland, M. (1993). *Advertising and the mind of the consumer.* St. Leonard's, Australia: Allen and Unwin.

Swayne, L. E., & Grego, A. J. (1987). The portrayal of older Americans in television commercials. *Journal of Advertising, 16*, 47–54.

Taflinger, R. (1996). *You and me, babe: Sex and advertising.* Retrieved January 7, 2002, from http://www.wsu.edu:8080/~taflinge/sex.html

Tanouye, E. (2000, January 19). US develops expensive habit with drug sector growth spurt. Retrieved December 1, 2002, from http://www.msnbc.com/ news/215163.asp

Taylor, C. R., & Stern, B. B. (1997). Asian Americans: Television advertising and the "model minority" stereotype. *Journal of Advertising, 26*(2), 48–60.

Taylor, P. (2002). *New nationwide coalition calls for free air time as next step in campaign finance reform.* Retrieved June 1, 2002, from http://www. bettercampaigns.org/press/release.php?ReleaseID=32

Teinowitz, I. (2000). Ad creates a "rat" problem for GOP. *Advertising Age, 71,* 4–5.

Teinowitz, I. (2001a). Congress eyes DTC ad threat. *Advertising Age, 72,* 3.

Teinowitz, I. (2001b). Supremes sink mass ad curbs. *Advertising Age, 72,* 3–4.

Teinowitz, I. (2002). Congress quite on issue of liquor ads. *Advertising Age, 73,* 2.

Templeton, J. (1997). Ad spending slights black consumers. *Advertising Age, 68,* 28.

The Search Engine Report. (1999). *Amazon paid placements raise ethics questions.* Retrieved February 15, 2002, from http://www.searchenginewatch.com

Thernstrom, A., & Thernstrom, S. (1998). Black progress. *Brookings Review, 16*(2), 12–16.

Thomas, M. E., & Treiber, L. (2000). Race, gender and status: A content analysis of print advertisements in four popular magazines. *Sociological Spectrum, 20*(3), 357–371.

Till, B. D., & Busler, M. (2000). The match-up hypothesis: Physical attractiveness, expertise, and the role of fit on brand attitude, purchase intent, and brand beliefs. *Journal of Advertising, 29*(3), 1–13.

Till, B., & Nowak, L. I. (2000). Toward effective use of cause-related marketing alliances. *Journal of Product and Brand Management, 9*(7), 472–484.

Tobacco Advertising in the United States. (1997). *Issue briefs.* Studio City, CA: MediaScope Press.

Try to keep it simple. (2002). *Advertising Age, 73,* s2.

Tsu, B. (2000). Time to get real: Teen girl survey rates advertising. *Advertising Age, 71,* 47.

Tung, J. (2002). Bigger bodies are back. *Good Housekeeping, 235*(1), 133.

Tupper, M. (1995). *The representation of elderly persons in prime time advertising.* Retrieved April 21, 2003, from http://www.geocities.com/lightgrrrrl/

Turner, S., Hamilton, H., Jacobs, M., Angood, L. M., & Dwyer, D. (1997). The influence of fashion magazines on the body image satisfaction of college women: An exploratory analysis. *Adolescence, 32*(127), 603–614.

Twitchell, J. B. (1996). *AdCult: The triumph of advertising in American culture.* New York: Columbia University Press.

Twitchell, J. B. (1999). *Lead us into temptation.* New York: Columbia University Press.

Underhill, P. (1999). *Why we buy: The science of shopping.* New York: Simon & Schuster.

Unger, R. K., & Crawford, M. (1992). *Women and gender: A feminist psychology.* New York: McGraw-Hill.

Ursic, A. C., Ursic, M. L., & Ursic, V. L. (1986). A longitudinal study of the use of the elderly in magazine advertisements. *Journal of Communication Research, 13,* 131–133.

U.S. Census Bureau. (1999). *Current population reports* (311). Washington, DC: Author.

U.S. Department of Health and Human Services. (1990). *Seventh Special Report to the U.S. Congress on Alcohol and Health.* Rockville, MD: Author.

U.S. Department of Labor. (2000). *Women at the millennium, accomplishments and challenges ahead* (Report). Washington, DC: U.S. Department of Labor, Women's Bureau.

U.S. General Accounting Office. (2002). *FDA oversight of direct-to-consumer advertising has limitations.* Washington, DC: Author.

U.S. Multicultural Advertising Agency Ranking. (2001, November 19). *Advertising Age, 72,* s14.

Utt, S. H. E. (1984). The effect of sexual stereotyping in print advertising on brand name recall, sales point recall and buying attitude: An experimental study. *DAI, 45*(5), 1231-a.

Valenti, C. (2001). *Patriot games*. Retrieved April 10, 2003, from the ABC News Web site: http://abcnews.go.com/sections/business/DailyNews/patriotic_ads_011019.html

Van Bakel, R. (2001, May). Do the taste test. *Creativity Magazine*, p. 4.

Vanden Bergh, B., & Katz, H. (1999). *Advertising principles: Choice challenge change*. Lincolnwood, IL: NTC Business Books.

Vasil, L., & Wass, H. (1990). Portrayal of the elderly in the media: A literature review and implications for educational gerontologists. *Educational Gerontology, 19*, 71–85.

Venkatesan, M., & Losco, J. (1975, October). Women in magazine ads 1959–1971. *Journal of Advertising Research, 15*, 49–54.

Voegele, J. (2002). *Recursive advertising—The joke's on us*. Retrieved April 15, 2002, from http://www.jvoegele.com/essays/spoofads.html

Vogt, S. (2001, July 2). RX advertising Redux. *Strategy*, 18.

Voigt, J., & Melillo, W. (2002, March 11). Rough cut. *Adweek*, p. 4.

Wake, B. (2002, March 12). How Big Tobacco got Hollywood to light up. *Ottawa Citizen*, p. A12.

Walker, C. (1993, January). Fat and happy? *American Demographics, 15*, 52–57.

Washington State Attorney General's Office. (2002). *Stomping out youth tobacco use*. Retrieved April 16, 2002, from the Washington State Attorney General's Office Web site: http://www.wa.gov/ago/tobacco/settlement.html

Wayman, R. (2000). *What is the Chinese Wall and why is it in the news?* Retrieved January 14, 2002, from http://www.investopedia.com/printable.asp?a=/articles/analyst/090501.asp

Weaver, D. T., & Oliver, M. B. (2000, May). *Television programs and advertising: Measuring the effectiveness of product placement within Seinfeld*. Paper presented at the meeting of the International Communication Association, Acapulco, Mexico.

Webb, D. J., & Mohr, L. A. (1998). A typology of consumer responses to cause-related marketing: From skeptics to socially concerned. *Journal of Public Policy and Marketing, 17*(2), 226–240.

Wechsler, J. (1998). DTC marketing issues fill up DDMAC's plate. *Business and Management Practices*, 10–12.

Weissman, R. X. (1998, October). But first, call your drug company. *American Demographics*, pp. 27–28.

Welch, M. (2000). *AOL, Time Warner and journalism: Life really ain't so bad*. Retrieved January 11, 2002, from http://www.ojr.org/ojr/business/1017966073.php

Welke, B. (1999). Why we should get rid of political advertising—now. Retrieved March 2, 2000, from http://www.salon.com/media/feature/1999/09/02/advertising/

Wells, M. (2001, October 29). Who really needs Madison Avenue? *Forbes, 168*, 131–132.

Wentz, L. (2001, November 19). Reverse English. *Advertising Age, 72*, s1–s2.

West Legal Directory. (2002). *Freedom of speech*. Retrieved April 19, 2002, from http://www.wld.com/conbus/weal/wfrspeec.htm

Whipple, T. W., & Courtney, A. E. (1985). Female role portrayals in advertising and communication effectiveness: A review. *Journal of Advertising, 14*(3), 4–17.

Wilcox, J. (2000). *Legal experts say merger OK likely.* Retrieved January 10, 2002, from the CNET News Web site: http://news.cnet.com/news/0-1005-200-1519200.html

Wilson, N. L., & Blackhurst, A. E. (1999). Food advertising and eating disorders: Marketing body dissatisfaction, the drive for thinness, and dieting in women's magazines. *Journal of Humanistic Counseling Education and Development, 38*(2), 111–122.

Wirthlin Worldwide. (1999, March). *Buying influences: Consider the source* (Research Report). Reston, VA: Author.

Wisconsin Public Television. (1996). *30 second candidate.* Retrieved April 1, 2000, from http://www.pbs.org/30secondcandidate/q_and_a/

Woellert, L., & Walczak, L. (2002). Campaign reform's dangerous aftershocks. *BusinessWeek, 3777,* 42.

Wolf, N. (1991). *The beauty myth: How images of beauty are used against women.* New York: William Morrow.

Wolszon, L. R. (1998). Women's body image theory and research. *American Behavioral Scientist, 41*(4), 542–557.

Wong, E. (2001, June 19). Nike trying new strategies for women: Company seeks merger of athletics and fashion. *New York Times,* p. 1.

Wood, D. J. (2002). *How to avoid false or misleading Internet advertising.* Retrieved February 15, 2002, from http://www.gigalaw.com

Wood, K. (2000). *Freedom of expression: Terms, dates and concepts.* Retrieved March 20, 2002, from http://kylewood.com/firstamendment/terms.htm

Woods, B. (2001). *Additional side effects.* Retrieved April 12, 2003, from http://www.promomagazine.com/ar/marketing_additional_side_effects/

Workman, J. E., & Freeburg, E. W. (1996). Consumer responses to fashion advertisements using models in wheelchairs: Is there a relationship to consumers' optimal stimulus level? *Family and Consumer Sciences Research Journal, 24*(3), 237–253.

Yoo, M. (1997). *Taming the TV.* Retrieved January 22, 2002, fromhttp://www.4children.org/news/300tv.htm

Zinkhan, G. M., & Carlson, L. (1995). Green advertising and the reluctant consumer. *Journal of Advertising, 24*(2), 1–7.

Zinkhan, G., Qualls, W. J., & Biswas, A. (1990). The use of blacks in magazine and television advertising: 1946–1986. *Journalism Quarterly, 67*(3), 547–553.

Index

About the Author

Kim Sheehan is Assistant Professor at the University of Oregon's School of Journalism and Communication. Her teaching and research interests include online consumer behavior, research methods, and advertising creative strategy. Her research has appeared in the *Journal of Advertising*, *Journal of Advertising Research*, and *Journal of Public Policy and Marketing*. Kim is coauthor of *Using Qualitative Research Methods in Advertising* (Sage, 2002); in addition, she contributed chapters to *Internet Marketing: Readings and Online Resources*, Paul Richardson (McGraw-Hill, 2000), and *Frontiers in Direct Marketing Research*, Joseph Phelps (Wiley, 1998). In 1997, the Advertising Research Division of the Association for Education in Journalism and Mass Communication awarded her Best Paper. In 1999, Kim was a finalist for Best Paper of the year in the *Journal of Advertising*. Prior to joining the academy, Kim worked as Associate Media Director and Media Supervisor for several advertising agencies, including Foote Cone and Belding in Chicago. Her clients included Budweiser, Coldwell Banker Real Estate, McDonald's, Laura Ashley, *People Magazine*, Bank of Boston, and Kraft-Miracle Whip.